Colorado's **TOP**
Fishing &
Hunting Maps

Colorado's TOP
Fishing & Hunting Maps

FAP

Colorado's Recreational Zones

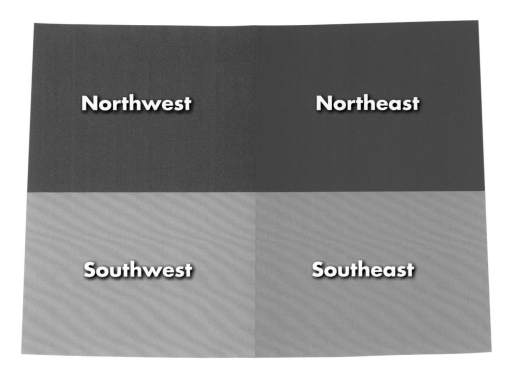

All inquiries should be addressed to:
Frank Amato Publications, Inc. • P.O. Box 82112 • Portland, Oregon 97282
503-653-8108 • www.amatobooks.com

ISBN-13: 978-1-57188-483-1
UPC: 0-81127-00325-9
Printed in China

Table of Contents

Getting Started!

Planning and anticipating future fishing or hunting trips is half the fun, but with so much information out there it can become overwhelming quickly. Hundreds of lakes and streams, and numerous fish and game species—Colorado's angling opportunities are endless.

Buying this book was a great start, *Colorado's Top Fishing and Hunting Maps* makes it a whole lot easier to plan and organize your upcoming adventures. The fishing and hunting information in this book comes from the long-time outdoorsmen in each area, this guarantees you the insider's scoop and puts you ahead of the game—even if you've never been there before. You will find everything you need: local accommodations and services, directions, fish and game species and where to find them, run timing, productive techniques, equipment and more.

It's time to call some buddies, pick a spot out of *Colorado's Top Fishing & Hunting Maps*, and start planning the fishing or hunting adventure of a lifetime!

Businesses and fishing/hunting regulations change frequently, confirm the information online before you finalize your plans.

Always Important Around Water!

- ALWAYS wear life vests when boating (legally required for children).
- Read CURRENT regulations book or check online.
- Haul out more garbage than you brought in.
- Look out for others and offer to help folks.
- Keep boat lines clear of objects.
- Never drag your anchor in a current on a short line.

This book and its maps are NOT FOR NAVIGATIONAL PURPOSES. All bodies of water are subject to change from strong currents, wind, erosion, soil deposition, etc. ALWAYS view maps with a critical eye!

NORTHEAST FISHING

Fish Rocky Mountain Arsenal for warmwater fun

COMMERCE CITY

by Mike Kennedy

The Rocky Mountain Arsenal National Wildlife Refuge, located just 8 miles northeast of downtown Denver, has opened two lakes — Lake Ledora and Lake Mary — to the public. The lakes are open to fishing from 8 a.m. to sunset on Saturday and Sundays from mid-April until mid-October. This year the lakes will close on Oct. 10.

Ladora has northern pike and largemouth bass; Mary offers largemouth bass, channel catfish, white and black crappie, bluegill and some northern pike and yellow perch.

The Rocky Mountain Arsenal was used as a chemical weapons facility during WWII and again during the Cold War. The U.S. Fish and Wildlife Service became involved at the Arsenal in 1986 when a roost of communal bald eagles was discovered. Public interest triggered a successful grassroots effort to have the Arsenal declared a National Wildlife Refuge. The refuge was established by an act of Congress in 1992. In April of 2004, the U.S. Army transferred 5,000 acres of land to the USFWS, officially establishing the refuge.

The refuge is restricted to 60 anglers at any one time, on a first-come, first-served basis. Wildlife Refuge Fishing Coordinator Ivan Vicente (303-289-0930) says that while only 60 anglers may fish at any one time, as many as 120 or more anglers may fish in any given day. This is because some anglers fish in the morning, then leave, returning their permit badge to the visitor center and allowing other anglers to fish after they've left. Early in the season they often have 120 anglers in a day, but now the number is closer to 50 anglers per day, leaving plenty of slots to fish.

Anglers must attend a 30-minute orientation class on safety and fishing rules and regulations before being allowed to fish. The orientation training is offered at 9 a.m. Saturdays and Sundays, and you have to call the visitor's center for training reservations. Normally you can fish on the same day as the training, but there is no guarantee.

The bite: Susan Echelberger of the USFWS at the Visitor's Center (303-289-0232, *rockymountain-arsenal.fws.gov*) says that many large fish have already been caught this year, including a 46-inch northern pike from Ladora and a 7-pound bass from Mary. One of the great things about the lakes on the old Rocky Mountain Arsenal is that the catch rate has averaged one fish per hour over the past 10 years.

Angler Tim Mossontte of Aurora has been fishing the Arsenal lakes fairly regularly and has been doing pretty well. Mossontte catches both bass and

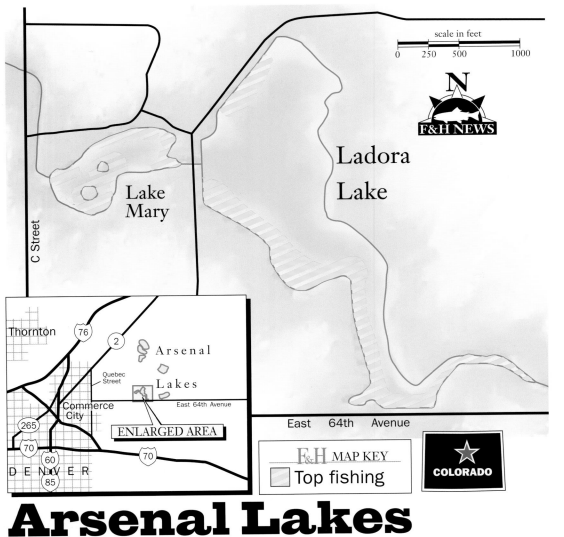

Arsenal Lakes

pike. On one recent trip, he caught a 22-inch pike on Ladora on 6-pound test and a Yamamoto Senko, then turned right around and caught a 32-inch, 9-plus-pound northern pike on a 6-inch swimbait.

Gearing up: When fishing Ladora, which has numerous northern pike, it's wise to use a steel leader. Pike can cut normal monofilament fishing line with their sharp teeth. Fish for pike in shallow water along weed lines and near other structure. Swimbaits, large crankbaits, spoons and spinners are good choices.

Crankbaits and plastics such as grubs, tubes, worms or Senkos are good for the largemouth bass. Use small $\frac{1}{32}$- to $\frac{1}{8}$-ounce jigs with tubes, grubs or hair jigs for crappie, bluegill and perch. All plastics must be at least 1½ inches long to meet the Colorado definition of artificial flies and lures. Fly fishermen should try a pike bunny or other large streamer on a 7- to 8-weight fly rod for pike, poppers for the bass and Woolly Buggers for panfish.

If the lakes have colored to muddy water after a severe rain or run-off, use brighter colors such as orange, chartreuse and fire tiger. Even if the whole lake isn't colored, but you're fishing the edge of a section of colored water, I'd still go with bright colors. I've had good luck with an orange, dark green and chartreuse Triple Threat plastic grub made by Kalin's. Fire tiger jerkbaits may also work well in off-color water.

In addition to bright lures, try lures that make noise or vibrate the water such as buzzbaits, spinners or rattlebaits. Often these bright or noisy lures attract pike even in clear water. However, if the lake or section of the lake you're fishing is relatively clear, you generally need to go with more natural colors and use a more subtle fishing approach. Select baits that match the natural forage in the lakes. At Rocky Mountain Arsenal I'd use bass, perch, shad and crawdad patterns.

Access: While most fishing is restricted to bank only, wading with chest waders in Ladora is allowed. No boats, float tubes, etc., are allowed on either lake.

Bank access on Ladora is restricted to the area from the dam down the rocky west shore, to the arm of the lake at the southern end. Restricted areas are well marked and basically follow the trails around the lakes.

Regs: Fishing is restricted to artificial flies and lures only. You must use barbless hooks, and all fish must be released immediately.

One exception to the artificial flies and lures rule, according to Vicente, is that vegetables such as corn or peas and even Power Bait can be used. I was told that some anglers catch catfish on these baits. You cannot use any form of live bait or cutbait.

An exception to the catch-and-release rule exists if you happen to catch a northern pike in Lake Mary. Mary is not supposed to have any northerns, but several have already been caught this year, and one in excess of 40 inches has been spotted but not yet landed. Vicente says that if you catch a northern in Lake Mary the best thing would be to carry it over to Ladora and release it. Short of that, just leave it on the bank.

A few northerns can eat a lot of the smaller panfish that Mary is known for. These smaller panfish and the fishing piers and walks around the lake make Mary a great place for kids to fish.

If you have any questions on the rules for fishing the lakes at the refuge, bring them up in the training session prior to fishing. Make sure you don't have any unauthorized baits or lures with you at the lake when you're at the refuge. Leave any questionable baits or lures at home or in your vehicle.

More activities: There are many activities going on at the refuge each weekend, with nature trails, guided tours and nature programs each Saturday and Sunday. It's a great place to take the entire family. With gas prices as high as they are, fishing nearby lakes and streams like the Rocky Mountain Arsenal NWR Lakes can be enjoyable and save you money.

An adult over 18 must accompany all youth, and everyone over 16 must have a valid Colorado fishing license. Entrance to the Rocky Mountain Arsenal is at the intersection of Havana Avenue where it dead-ends at 56th Street. After showing the guard your driver's license or other ID, continue for 1½ miles to the visitor's center and lakes. It costs $3 per day to fish; many other activities are free. **F&H**

IT'S SHORE FISHING ONLY at Lake Ladora and Lake Mary at the Rocky Mountain Arsenal NWR, but that doesn't mean you can't catch big largemouth like this one. (*F&H News* photo)

AT a GLANCE

What: Stay close to home and get in on some great warmwater fishing on smaller water at Rocky Mountain Arsenal NWR.

When: Lake Ladora and Lake Mary will be open until Oct. 10.

Where: Rocky Mountain Arsenal is at the intersection of Havana Avenue where it dead-ends at 56th Street just northeast of Denver.

How: Fishing is restricted to artificial flies and lures only; you must use barbless hooks; and all fish must be released immediately. Action is almost exclusively restricted to bank angling.

Who: Wildlife Refuge Fishing Coordinator Ivan Vicente (303-289-0930); Rocky Mountain Arsenal National Wildlife Refuge Visitor's Center (303-289-0232; *rockymountainarsenal.fws.gov*).

Aurora Reservoir: Peace, tranquility, oodles of fish

AURORA

by Mike Kennedy

Most metro lakes around the state are a blessing and a curse. They not only provide great fishing for a variety of species, they provide lots of traffic from pleasure boaters and skiers.

Just outside metro Denver is an exception to the rule in 820-acre Aurora Reservoir (park office 303-690-1286). It's just great fishing as your limited to wind-, manual- or electric driven craft only. You can take your gas-powered boat, but you have to raise the motor out of the water and remove any gas tanks you can. The result is a quiet fishery that you can enjoy without dodging the normal metro lake annoyances, especially on weekends or holidays.

There's a ton of great fishing on Aurora. It's the rare mix of quantity and quality fish. Spring usually proves a great time for both bank and boat fishermen to hit the water. During late May and early June, most of the fish available are in the coves or near shore.

Trout anglers can take advantage of some good fishing by focusing on the back coves like Marina, Senac and Lone Tree. The flats at the west end of the dam and coves along the east side of the lake also provide great spring action.

Shorebound anglers can keep it pretty simple. Just rig up some Power Bait and fish it just off the bottom. I like to tie four snap swivels spaced about 12 inches apart at the end of my line. I usually attach a No. 8 or 10 snelled hook to the top three and a ½- to 1-ounce bell sinker

SOAKING BAIT like worms, minnows or Power Bait is quite effective to catch big Aurora trout, as Timmy Schlewitz shows with this 20-inch, 3½-pound rainbow. Action is heating up from both shore and boat.

to the bottom. I like to put an orange, chartreuse and rainbow or pink Power Nugget on the hooks, cast it out and let it sink to the bottom.

Worms or minnows are also very effective, as 14-year-old Timmy Schlewitz can attest. He landed a 20-inch, 3½-pound rainbow off the west side of the dam by soaking a nightcrawler on the bottom.

As the summer months close in and water temperatures rise, expect trout to move out to the deeper water. Boaters do best during the summer as they're able to target those fish suspended in about 30 to 35 feet of water. Trolling is your best bet. Try pulling a variety of baits, inlcuding 'crawlers and smaller spoons.

When summertime arrives, bank anglers should shift their attention to other species.

Walleye: A lot of large walleye live in Aurora. Late spring and summer is a great time to chase them. Yes, "chase" is the appropriate term. You have to be mobile, as walleye tend to roam with baitfish or to find food. They aren't territorial like bass. Don't assume that because you caught fish in one spot last time, that they'll be there on your next trip. It's OK to check out the normal spots, but don't be afraid to move on quickly.

It's worth a little effort to cruise the lake looking for fish activity. While you're looking, troll a stickbait or worm harness behind you. You never know what you'll come across.

Worm, leech and minnow harnesses probably catch more walleye than anything else; however, don't be afraid to try new things. Trolling crankbaits, using planer boards or vertically jigging plastics, spoons or Northland Fire-Ball jigs with trailer hook and worm can also be effective.

If you find a likely walleye area, casting also works. I like to cast 4-inch grubs off rocky points or shorelines, which I admit you don't have many of at Aurora. The flats and coves between Senac and Lonetree, and the water along the east shore from Lonetree to the Scuba Beach are some of the best walleye areas.

AT a GLANCE

What: Enjoying Aurora Reservoir's abundant fishing opportunities without the mess of recreational boaters.

Where: To get to Aurora Reservoir, take Quincy Avenue 2 1/2 miles east of Gun Club Road. You can get to Quincy off Parker Road or off E470.

When: Some of the best fishing is going on right now. You should be catching the bass spawn. Walleye and wiper are both active. Trout should be close to shore and available to bank anglers. As summer temperatures heat things up, fishing will stay good, but move farther out in the lake.

How: Power Bait seems to be best for trout anglers, especially those on the bank. Trolling is a viable option for boaters chasing trout and walleye. Go with plastics and crankbaits for bass and wiper.

Who: All Pro Fish 'n Sport (303-795-3474); Valley Country Tackle (303-680-3544); park office (303-690-1286).

Bass: An abundance of big bass swim in Aurora; you just have to work a little bit for them. Cover is going to be the key. Search the shallower depth for cover. In late May it will be worth scouring the shallow weeds and logs hoping to find some late spawners. If that isn't successful, move out to the deep weed edges or the first drop-off nearby. Senac and Lonetree coves are a good bet for finding fish.

Don't expect fish to travel too far from their spawning grounds. Most likely they're cruising the area looking for a meal.

When fish are shallow, you'll do well to fish smaller plastics in natural colors. Spinnerbaits and crankbaits are a good bet as well. A good search bait is a baitfish patterned lipless crankbait like a Rat-L-Trap.

Wiper are fairly abundant too. It's hard to seek them out though. It's a good bet to watch for shad busting on the surface. Stick to the west side of the dam as well as the marina and swim beach for your best bet. Again, a shad patterned Rat-L-Trap is a good bet, as are white or silver crankbaits or plastics.

Getting around: As we noted earlier, you can't use gas propulsion on the lake so getting around can be difficult at times. It's a good idea to have at least two trolling motor batteries on hand, and three would be better. The wind can kick up pretty good on Aurora, so you need to have plenty of power and lots of thrust.

I've gotten stranded a couple of times. Now I fix a transom mount trolling motor on the back of my boat and use the bowmount to steer. When you feel your trolling motor start to wane, switch batteries.

Trolling motor fishing is quite effective as well. It's known that noise and vibration move fish away from your boat. Trolling with a quiet electric motor will keep fish in the strike zone better. And anyone who's fished the shallows with an electric motor knows the benefits it has in those conditions.

F&H

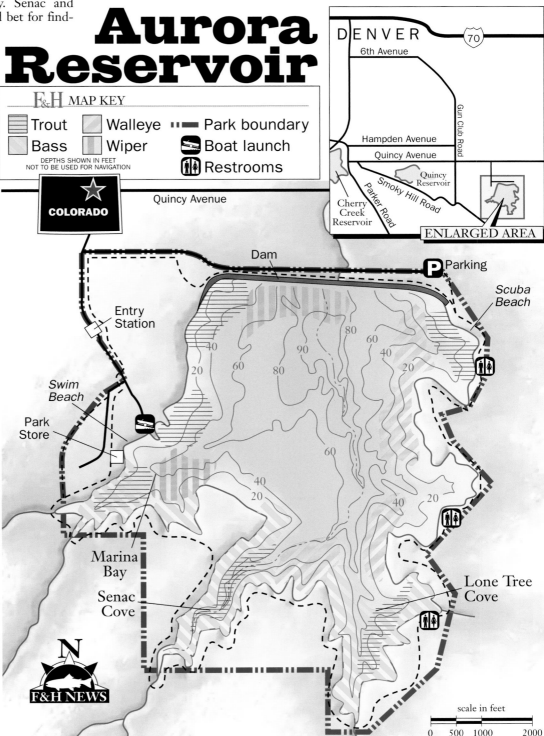

Aurora Reservoir

F&H MAP KEY

Trout
Bass
Walleye
Wiper
Park boundary
Boat launch
Restrooms

DEPTHS SHOWN IN FEET
NOT TO BE USED FOR NAVIGATION

COLORADO

DENVER

70
6th Avenue
Gun Club Road
Hampden Avenue
Quincy Avenue
Quincy Reservoir
Smoky Hill Road
Cherry Creek Reservoir
Parker Road
ENLARGED AREA

Quincy Avenue

Dam
Parking
Scuba Beach
Entry Station
80
90
60
40
40
20
60
20
80
60
Swim Beach
Park Store
60
40
20
40
20
Marina Bay
Senac Cove
Lone Tree Cove

N

F&H NEWS

scale in feet
0   500   1000   2000

Bear Creek Lake a wilderness oasis in urban jungle

LAKEWOOD

by Dusty Routh

Finding some good out-of-the-way fishing spots close to Denver is getting harder and harder every year. But around the Lakewood area you're in luck, because Bear Creek Lake Park (303-697-6159)

has a little bit of something for everyone who needs to shuck off the confines of big city life and get a little fishing in without having to drive for hours or traverse treacherous mountain passes.

The even better news is that the fishing here can be quite good, for a variety

of fish that range from rainbows and browns to monstrous perch, saugeye, tiger musky and even wipers.

Sometimes big fish: This year might be the winter of big perch and saugeye on Bear Creek, though big fish here

BEAR CREEK LAKE PARK

Coyote Gulch

Bear Creek

West Hampden Avenue

Turkey Creek

BEAR CREEK LAKE PARK

36
32
28
24
20
16
12
8
4

scale in feet

0   250   500   1000

MAP COURTESY OF BEAR CREEK LAKE PARK

COLORADO

F&H MAP KEY

Best fishing

Boat launch

DEPTHS SHOWN IN FEET
NOT TO BE USED FOR NAVIGATION

LAKEWOOD

Morrison

ENLARGED AREA

Bear Creek Lake

aren't always the norm. According to the park's naturalist Jode Morse, ice anglers so far this season have pulled in a 13-inch perch and a 21-inch saugeye. Both of these fish were caught in January.

Anglers should be aware, however, that the ice lid on Bear Creek tends to fluctuate with how much cold weather is hitting the metro area. Back in January Bear Creek had a nice, tight lid, with anglers drilling through as much as 10 to 14 inches of ice. But the warm weather fronts that came through in the latter part of the month and in early February put the kibosh on that lid.

"We had some really nice ice in January," Morse says. "We had 30 ice anglers at a time out on the lake, and the fishing was good. There was 10 to 14 inches of ice, very safe, almost ideal for ice fishing. But right now it's not really froze up as much as we'd like."

Morse says that in some places the lid has shallowed to as little as 2 inches close to the edges, and around 4 inches out towards the middle, and there's a small 2-foot ring of open water around the edges of the lake. But Morse has seen this happen before and she knows it's just temporary.

"Once we get some more cold blasts of weather, there will be more ice fishing," she says. "It's a long way from over for the year. We just have to be patient and wait for some more winter weather. It should lock up good again."

Morse points out that the rain and sleet really did a number on the ice lid. "It made a lot of places kind of soft and mushy," she says. Anglers intending to ice fish should be sure to call ahead to check on conditions before setting out.

More about those fish: Bear Creek receives regular plants of rainbow trout from DOW. The last planting was back in November, when the lake received 1,300 12-inch rainbows. There's also a very healthy population of perch, lots of saugeye, tiger musky and some wipers. The tiger musky will sometimes hit the same gear that you'd use for the trout, and you can expect some size from these fish.

"We gillnetted last summer," says Morse. "There was a 27-inch tiger musky that came out. We also found some very decent-sized browns. Now, we don't stock the lake with browns, so we're not sure how they got in there. Maybe from Bear Creek. But we found some real nice ones when we netted."

Morse says the trout bite for the stocker trout has held up well this winter, just so long as the ice conditions allow anglers to get over them. "The fishing was really relatively good when it was cold and when the ice is decent," Morse says.

Three lakes: The park actually offers three different lakes, with Bear Creek being the fishing hot spot. The other two lakes are "soda" lakes that are not stocked with fish.

Morse says the soda content of these two other lakes means there's not much of a freezing point, and the water has a different feel to it. "You can fish in those lakes, but we don't stock them and we kind of discourage fishing there," says Morse.

Christmas tree drop: Morse reports that she and her staff helped the fishery on Bear Creek along a bit by doing some Christmas tree drops on the southeast corner of the lake. "They seemed to have really made that into a hot spot over there," she says. But at 110 surface acres and with a maximum depth of 39 feet, setting up just about anywhere can produce fish.

One of the best ways to fish Bear Creek is with an ice jig tipped with a nightcrawler. Fished close to the bottom, this will produce lots of yellow perch. Fishing this rig suspended will entice the trout. For the tiger musky, consider using a larger jighead and sucker meat, as well as larger jigging spoons like Swedish Pimples. The winter saugeye bite is also good on jigs and nightcrawlers, as well as roundhead jigs and plastics.

Etc.: Bear Creek Lake Park requires a $4 entrance fee per car for fishing. If you intend to fish here a lot (as in more than 10 times per season) there's a $40 annual pass available, too. The park is located near the southwest corner of Lakewood close to Morrison along Highway 8. The lake and park are located on the east/northeast side of the park, which is owned by the City of Lakewood.

The park is open year-round. There's a campground that's open from April to October, plus a Visitor Center, picnic area and (come this summer) there's a swim beach. There's also an amphitheater for campfire programs in the summer. Morse says bring your camera because resident raptors and two bald eagles that call the lake home.

IT'S CLOSE to the Denver metro area, but Bear Creek Lake feels like it's in the middle of nowhere. Plus, you can catch nice fish there. Wyatt Chapman caught this 12-inch rainbow on his first ice fishing trip last January. His father Dave sent in the pic.

There are no special rules or regulations pertaining to the fishing on Bear Creek, Morse reports. Statewide fishing regulations apply. During open-water season, boats are allowed on Bear Creek with a 10-hp motor restriction. *F&H*

AT a GLANCE

What: Strapped for time? Bear Creek Lake offers close-in fishing and a getaway-from-it all prairie setting.

When: Watch the weather for a good, cold arctic blast that hangs around in the area long enough to firm up the lake's ice lid.

What: Bear Creek offers stocker rainbows, resident browns, yellow perch, tiger musky, saugeye, and even some wipers.

Where: Work the southeast side of the lake where plants of Christmas trees have added some structure.

Bonny hurt by drought, but still kicking out fish

IDALIA

by Tom Behrens

WIPERS like this one held by Victor Colaleo are a popular target at Bonny Reservoir, but you can also catch walleye, crappie, white bass and more.

Anglers heading for Bonny Reservoir might just want to call first before towing their boat out to the lake. Howard Paul, Park Manager for Bonny Reservoir State Park (970-354-7306), reports that the lake was down about 17 feet in the first part of April.

During the winter, work was done on lengthening and widening the boat ramp at the marina. Also, the turn-around area was reworked.

"Construction is finished, but we're waiting on the dredge right now," Paul says. The ramp is expected to be open for use, providing there are no hang-ups in dredging or weather problems by April 21. The ramp has been lengthened another 91 feet.

The area around Bonny has been plagued by lack of measurable rain in the last five years. "Three years ago we were just so bone dry out here on the plains that it just started pulling us down," Paul says. "Normally we can count on heavy rains of 4 or 5 inches. That can jump the lake up 5 or 6 feet over a two-day period. The rains we've been getting, like the last three years, have been ½-inch, 1 inch. When the ground is dry, the water soaks into the ground, and we don't get any kind of surface flow into the lake. We're so far east of the mountains, we don't benefit from any snowmelt runoff."

Although the water level is down, the good fishing continues. According to gill net surveys in 2002, walleye hogged most of the net space. Other fish counted were channel catfish, wiper, white bass and crappie. Gizzard shad are the food source.

"Low water can create good fishing, but it also has a negative impact on the fishery," says Mike Seraphin of the DOW. "It concentrates more fish in a smaller area, which increases the fishing success rates. But for fish, it doesn't provide the habitat that allows them to grow and flourish if there were the hiding spaces that normal water levels would provide."

To counter the affects of low water conditions on the fishery, DOW stocks Bonny. "Every year we add more channel catfish, not in huge numbers, but to continue the growth of the fish population. The same for wiper and walleye. Various years we've stocked a few largemouth bass and various other fish. We don't stock the crappie. They seem to do real well on their own."

One of those "various other fish" stocked in the lake is the tiger musky. These fish were initially placed in the lake in 2001-2002 to primarily control the rough fish, but will eventually provide a sport fishing opportunity as they mature.

"The fish that were put in were about 7 inches in length, so I think it will take a while for them to grow up," says Paul. "I imagine that by now they're putting up a little tussle if you get one on your line. The tiger musky is a sterile hybrid that will not produce on its own. They will not breed and will become fewer and fewer over time."

Crappie naturally reproduce well enough that stocking is not required. "At this time of year, most anglers' attention are going to be focused on walleye and crappie," says Raymond Niles, operator of Bonny Lake Marina (970-354-7339; 970-664-2219). The crappie are going to be found frequenting the rocks along the dam.

"Right now, with our water levels being down, you just gotta pick those spots," says Niles. "We've lost a lot of crappie habitat. Mostly they're along the rocks of the dam and in the mouth of North Cove. Right now the lake is low enough that we're lacking our boat docks, so we can't fish around them now."

Another good spot for crappie (and white bass) is a place along the north shoreline called Bird Island. "When you come out of the North Cove," says Niles, "head towards the middle of the lake. That's where we have real good luck on our walleye. It's been a while since we had some big wipers caught. Over in a corner of the dam is our hot spot for the big wipers. We do a lot of jigging. A lot of people have their best luck, sitting out from the rocks and fishing the lure off the dam toward them." Anglers with no boat can walk the dam to a spot where they will fish from.

Paul and his sons use minnows for

crappie. "A 2-inch minnow, using an open-face spinning outfit, is probably the most popular method and bait to use," Paul says. "Water depth is 15 or 20 feet deep at the dam, but you're not fishing that far from the dam, probably in about 5 feet of water. I like using minnows myself. I have two sons and it's easier when you're fishing minnows as bait. Otherwise you have to be able to feel the strike if you put them on under a float. It takes a little more finesse."

Niles and friends usually fish off the bottom for walleye, utilizing either bottom-bouncers or lures. "We like to use a deep diver as the lure," he says. "Rapalas and Shad Raps are really hot for the walleye. The first couple of years I was here, most of the walleye were taken while trolling. Now we do a lot of still fishing. If we're going to run lures, yes, we do troll about 2 or 3 mph. The lures we use will dive down to the

correct depth without adding any extra weight. A lot of people mistake the different types of diving lures. They just put one on. They don't know one will dive 15 feet and one 10 feet. If you put weight on, it will kill its action. Color choice on the lure is based on the color of the water."

"Wipers' delicacy are bluegills, so we try to stay close to bluegill colors," Niles says. "They really like Thin Fins and baits like that."

Niles trolls these baits. Paul states that the most successful wiper anglers are those who are following the bird action. "Watch for boils on top of the water. The trick is not to get on top of the fish, because you're going to drive the minnows back down. A lot of people make the mistake of trying to get too close to the boil and driving the fish back down. They'll catch one or two, but if they worked the edges with some type of Rat-L-trap, Kast Masters or soft plastic imitations, something that imitates the gizzard

AT a GLANCE

What: Wipers, crappie, catfish and more at Bonny Reservoir.

Where: From Denver, travel east on I-70. Take Exit 316 toward Byers. Continue until you reach the junction with 385. Turn south and drive until you see signs for the recreation area.

Who: Bonny Reservoir State Park (970-354-7306), Bonny Lake Marina (970-354-7339; 970-664-2219).

shad, they're more successful. If anglers find wipers on their fish finder, then it's vertical jigging."

Remember to call ahead to make sure the boat ramp is finished before coming to the lake this spring. According to Howard Paul, the ramp should be in use by the end of April.

The crappie, walleye and wipers are getting tired of waiting on you. Channel catfish, which I did not mention, are patrolling the bottom looking for something to eat. Buy them something nice and smelly on the way to the lake. **F&H**

Bonny Reservoir

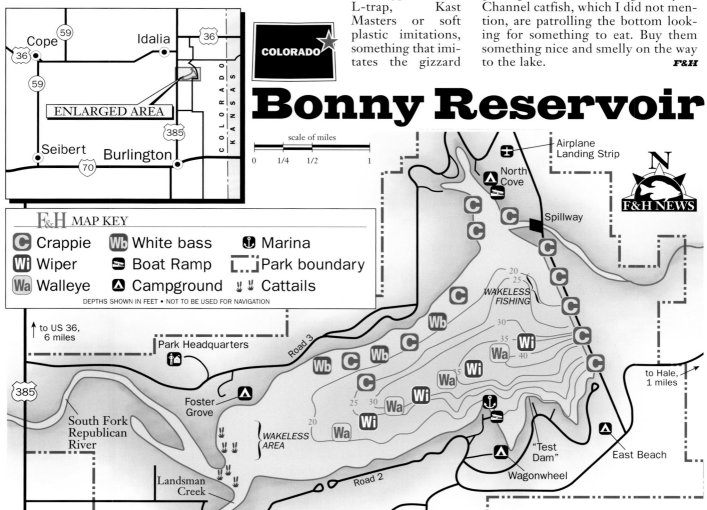

F&H MAP KEY

C Crappie   **Wb** White bass   **L** Marina
Wi Wiper   **≋** Boat Ramp   **⌐** Park boundary
Wa Walleye   **▲** Campground   **⥮** Cattails

DEPTHS SHOWN IN FEET • NOT TO BE USED FOR NAVIGATION

Carter Lake trifecta: Trout, bass, walleye

by Mike Kennedy

YOU'LL FIND stocker trout in Carter Lake as well as larger fish, plus bass and walleye. Kevin Corrington was age 5 when he caught this fish in 2003.

Looking for a little variety? Take a trip to Carter Lake in Loveland, where you can chase trout, bass and walleye.

Carter has many fishing opportunities, according to Sam Waldo of the Larimer County Visitor's Center. Waldo says that the trout fishing has been great with large numbers of stocker trout and larger added to the lake recently. A 23-inch rainbow was caught the day before I checked out the lake.

The best bet for trout fishermen is to fish the south shore around the Saddle Trailhead using pink or orange Power Bait, salmon eggs or worms. Another good summertime trout area is along the west side and at North Pines. Boat fishermen have luck slow-trolling Dick Nites, Triple Teasers, Little Cleos and Fiord spoons or other small spoons or in-line spinners behind a short string of Pop Geer or flashers.

I make my own mini-troll pop gear and have had luck with them. I space three small Colorado blades along 16 inches of steel wire, add a bead in front and back of each spinner and add swivels to the ends. Make sure to use clamps and crimp them on the wire so that the spinner has an inch or so to move but also stay evenly dispersed along the line. A quick-change clevis will allow you to test out different pattern blades without making a new rig. The mini-troll works well trolling but are also castable, which gives bank fishermen the ability to add pop gear to their arsenal of fish catching equipment. I've had good luck with both the perch and rainbow trout pattern spinners.

Bass: Carter has some huge bass; some even say a possible state record. Try surface lures around structure near the deeper water, or toss plastic tubes or grubs in browns and greens in the trees. Park Ranger Sol Miller says that bass are generally in 20 feet or less, and if you go out 20 or 30 feet from shore you're already over 20 feet, so most bass are in close to shore.

Miller recommends fishing the trees and brush south of Dam 1 on the southeast side of the lake. Fishing the brush along the west shoreline from the south shore boat ramp to the North Pines boat ramp can also produce fish. You'll want to use a little heavier gear around the brush. I use 10-pound P-line on my spinning reels and 12- to 15-pound P-line on my baitcasters. I lost a Lucky Craft Pointer 78 a few weeks ago using 8-pound test mono, and while the lure is well worth it's upper end price, you don't want to lose too many.

Besides the added strength of the easy-to-manage fluorocarbon line, I like the no-stretch factor that adds to sensitivity and hook setting ability. If I'm throwing a crankbait or spinnerbait where I'm concerned about the initial strike, I'll lighten up on the drag a little to compensate for the no-stretch. If I'm fishing cover with plastics, I'll have a pretty tight drag (just under the breaking level) so I can set the hook and yank the fish out of cover.

Try topwater lures around structure for bass in low light periods. Try a Chug-Bug, Torpedo, Zara Spook or Zara Puppy, or a floating stickbait like the original Rapala or Thunder Stick. In each case, let the lure sit after it first hits the water at least until the ripples settle, then bring the bait forward a couple of feet and pause again. When using a floating stickbait, just twitch the bait while leaving it in place. If you don't get a strike, slowly bring the bait back in. Just before you lift the bait out of the water, pause again for a few seconds. Often a fish will follow your lure back in, and that final pause will trigger the strike. Remember not to set the hook until the lure is underwater or you feel fish.

If you're getting strikes but missing fish, you may be setting the hook too early. You also want to have a floating worm, tube or Senko on another rod to follow up if you miss a strike. Sometimes you'll locate the fish with the topwater, then catch the fish on your follow-up cast with the plastic.

Small, salted plastic tubes in greens and browns are also good bass baits at Carter. Toss them around structure and

AT a GLANCE

What: Casting for quality trout, bass and walleye all in one day at Carter Lake.

When: From now through Autumn.

Where: To get to the lake, take I-25 to the Berthoud exit (Highway 56). Travel west on Highway 56 through Berthoud. After Highwayl. 56 turns to the north, watch for CR 8E and take it west to CR 31. Follow CR 31 to the lake.

How: Troll Dick Nites behind pop gear for trout, worm harnesses for walleye and pitch green or brown tubes for bass.

Who: Carter Lake Visitor's Center (970-679-4570); Betty's Bait & Tackle (970-484-7459).

work them back to the boat with a slight jerking motion of your rod tip. This gives the lure that dying minnow appearance. I like to use a tube jig with the jig head inside of the tube. You can also rig the tube weedless-style by Texas rigging a 2/0 to 4/0 Octopus or G-Lock hook and crimping a split shot to the hook under and to the front of the tube.

Several companies make hooks especially made for this technique. After a few casts, the salt starts to wear off, so I like to add scent to my plastics. When I'm trying to imitate a crayfish I'll add crayfish odor, and when I'm trying to imitate a baitfish I'll add baitfish odor. I believe anytime that you're fishing slowly, scent is a good idea.

When fishing for bass, I recommend practicing catch and release. If you do want to keep a fish or two for supper, make sure they're over 15 inches, the limit at Carter.

Walleye: There are a lot of walleye in Carter. Ranger Miller says that most of the fish caught are 22 to 25 inches. In an attempt to increase natural reproduction of walleye in Carter Lake, a slot limit has been imposed. Only one walleye can be kept, and it must be between 16 and 18 inches. All other walleye must be released.

Trolling harnessed 'crawlers, minnows, leeches or Erie Dearies sweetened with a 'crawler along the southwest side of the lake gives you your best chance. I've had a lot of fun experimenting and making my own harnesses. When you catch a fish using a fly, harness, pop gear, etc., that you've made yourself, it adds something to the fishing experience.

Making worm harnesses is very easy but there are a few basics that you must follow.

• Don't skimp on terminal tackle. I'd rather have a $10 fishing pole than fish with a cheap, dull hook. Buy good quality Gamakatsu, Owner or Eagle Claw Laser Hooks and use good 10-pound fluorocarbon line.

• Colored hooks can make a difference. I mostly use red Octopus hooks, but orange or chartreuse hooks can also be effective at times.

• Add an eye to your rig. Tom "Doc" Johnson of Matzuo Lures taught me that a walleye targets the head of a fish. A glass bead in front of the spinner reflects light like a fish's eye and pres-

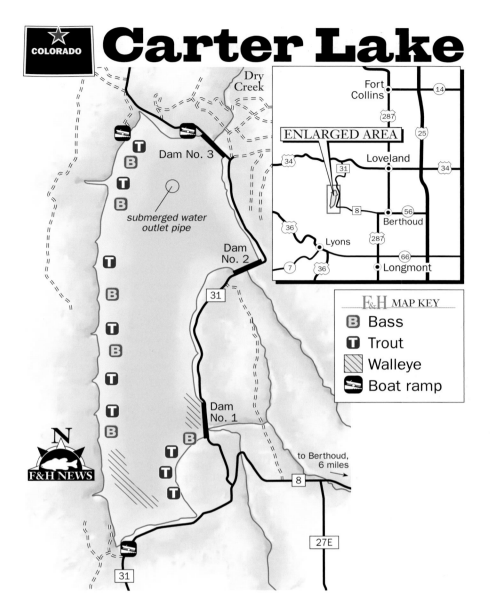

Carter Lake — COLORADO

Dry Creek
Dam No. 3
submerged water outlet pipe
Dam No. 2
31
Dam No. 1
to Berthoud, 6 miles
8
27E
31
N
F&H NEWS

ENLARGED AREA
Fort Collins
14
287
25
34
31
Loveland
34
8
56
36
Berthoud
Lyons
287
7
36
66
Longmont

F&H MAP KEY
B Bass
T Trout
▨ Walleye
🚤 Boat ramp

ents a target for fish. Johnson says that if you have an eye on your lure or spinner, you'll catch 85 percent of your fish on the front hook.

• Nose-hook your worm, minnow or leech. Whether fishing with one, two or three hooks, nose-hook your worm and let it trail flat in the water. Some anglers use a size 4 hook in front and a size 6 hook behind. I've experimented with different sizes and numbers of hooks, and I do OK with the larger No. 2 hooks.

• If fish are finicky, go simple. If you know you're trolling through fish but you're not getting bit, try to tone down your presentation. Sometimes just a red hook and red bead; chartreuse hook and chartreuse bead; or a hook and

piece of colored yarn (like a salmon rig) will get more action.

• Space your spinner. Make sure you use enough beads, floats, etc., that your spinner does not cover your hook. If your spinner is too close to the hook, you won't get a good hook-set.

Etc.: Carter Lake is owned and operated by Larimer County Parks, and the entrance fee on Monday through Thursday is $6 per vehicle and $6 per boat. On Friday, Saturday and Sunday ,the fee is $7 per vehicle and $6 per boat.

Editor's note: For more information, be sure to visit Mike Kennedy's Web site (www.coloradowarmwaterfishing.com)

F&H

April provides trout on ice or open water

GRANBY

by Mike Kennedy

MORNING'S THE TIME for Macks through the ice on Granby Lake. Terry Lane and Glen Straziar and their limit of lake trout from Granby. They caught their largest Mack — a 5-pounder — on a Storm Wild Eye Shad tipped with a piece of shiner meat.

For those of you that like to fish on hard water, April is about your last chance, except for those mountain lakes around 10,000 feet. Some lakes like Jefferson, Joe Wright, Big Creek, Chambers and others may still keep their lid into May, but you want to be very cautious. In April, even on our higher lakes, it's a good idea to fish in the mornings and get off the lake in the afternoons. On sunny days the thinner ice behind you, near shore, can weaken and cause problems getting off the ice.

Here are a few hard water and open water spots I recommend for April.

Best hard water trout

Lake John, in North Park near Walden, is one of my favorite hard water fishing locations. In mid-March the lake still had a lid of over 24 inches, and trout were cooperating for those willing to brave the snow and wind and who knew finesse ice fishing techniques.

Bill Willcox, owner and operator of the Lake John Resort said that anglers were bringing some nice rainbow "footballs" through the hole at Lake John. If you've never fished Lake John, you may not know what I'm talking about, but for some reason the fish are fatter there.

Willcox says that the morning bite is best, but some fish can be caught throughout the day. By the time this article hits the stands, the trout should be coming back up shallow — 6 to 8 feet or less. In late winter, with thick ice and heavy snow cover on this relatively shallow lake, oxygen can become thinner in the deeper water. The big fish will soon be moving to just off the shoreline.

Willcox also advises that instead of the subtle presentation that normally is best this time of year, don't be afraid to try aggressive jigging of a Kastmaster or Swedish Pimple. Some of the biggest fish caught in North Park at Cowdrey, Delaney Butte, and Lake John have been caught on spoons.

The best way to get to Lake John is to take Hwy. 9 (Exit 205 off I-70) to Kremmling. At Kremmling, turn west on U.S. 40 for 27 miles to Hwy 14. Continue east on Hwy. 14 for 33 miles to where 14 merges with CR125 then go north for ½-mile to CR 12W and follow the signs.

For more information on North Park fishing, contact Bill or Tish Willcox at the Lake John Resort (970-723-3226). It's a good idea to get a cabin or room right there at the resort and spend at least one night.

Granby Lake, in Middle Park just north of the town of Granby, is a late season favorite of many Colorado anglers.

I just today received an e-mail from longtime *F&H News* reader Glen Straziar who, along with his neighbor and fishing partner Terry Lane, caught 25 Mackinaw on a trip to Granby this week. Straziar's biggest Mack came in at 5 pounds and was caught on a Storm Wild Eye Shad tipped with a piece of shiner meat.

Straziar, who fishes Granby regularly, says that he's been having better luck on the shiner meat than with sucker meat. Many areas of the lake fish well this time of year. Other areas include Arapaho Bay, Dike 3 and the east side of Sunset Point. Straziar found his latest group of Macks stacked up on the 62-foot deep humps on the dam side of Deer Island.

Your best time of day, for both safety and fish bite, will be in the a.m. Make sure and be on the ice between 7 a.m. and noon. Macks are usually within 3 feet of the bottom when in water 50 feet deep or less, but out over the 60-foot-plus humps, fish were aggressively striking from 10 feet deep to the bottom. Watch your electronics and place your bait just over the fish.

Straziar likes to get his shiners from the tackle shop at 62nd and Wadsworth run by Brett Knight. If you're in the Granby area I recommend stopping in and seeing Richard or Margaret Crager, or Angie Kuczkowski at Budget Tackle 255 E. Agate (U.S. 40) in Granby, or give them a call at (970) 887-9344.

Best open water trout

Arvada Reservoir in the northwest Denver Metro area is a great place to fish in early spring. Arvada didn't open up until the first of April and the fish have been unpressured since last October.

Arvada Reservoir is owned by the city of Arvada and is restricted to bank fishing or hand propelled or electric boats only. No wading or belly boats are allowed. Rainbows in excess of 24 inches roam this relatively small 180-acre lake.

Trolling or casting spoons, spinners or small crankbaits can all be effective. I especially like to toss a Rapala Husky Jerk in the rainbow pattern. These baits work just about anytime, but they are especially good if you

---

AT a GLANCE

What: Pre and post ice-off at Lake John, Granby Lake, Arvada Reservoir and Jackson Lake.

How: Troll or cast spoons, spinners and jigs on open water and Kastmasters and Swedish Pimples on iced-over lakes.

Who: Arvada Ranger Station (303-420-7773), Jackson Lake State Park (970-645-2551), Granby: Budget Tackle (970-887-9344), Lake John Resort (970-723-3226).

Colorado trout fishing

toss them just after the DOW stocks a truckload of fingerling 'bows.

Fish the shallows; around the boat ramp; and, around the underwater humps in the southwest corner of the lake for your best early action. One of the nicest 'bows I've seen come out of the lake was a 24-inch hog caught by Boots Lewis on opening day a couple of seasons ago.

Arvada Reservoir is located 4 miles west of Ward Road on the north side of 64th Street. (64th turns into 66th street just before you get to the lake.) For more information, contact the park ranger station at (303) 420-7773 or call the Park Office at (720) 898-7400.

Jackson Lake, near Wiggins in northeast Colorado, opened to boating early this year and I've been getting good reports about the trout bite. One visitor to my Web site says that he's been getting good numbers of trout off the dam using Power Bait. Senior Park Ranger Brad Jackson tells me that the inlet canal on the southwest corner of the lake is the best area for trout in early spring, especially for bank fishermen.

The canal is only about a cast wide and you can only get a boat a little ways up into the canal. The rainbows will be in the canal until the water gets into the 55- to 60-degree range, then 'bows will move back into the main lake.

The deepest water in the lake is only about 24 feet and is located just in front of the white gatehouse on the dam that controls the irrigation gates. Jackson says that Power Bait and worms can work just about anywhere in the lake. Small spoons and spinners, such as Mepps, Kastmaster, Panther Martin or small crankbaits like Rapala Countdown or Jerk Baits in shad imitation 2½- to 3-inch size seem to work best in the canal. Forage in the lake is gizzard

shad, crawfish, and maybe some freshwater shrimp.

To get to Jackson Lake, take I-76 northeast to Exit 66 Hwy. 39. Turn north on Hwy. 39 for 7½ miles through Goodrich, then go west on Y5 (follow the paved road) for 2½ miles to the park. For more information, contact the park office at (970) 645-2551.

There are many other opportunities for spring trout in Colorado. Trout will be the most active species until waters warm to over 50 degrees. So while you're waiting for walleye to complete the spawn and for bass and wiper to wake up for the year, it might be worth your while to grab your ice rod, fly rod, or ultralight spinning rod and try for a Colorado rainbow trout. **F&H**

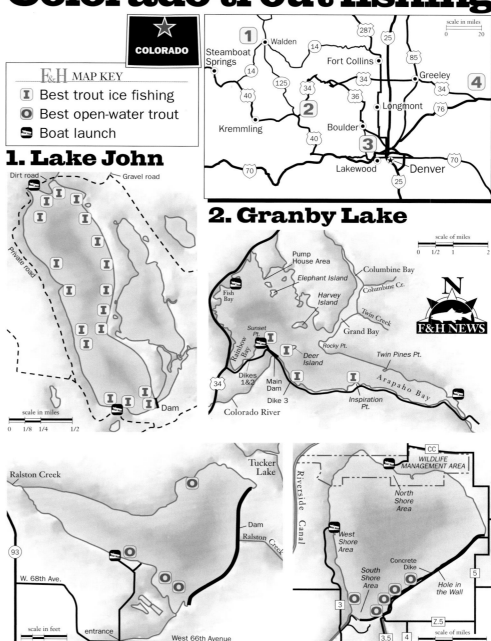

F&H MAP KEY
- **I** Best trout ice fishing
- **O** Best open-water trout
- **≈** Boat launch

1. Lake John

2. Granby Lake

3. Arvada Reservoir

4. Jackson Lake

Pike peaking at Elevenmile Reservoir

HARTSEL

by Jeremy Thruston

ake heed all ye who fish here — there be monsters in these waters. Brandishing mouths full of sharp teeth and stomachs that will digest most anything, they ply the waters of Elevenmile Reservoir in search of prey. Anyone who wants to hook one of these leviathans needs to make steel leaders and sure knots de rigueur.

Northern pike are the quarry and they grow to mythic proportions in the rich waters of Elevenmile.

"We had somebody bring in a 23½-pounder," says Eileen Collins, who owns the Eleven Mile Store (719-748-3424) with her husband Chuck "You don't get many chances to catch something that big outside of deep sea fishing."

Indeed, and if the trophy pike fishery isn't enough, the trout caught out of Elevenmile average 18 inches.

AT a GLANCE

What: Casting a variety of offerings at the monster pike that are all over Elevenmile Reservoir. There is also great trout and kokanee fishing.

Where: Elevenmile is an impoundment of the South Platte River south of Hartsel and west of Woodland Park. Concentrate on Stoll Mountain for pike. Hit Witcher's Cove for trout and kokanee. Elevenmile is about 115 miles southwest of Denver and accessible via Highway 24.

When: Action for pike picks up in late May and early June. Time to hit the water. Trout and kokanee started up when the ice came off and should remain good till late June.

How: Steel leaders are the key to the pike. They seem to bite anything, including flies. Trout and kokanee take the usual offerings.

Regs: The bag limit at Elevenmile is four trout, of which only two can measure more than 16 inches. No limit is set for pike.

Who: Eleven Mile Store (719-748-3424); Elevenmile State Park (719-748-3401).

Pike: Bait fishermen traditionally use 2- to 4-inch pieces of sucker to hook into pike. Spinnerbaits and other assorted hardware will also catch pike in good numbers. Fishermen have no way of telling just what a pike will decide looks good to eat. The 23½-pounder mentioned previously bit on green Power Bait.

"You should use steel leaders all of the time because you never know when a pike is going to bite," Collins says. Pike will tear regular monofilament line to shreds.

Pike fishing starts slowly right after ice-off, but picks up steam as time goes on. "They should start showing in greater numbers right around Memorial Day weekend," says Mark Young at Elevenmile State Park (719-748-3401). "It's really all dependent on the weather. If the weather stays cool the pike fishing might not pick up until the first week of June, but if it warms up early like last year, the pike fishing could get good during the third week of May."

Pike like to ambush their prey and their habitat reflects this tendency. They choose the very same weedy areas for feeding that smaller fish do for protection. Anglers should target these relatively shallow areas when going after northerns. In the early season fishermen can find the best fishing not at the crack of dawn, but during the hottest parts of the day.

"Stoll mountain on the north shore is very weedy and shallow, that's where they like to live," says Collins. "They really like the heat of the day."

If you like to eat pike, you're in luck. The Division of Fish and Wildlife has removed all limits on possession around the state. Fishers can keep as many pike as they please, although only so much can fit in a freezer.

Trout: Anglers have had no problem limiting out on trout during the early spring. Trout have a ravenous appetite after a long winter of meager pickings.

"People are throwing everything but the kitchen sink at them," says Young. "I tend to think that baits are better than lures at this time of year."

Dough baits in rainbow glitter, orange and green have provided consistent action. Nightcrawlers and salmon eggs will also catch their share of fish, although salmon eggs have been decidedly less popular now that the rainbow spawn is over.

In early May, Young says the fishing was better in Witches Cove and felt anglers would do well at Rogers Mountain, Rocking Chair and Rocky Flats. Fishing at Lazy Boy is fair and the trout fishing has yet to really pick up at Howbert Point and Stoll Mountain.

While major drawdowns at area reservoirs have really been tough on some of the fisheries, the fishing at Elevenmile has only improved. "It's fishing better with the low water," says Collins.

One doesn't have to look far for a reason. As reservoirs were lowered, the DOW captured some of the trout and moved them into other reservoirs. Elevenmile received a good number of these homeless fish. Young recalls watching more than 10,000 trout from Antero being released into Elevenmile.

"They came in all sizes," says Young. "There were hundreds of fish in the 18- to 20-inch range."

A definite pattern has developed for the trout fishing on the reservoir. Each year after ice-off the fishing will get real hot until around the second week of June, Young says. Then it slows down just slightly until July when there is a two- or three-week noticeable lull in catch rates. Inexplicably, fishing will pick up again right at the beginning of August, then taper off again until fall when the trout start putting on weight for the winter.

Kokanee: The kokanee fishing should be the best in several years if Young's predictions are correct.

"The salmon run on a four-year cycle and we should be seeing the end result of that this year," Young says. The reservoir didn't receive its normal share of kokanee for several years, but a healthy component of the population should be maturing this fall. The lack of a boat ramp has really constricted the amount of kokanee within reach of anglers. The one area putting out kokanee on a consistant basis is Witcher's Cove. The drop allows anglers to reach the deeper water that kokanee frequent.

Collins recommends Kastmasters in orange or blue-and-silver to pick up the kokes. Once the boat launch has opened, trolling traditional kokanee offerings like wedding rings will put fish in the boat.

Boats: The low water level on Elevenmile has put the main boat ramp out of commission. Anglers who wanted to get out on the water in the early season were restricted to hand launched boats. A temporary ramp should be in place by early May that will accommodate small to medium sized craft up to 21 feet, says Young. A permanent ramp is under construction and should be finished by May 30, although Young refuses to make any promises.

So get out on Elevenmile before the summer heat. This has become a primary fishing destination for Colorado anglers for a good reason. **F&H**

REGULAR READERS know that *F&H News* contributor Ed Marsh loves pike fishing. Well, if there was ever any doubt, here's the proof: An Elevenmile beauty.

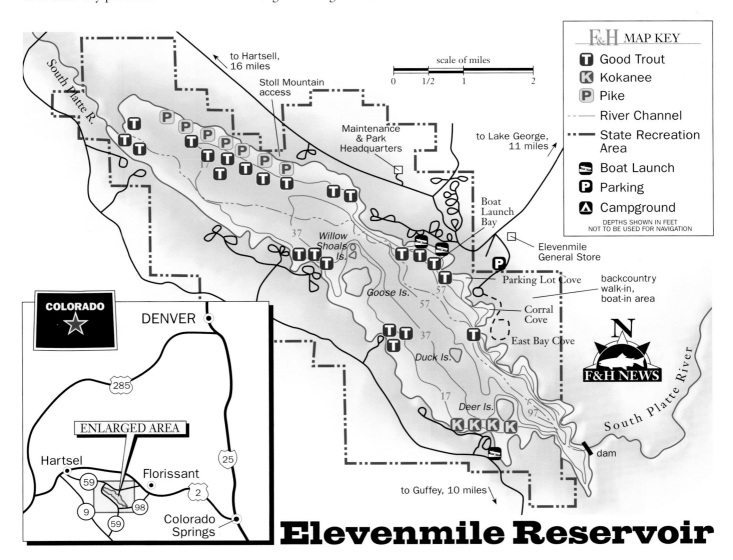

Elevenmile Reservoir

Bass, bluegill, crappie on tap at Frank Easement Ponds

WINDSOR

by Mike Kennedy

Two of the best warmwater ponds in the state are just a few miles north of Loveland at Windsor, says Brent Weaver, one of the managers of the Fishing Department at the Sportsman's Warehouse (720-858-1800) in Aurora.

There are two waters at Frank Easement Ponds,, a front pond and a back pond. Both have structure around the bank — trees, brush, concrete slabs, rock, etc. — and both have sand and gravel bars out in the lake that hold a lot of fish. You can reach many of the bars from shore, but would have access to more bars and the less pressured backsides of bars from a float tube or pontoon.

I wouldn't recommend trying to wade these ponds; there are too many deep holes. We did see one angler who was wading, but he was standing inside of his float tube. I guess his tube would carry him across the deeper water, but he could stand up when he got to the gravel bars and shallow flats. Using a float tube on these ponds is definitely safer than trying to wade.

This would be a great place to take young anglers or anyone who wants to make sure they catch something. There are so many fish in these ponds and the locations are so predictable that I think you'd have to really try hard to not catch something. The key seemed to be using small lures or flies and not fishing too fast.

Bass: John Grimland of Loveland and I were catching both bass and bluegill on topwaters such as Heddon Torpedos and also on tiny spinners, Senkos and just about everything we threw at them. Most of the fish we caught were small, with bass from 10 to 12 inches. a couple near the 15-inch mark. Bluegill were usually 6 or 8 inches, but there were a lot of fish and they were fun to catch.

I'd met Grimland earlier in the morning at the Big Thompson Ponds in Loveland, and we didn't get to the Frank Ponds until nearly midday. Even in the heat of the day we were able to catch a lot of fish using small baits.

The gravel bar out from the south shore held a lot of fish. Running a tiny green Torpedo over the ends of the bar or in the northeast cove was very effective for bass. Casting tiny ⅛-ounce spinners off the sides of the bar also caught fish. Throwing 4-

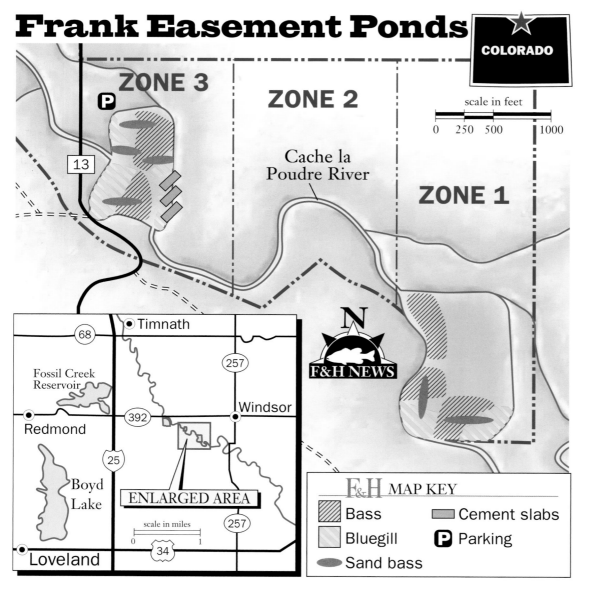

Frank Easement Ponds

COLORADO

ZONE 3

ZONE 2

ZONE 1

scale in feet
0   250   500   1000

Cache la Poudre River

13

P

N

F&H NEWS

Timnath

68

257

Fossil Creek Reservoir

392

Windsor

Redmond

25

Boyd Lake

ENLARGED AREA

257

scale in miles
0   1

34

Loveland

F&H MAP KEY

Bass   Cement slabs

Bluegill   P Parking

Sand bass

inch green or 3-inch chartreuse Senkos off the edge of the concrete slabs at the east side of the front pond or off the sides of the gravel bar dividing the front pond into two sections was also very effective for both bass and bluegill.

I caught fish both with Texas rigged and Wacky rigged Senkos. These ponds are warmer than many Colorado ponds because they're shallow. The ponds only have warmwater fish like spotted and largemouth bass, crappie, bluegill and perhaps catfish. There's no trout in these ponds, so leave your Power Bait at home.

I was surprised to find scrappy spotted bass in these ponds. A spotted bass fights like a smallmouth, but looks like a largemouth. You can tell a spotted bass because even though it has the black line down the side like a largemouth, their mouth is small like a smallmouth. They also have tiny teeth on their bottom lip that won't hurt you, but you can feel them when you thumb the fish.

Bluegill: I saw some huge bluegill and crappie myself when I spent a few hours at the Ponds recently. As I parked my car in the parking area, Jacob Valasek of Fort Collins was just returning to his car with a stringer of bluegill and crappie. One of the bluegill was just over 10 inches, which can earn Valasek a Master Angler award. Both crappie and bluegill were caught on dry flies and a clear casting bubble. These were some of the biggest bluegill I've seen in Colorado. There are also zillions of smaller bluegill.

I'm sure live bait would also be effective. I didn't have any flies or bait with me the day I was there. If you're going after bluegill or crappie with a worm, use a small hook and just a small piece of a nightcrawler, or the panfish will

rob you and drive you nuts. If you're missing hits, put on smaller bait.

I caught most of my bluegill off the sandbars on the back pond. Casting the 3-inch chartreuse Senko right at the edge of the bar and letting it fall off the side got a bite about every other time. I must have caught 30 or 40 fish off the only two 3-inch Senkos I brought with me. When my last one wore out I broke it in half and started catching bluegill on just a 1½-inch piece.

To get to the Frank Easement Ponds from Denver, go north on I-25 to Colorado 392, Windsor, exit 262. Head east on Highway 392 to County Line Road at the stoplight at the bottom of the hill. Turn south, go just a ½-mile to the parking lot. To get to the Big Thompson Ponds take exit 255 off I-25, Colorado 402, get on the frontage road east of I-25 and head north about a ½-mile to the underpass. Go west through the tunnel and turn right at the end of the tunnel. Continue down the gravel road ¼-mile to the ponds.

Big Thompson Ponds: Another good place to fish in the area is the Big Thompson Ponds just south of Windsor at Loveland. Some anglers fish for catfish in the first pond, but you're better off to pass by the first two ponds and park where the road stops at the second pond. Then walk back and fish the third and fourth ponds.

Grimland and I had luck on the shallower and warmer third pond fishing from the southeast shore with Torpedos, spinners and Senkos. We'd

IT'S SIMPLE FISHING for bass, bluegill and crappie at the Frank Easement ponds. Jacob Valasek of Fort Collins shows off a stringer that includes a 10-inch bluegill.

cast right along the side of structure like reeds, cattails and brush. Watch your line closely, especially with Senkos, as bites can be tough to detect.

This was the first time Grimland had ever used topwaters, but I'm sure it won't be the last. There's something about seeing fish come up and take your lure. One thing you do have to learn when fishing topwaters is to not set the hook too fast. Often the fish will swirl near your bait, or even hit it before it actually bites the lure. Some believe that the bass is trying to injure or stun the fish by ramming into it before they try to eat it. In any event, make sure you feel the fish before you set the hook.   *F&H*

AT a GLANCE

What: Taking advantage of fast bass and bluegill action at the Frank Easement Ponds in Windsor.

Where: The ponds aren't difficult to fish. Structure is obvious. You can even fish the sandbars from shore. Both the Easement Ponds and Big Thompson Ponds aren't too far from Denver and just a few miles from I-25.

When: With the water getting well into the 60s, you'll do well chasing postspawn bass. Bluegill are incredibly active. And both should continue to bite into fall.

How: Flies are really a great bet for bluegill. But you'll catch them on crankbaits, Senkos and any other bass offerings. Bass will bite a lot of things with crankbaits, Senkos and spinners at the top

of the list. You'll have a lot of fun fishing topwaters early and late in the day as well.

Regs: The Easement Ponds are hand-launch only, and you can make no wake. If you want to get out on the water, you'll need to take a float tube or pontoon boat.

Who: Sportsman's Warehouse (720-858-1800), Alkire's Sporting Goods (970-352-9501).

Five Front Range walleye hot spots

by Mike Kennedy

In just a quick survey of my fishing records, I found at least 30 locations in eastern Colorado that have walleye. There are probably many more than that. There are at least 10 walleye waters on the Front Range alone. Some Front Range walleye hot spots include Aurora, Boyd, Chatfield, Cherry Creek and Horsetooth.

Aurora Reservoir: Located 2½ miles east of E-470 on Quincy Avenue. Aurora Reservoir is a quiet place to fish for walleye. The reservoir is restricted to manual, wind, or electric propelled vessels only. It's good to have at least two batteries with you just in case you run into a lot of wind. I use both a transom mount and bow mount trolling motor. The transom mount helps in loading and unloading the boat and can be used in addition to the bow mount to bring the craft back home in windy weather.

Drifting with a worm or minnow harnesses or slow-trolling a spoon, shallow running crankbait or jerkbait early or late in the day can be effective. Vertical jigging, using a worm harness, or trolling deep running crankbaits during the middle of the day also works well.

To get your worm rig or crankbaits down deep use a bottom bouncer, clip-on weights or leadcore line. Fish along the flat between Marina and Senac coves or along the points from Lonetree Cove to the Scuba Area. Walleye must be 18 inches, and they will check you.

For more information, contact the park office at (303) 690-1286

Boyd Reservoir: Located near Loveland off US 34 (exit 257 on I-25). Boyd State Park runs along the west side of Boyd Reservoir. The rest of the land around the lake is privately owned. You must have a Colorado State Parks pass to enter through the state park.

Use jig and minnow, a minnow under a slip bobber, or a slowly worked jerkbait early in the season. Troll or drift worm harnesses or crankbaits in the lower end of the lake near the riprap at the dam and off points as the water warms. The points along the east shore often hold walleye. Trolling jointed Rapala Shad Raps or other minnow baits in the perch, crawdad or shad patterns can be effective. When trolling over shallow flats you may want to use planer boards to get your lures out away from the path of the boat where

HEAD TO THE FRONT RANGE to catch walleye like this 9-pounder Tom Zacchini of Aurora caught at Horsetooth Reservoir last spring.

fish might be spooked. Walleye at Boyd need only be 15 inches to be legal.

For more information, call the park visitor center at (970) 669-1739.

Chatfield Reservoir: Located in Littleton in the southwest Denver Metro area on Wadsworth about a mile south of C-470. Chatfield is in Chatfield State Park and requires a State Parks Pass. Chatfield is one of, if not the best, walleye lake in the state. It sees a great deal of fishing pressure, but savvy anglers can still catch a lot of nice fish. The key is adjusting to more subtle techniques.

The use of planer boards, long-line trolling, zigzag trolling, slow drifting with drift socks or vertical jigging can all produce at times. Your trolling motor can spook fish on a highly pressured body of water, so try to drift if possible until you locate fish then anchor.

Chatfield is a place where the wind can really improve the bite. The wind can make it hard on the fishermen, but if you learn to control your boat by the use of anchors or drift socks to stop or slow down the drift you have a chance for some good fishing. Fishing over midlake humps out from the boat ramp and near the midlake buoys can be very effective.

Perch and shad-colored baits or minnow or worm harnesses work best. A curly tail grub tipped with a half a night-crawler slowly jigged within 6 inches of the bottom on midlake humps is hard to beat. The slower you fish, the more important live bait or scent on your lure will be.

For more information, call the park office at (303) 791-7275.

Cherry Creek Reservoir: Located about 1 mile south of I-225 on Parker Road in Cherry Creek State Park. Cherry Creek is relatively shallow and only 880 acres.

This lake is also highly pressured but the water is not as clear as other metro lakes. You still need to use subtle techniques such as drifting, still fishing, vertical jigging or use live bait under a slip bobber. When using a slip bobber, remember not to set the hook as soon as the bobber goes down. You need to quickly take up slack until you feel the fish, then set the hook. In low-light periods fishing along the dam can be effective. Often trollers miss out on many shallow fish that can be caught casting in the 3 to 8 foot range.

Use at least 10-pound test; I lost a couple Lucky Craft Pointer 78s up shallow where I couldn't go get them before I learned to go to heavier line. You can also use LureSaver Split Rings that flex open similar to you unfolding your arms to release the hook before your line breaks. With this product you will get your lure back and the LureSaver and only be missing the hook. Much cheaper than buying a new lure.

For more information on Cherry Creek, call the park office at (303) 699-3860.

Horsetooth Reservoir: Located west of Fort Collins. Take I-25 to the Harmony Road exit. Turn west on Harmony Road to Taft Hill Road and continue for about 1 mile to CR 38E and follow the signs to the lake.

Horsetooth is in a Larimer County Park and requires a $6 per day car pass and $6 per day boat pass. Fees are $7 each on Friday, Saturday and Sunday during open water season.

Troll shallow running shad-imitation crankbaits along the face of the dam early, late or on cloudy days. Also fish along the rocky shore on the east side from the second dam north to the main Horsetooth Dam. Trolling a curly tail grub tipped with a half a 'crawler or casting curly tail grubs or jerkbaits can be effective. When fishing deep you can use leadcore line, bottom bouncer or Lindy Rig. A Lindy Rig is a boot-shaped weight that slides up and down your line ahead of your swivel and has a flat bottom that is less prone to hanging up. I like to use a sinker slider, which is a plastic tube with a snap on the bottom that also slides up and down your line. When using a sinker slider, you can change the size and style of your weight without cutting your line. My fishing partner, and long-time trolling expert, Ray Romberger taught me to use this device a couple of years ago and it really makes changing weights and depths easier.

For more information on Horsetooth, call the park office at (970) 679-4554.

F&H

AT a GLANCE

What: Spring walleye options in Colorado.

When: As soon as the water warms enough for the fish to become active, usually in early April.

Who: State Parks: Aurora Reservoir (303-690-1286), Boyd Reservoir (970-669-1739), Chatfield Reservoir (303-791-7275), Cherry Creek Reservoir (303-699-3860), Horsetooth Reservoir (970-679-4554).

1. Horsetooth Reservoir

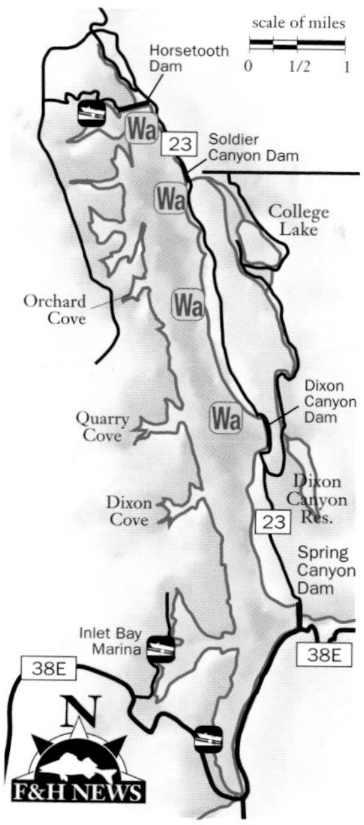

2. Boyd Lake

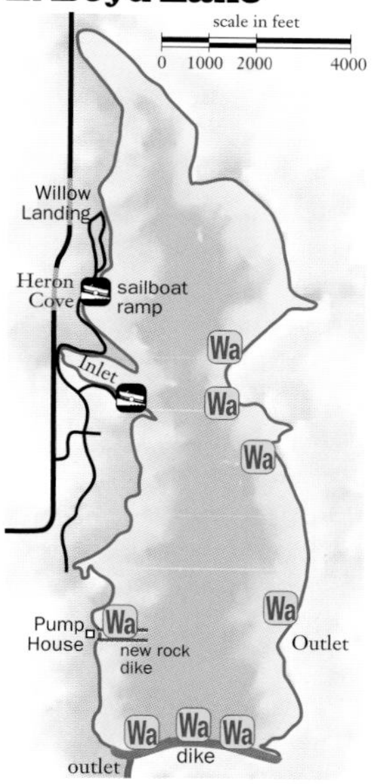

3. Chatfield Reservoir

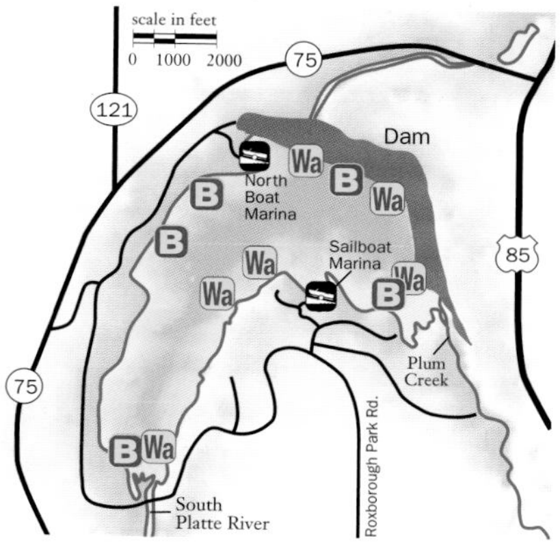

4. Cherry Creek Reservoir

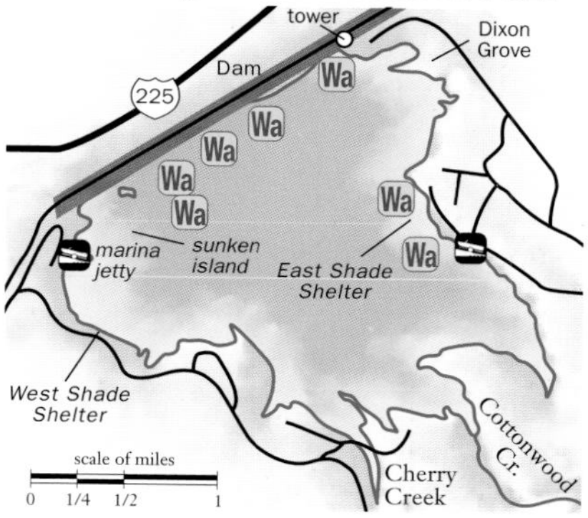

5. Aurora Reservoir

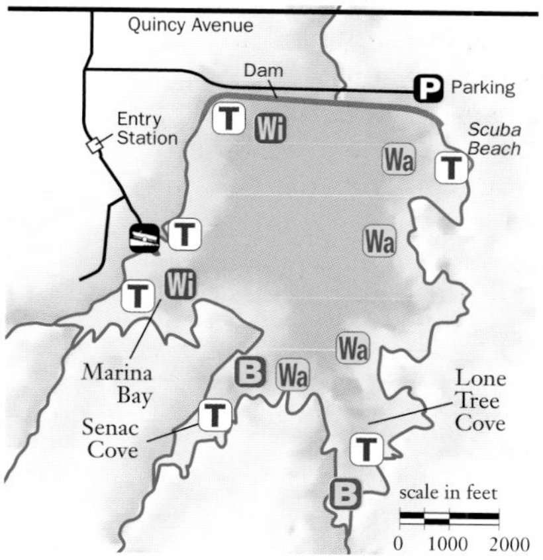

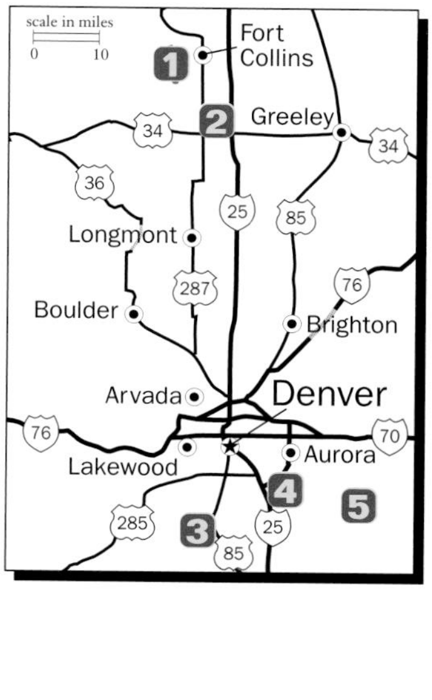

F&H MAP KEY

- **B** Bass
- **Wa** Walleye
- **T** Trout
- **Wi** Wiper
- Boat launch

Front Range

Horseshoe Reservoir muskie: 50-inch fish possible

WALSENBURG

by James Smith

Ken Karbon, former president of the Colorado Chapter of Muskies, Inc., is one of a few very good muskie fishermen in Colorado. He and other members of the Colorado chapter consider 160-acre Horseshoe Reservoir one of the top two muskie reservoirs in Colorado, along with Big Creek Lake near Cowdrey.

Why is Horseshoe considered one of the top two? To date, there have been 31,525 hybrid tiger muskie stocked in Horseshoe Reservoir. The first stocking occurred in 1986. The Colorado Division of Wildlife considers a normal stocking rate to be approximately five fish per acre. Some years Horseshoe has been stocked with 10 muskie per acre, and other years they've stocked 20 muskie per acre. In other words, the DOW has been stocking Horseshoe with more than twice their normal muskie stocking rate. This will promote an excellent number of muskie in this reservoir. In addition, any reservoir that has been stocked for six or more years has the potential of holding 50-inch muskie. Any 50-inch fish will get my attention, and a bunch of them is even better.

The DOW has had a philosophy of

KEN KARBON with a nice muskie he pulled from Horseshoe Reservoir. Horseshoe's been stocked with muskie for nearly ten years, and have had a chance to grow to truly trophy proportions.

AT a GLANCE

What: One of the top two places to catch big muskie in Colorado.

When: From now through autumn at dawn and dusk.

How: Throw natural-colored Buchertails. Shallowraiders and 9- to 12-inch jerkbaits in bays and on humps in 5 feet of water or less.

Where: Go south on I-25 to Walsenburg and take Highway 160 west for 3 miles to the park entrance.

Contacts: Lathrop State Park (719-738-2376) or Erin Jerant, owner of the Hollowpoint Gun Shop (719-738-3426) in Walsenburg. Hollowpoint is 2 miles east of Lathrop and carries bait and equipment.

using the tiger muskie as a "control" fish. Many of the reservoirs where they've stocked muskie have been over populated with suckers. With the introduction of muskie, the sucker population is reduced considerably. Reducing the biomass of suckers in a reservoir leaves more food and less competition from the suckers, thus allowing other sport fish to grow and prosper. It's not just the muskie that benefits, all species do.

In addition, the muskie create a sport fishery with few equals. They call this "the fish of 10,000 casts." But once you hook one, you'll know why you made casts No. 1 to 9,999. Further, you'll become so caught up in the excitement and thrill of catching this awesome fish that I'm sure you'll become afflicted with that phenomenon called "muskie fever."

The basics: Horseshoe Reservoir is located just west of Walsenburg on Highway 160 at Lathrop State Park. The reservoir has a wonderful concrete boat ramp on the north end, great campgrounds and muskie. I would suggest fishing here in the spring and late fall. The weather gets very hot beginning in June and throughout the summer.

Horseshoe has been designed for fishing, with five fishing piers along the dam. In addition, the entire reservoir is a no-wake zone, so it encourages fish-

ing. The adjacent reservoir, Martin, sees more of the water-skiing crowd.

There are several good bays in Horseshoe. There is a great hump in the middle; it's not hard to find. It's right between the rock and the northernmost pier. Although I've never raised a fish there, I have seen some nice muskie holding on that structure. The park rangers tell us a number of muskie are being caught on the north side of the island. I did pick one up on the northeast corner of the island, but again, I would direct you to what I consider the more likely spots.

Most of my bigger fish have been seen at the ends of the fishing piers and in the bays on the west side. I wouldn't spend any time in the south third of this reservoir, from the rock south. I've never seen any muskie in that area.

This is a nice, clear lake, so my suggestion is to throw natural colors and patterns. Some good choices might be Buchertails, Shallow Raiders, Baby Depth Raiders or the new Mepps Maribou Tails. Anything in the prism/holoforms finish will do the trick. Smaller and jointed lures work best in the spring and early summer. By late summer and early fall I would recommend larger (9- to 12-inch) jerkbaits like the Suicks. I suggest shallow running lures because most of your muskie will be caught in less than 5 feet of water.

This is a perch- and trout-based system, so I suggest darker colors, like browns and greens with yellow accents. Black-and-yellow is also good.

The best times to fish Horseshoe are going to be in the early morning (before 9 a.m.) and later in the evening (after 5 p.m.). This will keep you out of the heat of the day, and you'll appreciate that. In the early evenings you may be lucky enough to see some muskie "porpoising" along the surface. I've never heard of a muskie hitting a lure at this time, but Lord knows plenty have been thrown at them. The best thing I can suggest is to mark their location and return at another time.

The park has a visitor center run by Park Manager John Brandstatter. He does a great job managing these parks, and generally has muskie information available at the visitor center. In the summer he offers a variety of seminars in the campground in the evenings. Check the schedules.

As I said earlier, Horseshoe Reservoir has the potential for very large fish. I'm talking whoppers in the 50-inch range. I haven't heard of any fish from there over about 46 inches, but that doesn't mean they don't exist. Ken Karbon is pretty proud of his 43-inch Horseshoe muskie.

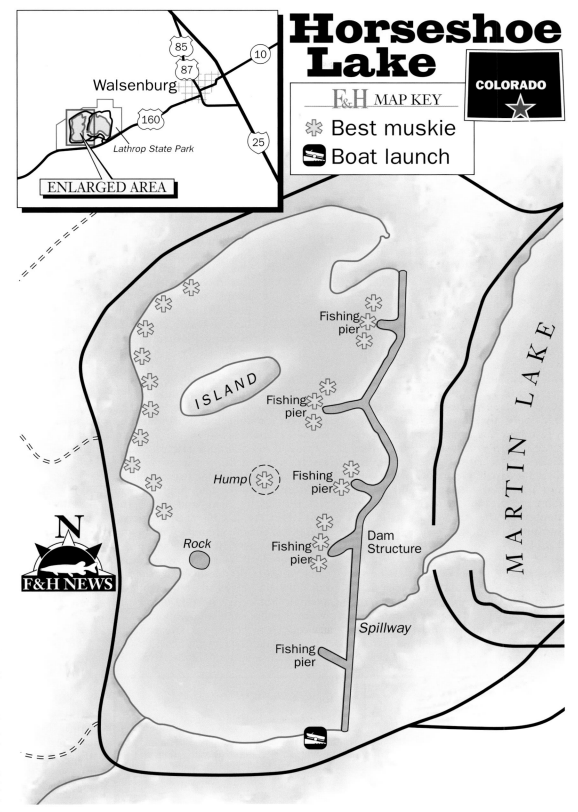

Horseshoe Lake

F&H MAP KEY

❄ Best muskie
🚤 Boat launch

COLORADO ★

Walsenburg

Lathrop State Park

ENLARGED AREA

ISLAND

Fishing pier

Fishing pier

Hump

Fishing pier

Rock

Fishing pier

Dam Structure

Spillway

Fishing pier

MARTIN LAKE

N

F&H NEWS

In recent years muskie have taken the country by storm. Today 37 of the lower 48 states have muskie programs. For additional information, check out the Muskies, Inc. Web site (*www.muskiesinc.org*). **F&H**

Hit full North Sterling for walleye, wipers, crappie

STERLING

by Mike Kennedy

JEFF HESTER shows two walleye like the ones you can find at North Sterling Reservoir, where you can also find crappie and wipers.

North Sterling Reservoir is 100 percent full and the water is warming, according to Park Tourist Assistant Irene Gomez. Gomez says that wipers are being caught at the inlet, crappie and rainbow are being caught off the dam and catfish are starting to be caught on cut bait near the inlet.

Walleye fishing was a little slow in late March but should really start picking up the end of April and through the month of May. One of the reasons that early walleye numbers may be down is that there have not been very many boats on the lake so far this year,

according to Gomez. North Sterling has a lot of walleye and while you don't hear about a lot of huge hogs coming out of there, it's a good place to fish if you just want a couple walleye for supper. While you might have a better chance of catching a larger walleye at Chatfield, Horsetooth, Cherry Creek or Pueblo reservoirs, you're more apt to catch supper at North Sterling. The size limit for walleye at North Sterling in only 15 inches.

I've had my best luck catching walleye by slowly drifting a worm harness along the bottom off the main points at the deep end of the Cunningham Arm and the Darby Arm, and along the dam. Also try fishing around Goose Island and off the secondary points up the Darby and Cunningham arms. I make my own worm harnesses and used to use a double-hook worm rig, but in recent years I've gone mainly to a single-hook rig, nose-hooking the worm. I believe the single hook allows the crawler to flow more naturally.

If you make the worm harness, use a glass bead, a spinner blade, five col-

ored beads and then a single No. 4 red hook. Place five small colored beads in front of the hook, to assure that the spinner blade doesn't hide the hook while it's spinning and interfere with hooking the fish. In front of the blade put a glass bead that will resemble a fish eye. Walleye normally target the eye of their prey because they want to eat them headfirst. If you're fishing murky water or fishing deep, an orange or fire tiger blade might work best as walleye see orange better than any other color. If you're fishing clear water, more natural color blades such as perch or rainbow trout often work best.

Trolling stickbaits — like Rapala Husky Jerks, Lucky Craft Staysee 95s, Smithwick Rogues, Walleye Divers or Storm Thunder Sticks — or drifting a shiner under a slip bobber can be effective. There are no restrictions at the dam or riprap at North Sterling, but more walleye are taken on the main lake points and up the two arms of the lake than at the dam. Casting near rocky shores or trolling shallow-running crankbaits behind a planer board is effective during low light periods. During the day, when fish are deeper, switch to a bottom-bouncer, sinker slider or Lindy Rig and troll a worm, minnow or leech harness in the same general areas but in deeper water. Start trolling minnows when the water is still below 50 degrees, then switch to worms and minnows and only go to leeches later in the year.

Many anglers are not familiar with a sinker slider. It's a small plastic tube with a snap on the side. Your line goes through the tube, you add a bead to keep the tube from crawling up onto your swivel, then add the swivel and worm, minnow or leech harness. You can put any size weight on the sinker slider and change weights without cutting your line. Also, it's not fixed like a bottom-bouncer, so the fish feels less resistance. One caution: If you use Fire Line or any line with a coating, keep an eye on the line just above your swivel because the sliding back and forth of the sinker slider will wear off the coating and weaken your line after a while.

AT a GLANCE

What: Aggressive wiper, supper size walleye and crappie at North Sterling Reservoir.

Where: Fish for wiper at the inlet in the southeast corner of the lake and other areas that warm first in the early spring. More walleye are taken on the main lake points and up the two arms of the lake than at the dam. Look for crappie off the dam and in Marina Cove.

Who: Bayside Marina (970-522-1511), Park Office (970-522-3657).

Directions: To get to North Sterling, take I-76 northeast to Sterling, exit 125. Go over the bridge into town and continue on Chestnut Street/US Highway 6 a few blocks and jog left onto Platte Street. Go two blocks to N. 7th Avenue, County Road 39. Turn right and go 12 miles to the reservoir.

Leadcore line is another way to get your lure down low. I use a Penn 209 that just barely holds 100 yards of 18-pound leadcore. The leadcore will track more directly behind your boat if you're fishing a zigzag pattern or following a break line than monofilament lines will. If wind will allow you to drift very slowly or you want to fish a likely point, you might try a variation of the Carolina Rig. Instead of using a plastic worm or grub as bait, use a live nightcrawler and inject it with air so that it will float. It can be deadly even when fish are inactive.

Remember, when walleye aren't aggressive and you feel a light tap, you need to give them some line, and time to fully take the bait before you set the hook. If you're using a spinning reel, hold your finger on the line with the bail open. When you feel the fish release some line, lower your rod tip, close the bait, and when the slack is out of the line, set the hook.

Crappie fishing should be good this year. Gomez says that the DOW recently stocked an additional 50,000 crappie into the lake. Fishermen are already picking up crappie off the dam and in Marina Cove on crappie jigs or minnows.

Crappie fishing should really heat up as fish move into the shallows to spawn as the waters get closer to 60 degrees. If you want to use minnows, bring them with you. In prior years the Bay Side Marina (970-522-1511) at North Sterling only carried shiners. They will be open weekends until Memorial Day, then open full-time until fall.

Wipers are my personal favorite at North Sterling. They're one of the hardest fighting fish in the state. Some wipers are being caught now in the inlet area, but the most active wiper fishing will be in May and June. A couple of years ago there was a big shad kill-off at North Sterling due to a harsh winter, but the million or so shad that were stocked into the lake after that seem to have fared well this winter. That means that the wipers should be fat and active.

You can troll for wiper with worm or minnow harnesses or crankbaits, but always have a pole with a topwater or shallow-running bait on in case you see the wiper boiling to the surface chasing shad.

North Sterling Reservoir

COLORADO

Fish for wipers at the inlet in the southeast corner of the lake and other areas that warm first in the early spring. Warmer water will attract baitfish, which will attract the wiper. Try shad-imitation crankbaits and minnow rigs. Blue-back Rat-L-Traps get good results. Topwater lures such as Zara Spooks and Zara Puppys are effective when the wipers are chasing shad to the surface. Silver Kastmaster spoons and white or shad-color plastics can also produce.

Don't be afraid to use live bait either. Nightcrawlers, cutbait, crawdad tails, shrimp or minnows have produced nice fish. Drifting live bait can be a good way to locate schools, but then switching to lures may produce more fish. When you've found a school you want to be able to cast a long distance so you don't come right up on and spook them.

Catfish can be found near the inlet in early spring, but the best locations most of the year are near the west trailhead in the upper end of the Cunningham Arm. Use heavy gear and cutbait, stinkbait or chicken or turkey liver for best results.

To get to North Sterling Reservoir, take I-76 north to Sterling, exit 125. Go over the bridge into town and continue on Chestnut Street (US Highway 6) for a few blocks. Take a left-hand turn onto Platte Street. Go 2 blocks, turn right onto North 3rd Avenue and go 4 blocks to Broadway. Turn left and go 4 blocks to N. 7th Avenue (County Road 39.). Turn right and go 12 miles to the reservoir. Watch for signs.

For more information on North Sterling contact the Park Office at (970) 522-3657. **F&H**

South Platte sees annual migration of German browns

HARTSEL

by Steve Nelson

very fall, large German brown trout in Antero, Elevenmile and Spinney Mountain reservoirs are compelled to leave their deep-water sanctuaries and swim upstream to spawn. It's during this annual migration that they are most vulnerable to fishermen. The browns begin to move into the river in mid-September, and they will continue to run upstream well into November. The trick for fishermen is to be there when they are moving through — a feat that's easier said than done.

"I'm already hearing reports of browns moving up into the Middle Fork from Spinney," says DOW biologist Greg Gerlich (303-297-1192). "Several anglers have reported browns in the 20- to 23-inch range on the Tomahawk SWA, but we really don't start seeing them in higher numbers until the end of the month."

Brown trout in all three reservoir can run large. Twenty-inch-plus fish

ERIC JOHNSON of Colorado Springs shows off a beautiful South Platte River brown trout.

AT A GLANCE

Location: South Park between Elevenmile Reservoir and Spinney Mountain Reservoir; above Spinney Mountain Reservoir to the confluence of the South Fork and Middle Fork; and the South Fork above Antero Reservoir.

Species: German brown trout, some rainbows and cutthroat.

Timing: The brown trout run has already started and should continue through October — which has the best fishing — into early November.

Regulations: The South Platte River has many and complicated regulations. Study them carefully before going.

Facilities: Camping is available at Elevenmile State Park and at Chaparral Park General Store. There are restaurants and motels in Lake George and Florissant.

For information: Contact the Chaparral Park General Store (719-836-0308).

are common, and it's not unusual to see 4- to 7-pounders landed. And every season a few lucky anglers get into a 10-pounder. The chance to do battle with one of those truly trophy fish is one reason why many anglers make this their must-fish trip of the year.

Where to go: The South Platte River drainage is one of the most heavily regulated waters in the state. It also has a great deal of public access through state wildlife areas and fishing easements. They are listed in the 2001 Fishing Regulations and Wildlife Property Directory available at DOW offices and most sporting goods stores.

There are several key places to fish: the river between Elevenmile and Spinney Mountain Reservoir, which has a mix of resident rainbows and browns; the river above Spinney Mountain Reservoir to the forks, the South Fork and Middle Fork; and the South Fork above Antero Reservoir. The Middle Fork has the best spawning habitat and typically holds more browns, and it has excellent public access here.

But with all that public access, you can expect plenty of company. Your best bet would be to fish during the week if possible or be on the water at first light and again at dusk. Those

early and late hours often produce the most action, as browns are very active in the dark.

When and how: "By the end of November most of the run is over," says Gerlich. "I've seen times on the South Fork when it's been fishable in early December, (with) guys in there nymphing. But I didn't see any spawning activity then."

So the window of opportunity is wide open and will stay that way for at least another 6 weeks, maybe longer. But since you can't predict exactly when those fish will be moving — and a lot of them do their traveling at night — you have to take your chances.

Bob Hix at All Pro Fish-N-Sport (303-795-3474) is an expert brown trout hunter with many years of experience fishing these waters. His advice is worth heeding.

• If you're there on a bright and sunny day, your chances are not good unless you fish at the crack of dawn or after the sun goes down. Ideal conditions for brown trout are an overcast day, with some wind and hopefully some rain or snow. Hix says his best day ever on the South Platte was during a snowstorm and the browns were hitting everything he threw at them.

• When the water is low and clear, the trout can see you as easily as you can see them. This calls for a stealthy approach. Some anglers crouch down or go as far as to crawl carefully down to the river's edge keeping a very low profile. The clothes you wear can make you blend in or stand out. Wear light, muted earth-toned colors. Don't wear bright colors or bright jewelry. Some anglers even remove their wristwatches.

• First you have to spot a fish, then get yourself into position so you can cast to it. The trout may take it on your first cast, or it may simply ignore it. If he ignores your fly, give him something new to look at.

• Come often and cover a lot of water. Successful brown trout anglers are on the river at least once a week through October. Keep moving, don't stand in one spot. You have to actively search out and locate those bigger browns. Be stealthy.

Tackle: The majority of fishermen who come to the South Platte after these browns are fly fishermen. Ideally, you need a 7- or 8-weight outfit, and don't go any lighter than a 3X tippet. If you go lighter, chances are you'll be broken off or you'll have to play the fish to exhaustion before landing it. Hix prefers to fish large streamers like a Zonker, Twentyincher, Halfback or a Woolly Bugger in sizes 2 to 6. If those aren't working, he suggests a Grizzly Shrimp or an egg pattern. If all else fails, it's time to go with a San Juan Worm or Bob Good's Colorado Caddis.

Go big, black and ugly is Giles Alkire's of Alkire's Sporting Goods (970-352-9501) advice, and he's an old brown trout hunter from way back. He also favors Halfbacks and stoneflies when fishing for browns.

Spin fishermen can also get into the browns, though it is a little tougher. "I haven't had a lot of success on those bigger browns with spinning tackle," says Gerlich. "You usually only get one shot at them. My recommendation is a spinner, and go small, like a No. 1 or a 0. Use the tiny stuff and cast upstream so the current brings it down through the runs. I would also suggest fishing a Marabou jig, just bouncing it along the bottom. I've seen browns come flashing out from the bank to hit those. You might even try a tube jig."

Care and handling: When you do hook a fish, bring it in as quickly and carefully as possible, then handle it gently when you release it. "Minimize your handling of the fish, release it quickly, and don't walk on the redds," says Gerlich. ***F&H***

South Platte Browns

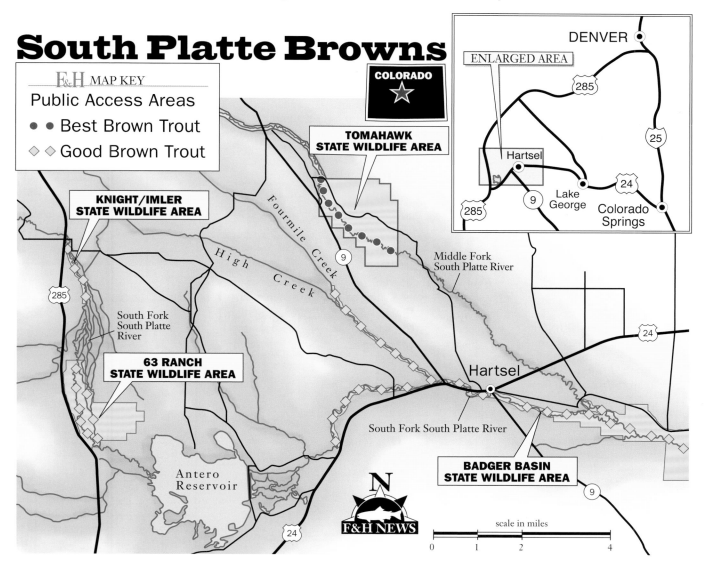

F&H MAP KEY

Public Access Areas
● ● Best Brown Trout
◇ ◇ Good Brown Trout

COLORADO ★

DENVER

ENLARGED AREA

285

25

Hartsel

285 9 Lake George 24 Colorado Springs

TOMAHAWK STATE WILDLIFE AREA

KNIGHT/IMLER STATE WILDLIFE AREA

Fourmile Creek

High Creek

9

Middle Fork South Platte River

South Fork South Platte River

63 RANCH STATE WILDLIFE AREA

285

Hartsel

South Fork South Platte River

BADGER BASIN STATE WILDLIFE AREA

Antero Reservoir

24

N

F&H NEWS

9

24

scale in miles

0   1   2   4

Trout lead variety of options at Union Reservoir

LONGMONT

by Mike Kennedy

Rainbow trout are the best early-spring bite at Union Reservoir, says Senior Park Ranger David Mohr (303-772-1265). Some nice trout have already been taken this season on Power Bait, worms, Woolly Buggers and Pistol Petes (Woolly Buggers or other nymphs with propellers).

The best location for shore-bound trout fishing is from the boat ramp southeast to the windsurf beach. Trout were also being caught off the pier on the west side of the lake the day I was there. Power Bait seemed to be the bait of choice for trout fishermen.

Union has been rising from its winter low and should continue to rise as snow runoff flows into the lake. Union also warms quicker than many Colorado lakes because it's somewhat murky and relatively shallow. All these factors help to get the fish going early in the year.

Union Reservoir, owned by the city of Longmont, has many warm-water species such as wiper, crappie, catfish, walleye and even a few bass. Wiper are the most sought-after fish in Union, but all the species should start to bite in mid-April. Look for a good pick-up in action as April gives way to May.

Wiper: The hybrid between a white bass and a striped bass is the most prized fish in the lake. I talked to fishermen who said they'd seen or caught several fish over 25 inches last season.

The best place to fish for wiper in the spring is at the tiny inlet between the fishing pier and the boat ramp. There is just a small canal about 6 feet wide coming into the lake, but the warmer and oxygen-rich water attracts baitfish, which draw wiper and other game fish.

Another good location is over on the east side in front of the pump house. Trout flies are some of the most effective artificial lures for wipers. Try a Pistol Pete or Woolly Bugger in brown, black or olive.

Jerkbaits, crankbaits, spoons or spinners will catch fish in open water later in the season, but bait such as shrimp, mussels, a crawdad tail or worms catch fish all year.

Fish live bait suspended under a slip bobber on or near the bottom, or troll them on a harness. Boat fishermen have the advantage because they can chase the fish around the lake and watch for offshore boils.

Other bites: Chase crappie with your typical crappie jigs or minnows. The fishing pier is one of the more popular locations to fish for crappie because it's difficult for bank fishermen to reach deeper water unless they're on the pier.

Boat anglers find crappie in the deeper holes most of the year, but they'll be moving onto any shallow structure as the water warms.

Catfish are also a popular bite at Union. One fisherman I talked to said he has caught several over 10 pounds. The northwest section of the lake, which you can only get to by boat, is the best area for catfish. Cutbait, stinkbait and worms are the most productive offerings. I like to use a clicker reel so the big whiskers can move with my bait without knowing that I'm there until I'm ready to set the hook.

Walleye are in the lake, though they were never stocked. Rangers believe they must have come in from the inlets or were dumped by fishermen, which is illegal. Many walleye have been caught offshore in the southwest corner of the lake.

Logistics: You can use a gas motor on Union, but it's wakeless boating only. Wipers must be 15 inches and crappie must be 10 inches. There is a $5 per car and $5 per boat Longmont City fee for using the park. Park hours are 6 a.m. to 6 p.m. March 1–April 30; 6 a.m. to 9 p.m. May 1–Sept. 1; and 7 a.m. to 7 p.m. Sept. 2–Oct. 31. The park is closed in the winter. Camping is available in the park after May 1.

Editor's note: For more information visit Mike Kennedy's Web site (www.coloradowarmwaterfishing.com).

F&H

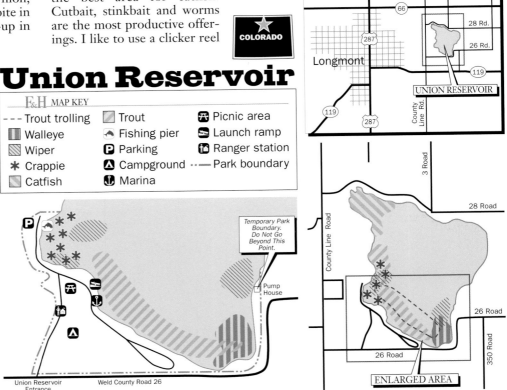

SOUTHEAST FISHING

Swing into early-season bass, wipers on John Martin

HASTY

by Dusty Routh

The great thing about John Martin Reservoir in southeastern Colorado near the little town of Hasty is that it's far enough away from anywhere that the fishing pressure isn't all that great. It's a wide-open prairie reservoir, an oasis in an otherwise desolate plains area. Here you can find largely undisturbed largemouth bass, some smallmouth and wipers that can approach 20 knuckle-thumping pounds.

The bad thing about John Martin Reservoir is it's a wide-open prairie reservoir, an oasis in an otherwise desolate plains area. To wit, the wind that blows here in the late spring can put the kibosh on what might have been an otherwise thoroughly productive day spent casting for largemouth bass, which can hit the 7- to 8-pound mark.

"I'm not a big fan of John Martin," says Colorado bassing expert Jim Bliss. Bliss is based out of Ft. Collins, and has managed more than his share of club bassing tournaments around the state. "I mean, for tournament angling, it's a tough lake. The ramp and facilities are rough, at least in terms of trying to get 60 boats in and out of the water. And the wind can be deadly. Just deadly."

Bliss points out that if you're going to fish John Martin, be prepared to let the wind dictate whether your day happens as planned or not. "The wind will blow you right off the lake," Bliss says. "There aren't too many places where you can hide to get out of it. And if you do hide, you'll be stuck there. The wind won't let you get home."

And how about when the wind's laid down some? "John Martin has got great wiper fishing, just great wipers. The bass fishing isn't bad. There's good walleye," Bliss says. "There are good fish all over that lake. You just have to know the lake real well, and where to go on it. At John Martin, different things work at different times."

Wind, wind, and more wind: OK, so you've been warned about the wind. But here's further insight: If the wind is blowing out of the northwest, you can be protected somewhat. Any other direction, and this big impoundment of the Arkansas River can see rollers to 9 feet. That's "9," as in 5-foot rollers plus 4 feet more on top of those for your horrific pleasure.

"You really have to watch yourself," Bliss says. "John Martin is wide open and flat. There's really no place to hide unless that wind is coming from the northwest."

Bliss says that if you pay due respect to the weather, you should be OK. "That's the biggest thing," he says. "Watch the weather. It can get deadly. I've seen people go out there in smaller boats and they're in 6- and 7-foot rollers. They have no idea what to do. That's when it can turn deadly."

Fish early, fish slowly: If it's big bass you want to target at John Martin, keep in mind that these bass are particularly sensitive to water temperatures. If you're fishing in the spring, which is essentially anytime before June, slow presentations are the way to go.

"Don't pull out your spinnerbaits if the water's still cold," Bliss says. "And not much in the way of plastics, either. When it's slow, throw a jig-n-pig. If the water's clear, use natural colors for your jigs. If it's not clear, go with darker col-

ors. Darker water on John Martin equals darker lures."

Another s-l-o-w presentation that works well here is a suspending Rogue minnow jerkbait. "They work really, really well," Bliss says.

Where dem bass at? One place to start your search for John Martin's bodacious bucketmouths is in the cove behind the railroad bridge, and then all around the lake's islands. While nothing in bass fishing is sure-fire, naturally, this is as close as you'll get. If the bass are in a biting mood, these are top places to find them.

Same goes for the distinct underwater humps down by the dam. "Bass fishing on those humps is good in the spring," Bliss says. Fishing a jig-n-pig tight to bottom on the humps should get you a nice catch for the day.

About those wipes: John Martin has an awesome wiper fishery (wipers being a cross between white and striped bass). If you aren't targeting wipers on purpose, you may just catch a few while you're bass fishing. "We catch them a lot when we're bass fishing, especially with spinnerbaits, Rogues and fishing topwaters," says Bliss.

The lake also has some smallmouth, and there may be some spotted bass as well, Bliss points out. But it's those wipers that are the most fun, with fish running as big as 20 pounds. A lot of anglers fish for them with live shad or smelt on a balloon rig.

It's not uncommon to run across big wipers boiling right on the surface of the lake. If you encounter that and you'd rather be catching bass, don't be discouraged. Boiling wipers means there are baitfish in the area, and the largemouth can be in the same vicinity chomping down on the remnants of the wiper attacks.

Bliss says wipers are delicious table fare. "Wipers are good to eat, provided you clean out the red line when you fillet them," he says. "If you don't, that makes them taste fishy. If you cut out that red line, it's hard to tell a wiper from a walleye; the fillets are that good. Let me just say this:

AT a GLANCE

What: Good fishing at John Martin Reservoir in May for largemouth bass and wipers.

How: Check the water temperatures. If the water's still cold, fish a slow jig-n-pig presentation or a suspending Rogue minnow imitation. If the water's warming up, throw white and white/chartreuse spinnerbaits.

Where: Be sure to check out the underwater humps down by the dam. Also fish around the islands. And if you can find submerged brush, buzz these with buzzbaits and spinnerbaits.

When: John Martin fishes well from spring on through summer.

Who: John Martin Reservoir State Park (719-829-1801).

I've enjoyed every one I've ever eaten. I don't throw them back."

Back to bass: Bliss says that you can have some very good fishing days on John Martin, and you can have some very poor fishing days. It's that kind of fishery. "It all depends on the day," he says. "It's a very unusual lake."

Bliss relates how he fished it once during the summer. "It was in the heat of summer, something like 97 degrees out. The water was very clear. I was finding big bass off submerged brush piles with buzzbaits and spinnerbaits in a foot of water, fishing small bushes in super clear water. Other guys were running other patterns, but I got on this pattern and it was just a very, very strong pattern."

Pueblo possibilities: The bass fishing at Pueblo should be heating up right about now, too. Most of the

A JIG-AND-PIG is a great way to chase down John Martin largemouth early in the season. But when the water warms, think about slinging a spinnerbait or crankbait.

camping sites there opened up on April 1. To make a reservation from Denver, call (303) 470-1144. Outside Denver, call (800) 678-2267.

You can reach John Martin Reservoir State Park at (719) 829-1801. **F&H**

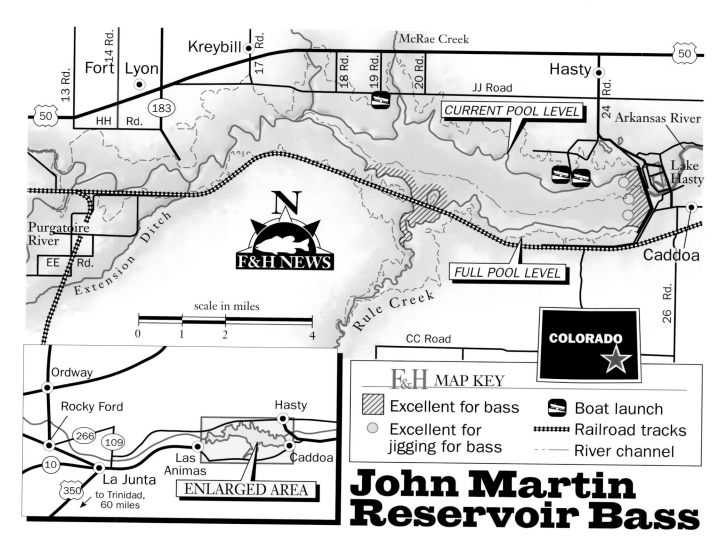

John Martin Reservoir Bass

MAP KEY: Excellent for bass, Excellent for jigging for bass, Boat launch, Railroad tracks, River channel

Northwest
Fishing

Fine high-country trouting at the (other) Arapaho Lakes

──────── WALDEN

by Giles Alkire

'know, once upon a time, 'bout 13 years ago, I swore to myself I'd never mention this cluster of high country lakes in print ever again. I sincerely meant it, and I've kept my word But things have changed. I've watched a bad situation turn sour, and the very area I'd tried so hard to keep a dream fishery forever finds itself in real trouble.

Nah, I don't mean the fishin's gone punk; it hasn't really taken a change for the worse at all! It's the conditions 'round the lakes and the blatant overuse of ATVs, off-road machines and irresponsible bikers that have left a bad taste in a lot of people's throats. And *there*, my friends, is where *you* come in.

I'm gonna send you to what can be some of the sweetest fishin' you may have ever seen in Colorado! If you hit it when the Fishin' Fates are smilin' on you, I promise you'll never forget it. A few catches will tug the scale to the double-digit mark (but I'll admit some days you couldn't buy a decent trout with a bushel of bullion!).

OK, quit slobberin', I'm gonna tell you where they are, but I'm gonna lay an onus on you, too. *please* take your camera with you — or even better, a video camcorder — and your handy-dandy cell phone.

If you see trailriders, fishermen or anyone else cut shenanigans in the manner of habitat disruption, trash tossin' or really rowdy behavior, try to get a pic of the perp and take note of the incident. But don't stop there; report it to Operation Game Thief (800-332-4155). You don't have to identify yourself to OGT. If you see somethin' really bad, call the Walden Sheriff's Office (970-723-4296).

If that's a deal, let's head out to Arapaho Lakes?

Getting there: No, not the Arapaho Lakes west of Boulder. Nope, these are nestled in the tall timber, watched over by towering rock formations and fields of wildflowers. Twelve lakes in all; take your pick and make your play! In some you'll find mostly pansizers, but others harbor some real hogs.

You're gonna need two things to do this right: A Routt National Forest map and USGS Topo Quad of "Buffalo Peak," *not* Buffalo Pass! Without them you're gonna be one confused puppy. If you call me to talk and don't have the maps by the phone, I'm not gonna be much help.

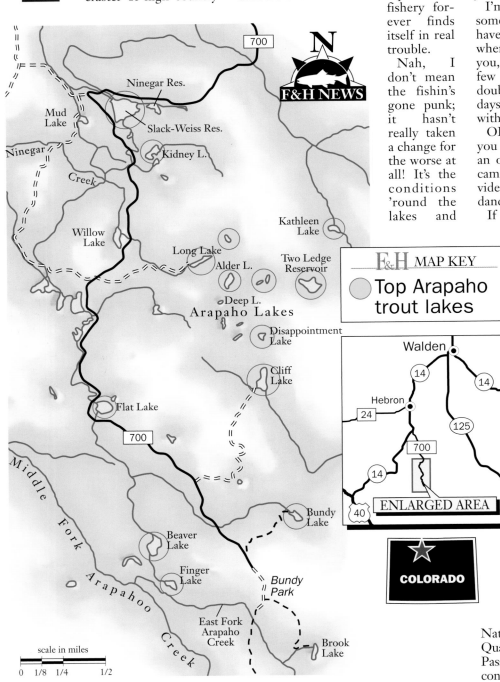

Arapaho Lakes

Head west out of Walden 15 miles on Highway 14 to JCR 28 and turn east on the paved road. Go a mile, turn south on JCR 11 and you're on your way. Go 5 miles past Slack Weiss Reservoir and keep right on runnin' south on FSRD 700 to a three-way junction in the road. There, RD 705 goes ahead to the East Fork of Arapaho Creek, RD 700 goes to the right and a sharp left-hand turn is signed "Cliff Lake, 2 miles." Wrap yer mitts 'round that steering wheel and hang a left!

When you get to the end of the road you'll find a nice parkin' lot and probably a few cars, but no lake to be seen anywhere. But with a map, a compass or good sense of dead reckoning once you get oriented, you've got it made, and the key to the whole thing is Cliff Lake.

Cliff's about 400 yards due north, down the hill. Or you can head straight west, over the side, and pick up an old two-track road that'll take you right to the lake.

(Those old roads are part of the problem. Seems a lot of folks aren't content to stay on 'em! So if you see unsportsmanlike conduct, do your best to help stop it.)

The lakes: As noted on your topo map, all the rest of the lakes are within easy walkin' distance. Anglers can hit 'em all on a single weekend if they're of a mind to. Just a few hundred feet north of Cliff is a real cantankerous cuss: Disappointmant Lake. Appropriately named, it's more often than not just that, a disappointment — but not always. I have pictures of an 8-pound, 2-ounce rotund big ol' 'bow that met it's doom there, and other pics of 3- to 8-pounders taken at Cliff. Lots of experienced anglers get many 3- and 4-pounders. But fairly put, the last four lakes I'm gonna mention seldom relinquish a large fish.

Less than a mile west is Deep Lake; a bit north of it are Long and Alder lakes, all of which cough up some impressive catches from time to time. A ¼-mile east and a bit over a ½-mile north of Cliff is Two Ledge Reservoir, and a ¼-mile further north is Lake Kathleen. Now, if that wasn't enough, there are more!

Just a little over halfway between the junction on the roads and the parking lot, Bundy Lake lies hidden in the timber a few hundred feet to the east. A mile south, on RD 705, Brook Lake is a stone's throw from the road. A mile

HEADING TO THE HILLS and fishing small high mountain lakes can produce big fish. Flinging flies or casting lures will produce nice trout on the Arapaho Lakes.

west of Bundy Lake, RD 704 will take you to Finger and Beaver lakes. Had enough? Don't quit on me yet!

Located behind (southeast) Slack Weiss Reservoir is Kidney Lake, and 2 miles south of Slack Weiss right alongside RD 700 is Flat Lake — and *that*, laddies and lassies, by my count is an even dozen! None of 'em are large and few of 'em are deep, but due to their peculiar structure and location, they rarely suffer a winterkill. All of 'em except Finger and Beaver are stocked by Division of Wildlife workers with fingerlings that grow very rapidly and occasionally attain massive size.

The lakes' main food base is freshwa-ter shrimp, backswimmers, leeches and all sorts of squiggly li'l critters I'm not even gonna take a guess at. I've had excellent success using Hank Robert's Yellow Drake Nymphs, Prince Nymphs, Halfbacks and Black Carsons. An extremely effective metal lure offering is a black ¼-ounce Thomas Eel or Al's Goldfish Helgy or a ¼-ounce Kastmaster, painted black.

Fly flingers do well with large (I mean size 2 or 4) black or dark olive Matukas or Woolly Buggers. Don't be bashful! Toss out a big 'un; you ain't fishin' for minnows. Myself, I consider a fish under 3 pounds a "go-backer." Treat 'em right, please! **F&H**

AT a GLANCE

What: Appreciating one of Giles Alkire's little high-country gems. A dozen or so lakes in the area provide great trout fishing and, at times, too many rogue off-roaders.

Where: These are not the Arapaho lakes just west of Boulder. Rather, they're some high-country tarns south of Slack Weiss Reservoir.

When: Now is as good a time as any. You'll want to get out there while the water is still cool and conducive to a great trout bite. This makes sure the fish aren't out deep in the middle of the lake where you can't cast at them.

How: Just bring your favorite offering. Flies are Giles' favorite, but you'll be just fine toting some spoons and spinners.

Who: Call Giles Alkire (970-352-9501), or stop by 1211 9th Street in Greeley from 10 a.m. to 4 p.m. any weekday.

Bugs bring June splendor to Colorado River

KREMMLING

by Dusty Routh

If there's a consistent theme you hear throughout the month of June about the best place in Colorado to throw a bug for aggressive river trout, that theme always seems to include the Colorado River and its many tributaries.

"The Raddy," as it's affectionately known by the army of fly anglers who spend time on it, is truly one of the more classic rivers in the state, if not the entire country, to fish, says Marty Bartholomew, author of "The Flyfisher's Guide to Colorado." He devoted almost 20 pages to the river in his book. "The Colorado River is among the top trout streams in Colorado," he says.

That may be an understatement. With Gold Medal status on the Windy

Gap to Troublesome Creek area, the river has become a shrine to selective gear catch-and-release fly purists and a playground for guides from fly shops up and down its length.

Bug on, bug off: One significant reason for the unrelenting adoration directed toward the Colorado River is the abundant insect life fly anglers usually find on it. In fact, June is one of the top months of the year for properly matching a hatch, leading to incredibly productive trout action.

Anglers will find evening caddis hatches, solid midday blue-winge olives coming off, consistent midge activity all summer long, stoneflies starting in mid-June and pale morning duns as the river settles into summer shape by late

June. Golden stoneflies, red quills, and terrestrials are on tap for later in summer. Bartholomew also recommends scuds during all months of the year as a steady go-to fly. Because the Colorado can be such big water, streamers can work at almost all times of the year, except possibly in winter. Woolly Buggers are the choice du jour for a lot of the streamer work.

In the early part of the summer season — as in late May and very early June — anglers can also expect to see hordes of baetis activity as you would on other rivers in the area.

Guidespeak: "If you don't fish the Colorado, or you haven't fished it yet this season, that's where I really recommend people going," says Jonathan

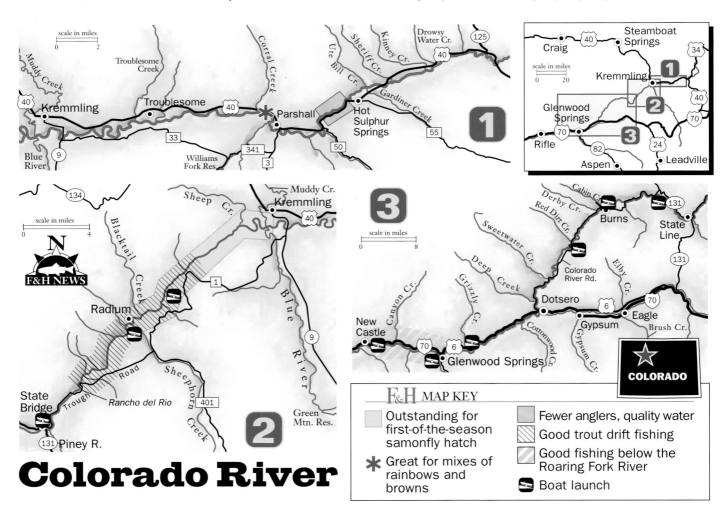

Colorado River

F&H MAP KEY

- Outstanding for first-of-the-season samonfly hatch
- ✳ Great for mixes of rainbows and browns
- Fewer anglers, quality water
- Good trout drift fishing
- Good fishing below the Roaring Fork River
- ⛴ Boat launch

Engle with Breckenridge Outfitters (970-453-4135). "Especially since other rivers, like the Blue, get hit so hard in June."

Adam Cuthriell with Summit Guides (970-468-8945) is another big proponent of fishing the Colorado in June. "If I had to pick my three favorites, they'd be the Colorado, the Blue and the South Platte," he says.

Cuthriell's been guiding steadily for the last four years, and he's definitely a fan of what the Colorado River has to offer. "The upper part of the Colorado has been fishing well so far this year," Cuthriell says. "The stoneflies aren't up there yet, but we've been doing well on Hare's Ears, nymphs, Pheasant Tails and the small Adams for risers. But it's mostly subsurface action so far."

The Gold Medal section, from Byers Canyon on up (east of Kremmling, near Hot Sulphur Springs), doesn't have a lot of public land where everyday anglers can access the river. But the hot fishing makes the limited water more than worthwhile.

"There's not a lot of public access," Cuthriell says, "but there's enough."

Which is to say, there are some private lease ranches along that stretch, where you'll have to pay to play, but there are also a few public access points as you drive along the river where you can pull in and get some line-on-the-water time without having to take out a loan.

Not one to fish in crowds, Cuthriell likes the Colorado right where it starts to turn to public Gold Medal water. "It never gets too crowded there," he says. "It's not like the Parshall/Breeze/Sunset unit areas down further (these are the units clustered near the Colorado's confluence with the Williams Fork). Those are supposedly such famous places to fish, but I'd rather go up higher to get better water that's less crowded."

Mark Johnston with Cutthroat Anglers (970-262-2878) in Silverthorne agrees. He points out there are fewer anglers in the Gold Medal area, but still lots of solid trout action, mostly for browns.

"I really like the browns and even the whitefish," he says. Johnston also likes to fish the Colorado down near the Pump House area, which is located below Gore Canyon, south of Kremmling and north of State Bridge. "There's been good flows this year, down just a little bit, but for this time of year just about average," he says. "We've been picking up mostly browns, throwing small dry fly caddis. That's mostly been an evening deal."

And it's not just brown trout that are drawing anglers. Johnston says the peak for whitefish should happen soon. "Whitefish angling gets really good starting in the spring," he says. "I think it usually peaks around June."

Harry Portland at Fryingpan Anglers (970-927-3441) in Basalt agrees the Colorado is the hot spot come June. "I've heard it's been fishing great," he says "It's where all the guided trips are going now. It's the place where people who really know trout fishing tend to wind up."

Portland says that blue-winged olives and caddis are coming off the Colorado now. "There'll be pale morning duns by early June or mid-June," he says. "It's a great river, a really excellent producer."

Most of the activity he sees is on the lower stretch of river, on either side of Kremmling. "Lots of blue-winged olives and caddis in that stretch," Portland says. "We usually fish from State Bridge on upstream to Kremmling. We've been getting great hatches in the evenings — those are caddis — and the blue-winged olives have been real consistent this year between 10 a.m. and 2 p.m., depending on water temperatures. The fish are loving those small mayflies, and streamers are working well too."

Making sense of the geography: The Colorado is big water, a long river fed by a plethora of feeder streams and other rivers. Mostly, you can divide it up into three good central state sections:

Windy Gap Reservoir to Kremmling: This is the most-fished section of the Colorado. Here you'll find the "classic" river sections including Hot Sulphur Springs, Byers Canyon and the Gold Medal section, then the really popular locations around the Kemp Breeze and Sunset units. This stretch also contains the confluence of the Williams Fork (offering excellent trout action and decent public access), and the private water down near Elktrout Lodge.

Kremmling to State Bridge: This sec-

BIG FLIES, nymphs and even dries are a great bet for catching healthy rainbows like this one. There's a chance to catch a lot of nice fish in the coming months in the upper Colorado River.

tion contains foot access into Gore Canyon, a good drift from the Pump House down to Radium, and access from Rancho Del Rio to State Bridge.

State Bridge to New Castle: This 130-mile stretch of river offers access at State Bridge, Catamount Bridge, Burns and just below Posey Creek before hitting Dotsero and the confluence with the Eagle River. From there anglers will find treacherous Glenwood Canyon, which is mostly a whitewater rafting stretch. Bartholomew, however, recommends hitting the Grizzly Creek area at the campground for a peek into this section. Access points in this part of the river include Grizzly Creek, Glenwood Springs and New Castle. **F&H**

AT a GLANCE

What: June is a prime month to get on the Colorado River for rainbows and browns, and the peak of the whitefish summer fishery.

When: Most of the runoff on the lower portions of the river will be wrapped up by the end of May or early June. The upper river may still have some nasty left to it until later in June.

How: This is classic match-the-hatch fly fishing. Expect to see PMDs and BWOs in the daytime, along with some baetis, and lots of caddis action in the evenings.

Where: All sections are fishing well. For fewer people, head up into the Gold Medal section. For rainbows and browns, fish around the Williams Fork confluence. For mostly browns, fish below Kremmling.

Who: Breckenridge Outfitters (970-453-4135); Summit Guides (970-468-8945); Cutthroat Anglers (970-262-2878); Fryingpan Anglers (970-927-3441).

Stick close to dam for winter trout on Fryingpan

BASALT

by Dusty Routh

THE FRYINGPAN RIVER below Ruedi Reservoir is dam tailwater, and can be fished all year long. This time of year, you can sleep in and catch fish during the warmest part of the day.

There was a time before Ruedi Reservoir was built, when the Fryingpan River was as esteemed a trout river as any in the country. With the construction of the rock and earthfill dam and reservoir between 1964 and 1968, that esteem was put on hold, pending future judgment on how the fishing would hold up once the river was turned into two rivers: the upper river, above the dam, and the lower river, which became a tailwater fishery.

The 285-foot-tall dam now sits in all its manmade splendor about 15 miles east of Basalt. Ruedi offers nearly 1,000 acres of prime seasonal fishing of its own, with everything from Mackinaw to rainbows to browns. The river above Ruedi is seasonal too, depending on road and weather conditions like ice and snow. But below the dam, the value once ascribed to the Fryingpan still exists, if not even more so, as this has become one of the most popular and productive tailwater fisheries in the state.

All-season fishing: Because the lower water is dam tailwater, the Fryingpan can be fished 12 months out of the year. And boy howdy, does it ever get fished. It's an extremely popular winter fishery, for example, because it doesn't ice up, because the roads are maintained and — most importantly —

because it can offer incredible fishing for fly and lure anglers. There are healthy populations of rainbows and browns, with some of the 'bows reaching excellent sizes because of feed like mysis shrimp coming down the river from the reservoir.

Fishing the 'Pan in the winter is a hardy exercise, because temperature ranges can run from nasty to nastier. During a recent week on the river, for example, highs went anywhere from 15 to 20 to 30 to 35 degrees, and lows sunk as far as −10 degrees. Late December and early January are typically the coldest times on the river, but mid-January can show glimpses of warmer daytime temperatures.

"December is usually the coldest month of the year here," says Art Rowell at Fryingpan Anglers in Basalt (970-927-3441). "But we usually get a thaw around the second week in January. We're looking forward to that."

When it does stay bitter outside with these kinds of cold temps, midday fishing is your best bet.

Banker's hours fishing: During the cold snap that hit the river near the end of December, the fishing really slowed down, naturally. "It just got so cold," says Rowell, "that the fishing has been tough. Some guys went out and caught a few fish, but it's really tough when it gets below zero. The fish are

sluggish, not to mention your fingers."

Rowell suggests sleeping in and staying warm, and not fishing until at least 11 a.m. or noon. "When it's really cold, don't go out before noon," he says. Let it warm up, and then plan on hitting the river for just a couple of hours. This way, you're fishing the "warmest" part of the day (that term used loosely when highs only reach 15 degrees).

When it gets cold and stays cold, anglers bunch up just below Ruedi out of necessity. The lower, mainstem part of the Fryingpan can get really icy, with chunks of ice flowing past. And the Roaring Fork downstream can get so icy that it's unfishable. "Fishing close to the dam, that's the only places that's not iced up when it gets really cold," Rowell says. "The Roaring Fork has been unfishable on some days, all day long, with big ice chunks in it. Usually, the Fork clears off by noon. But not when it's really cold."

Shrimping for trout: As the mercury climbs, however, look for the Fryingpan's resident rainbows and browns to get just active enough that you can tempt them with mysis shrimp patterns. "All that mysis shrimp in Ruedi Reservoir, that's how these fish get so big," Rowell says. For fly anglers, that means learning to effectively fish mysis shrimp patterns in both the deep water up close to the dam, and on the shallower flats just down from the dam.

"We have a half a dozen mysis patterns that are effective," Rowell says. These include shellback shrimp, the BTS Mysis, Reed's Ultra Mysis, the Live Mysis, and the Umpqua Lite Brite Mysis.

Mysis patterns are most effective when you fish them like a nymph, stumbling and bumbling the shrimpy fly along the bottom at the prevailing speed of the current. Just below the dam, the name of the game is to get that pattern on the bottom, which isn't always easy. "Below the dam, put a lot of weight on when you're fishing the plunge pool, the Toilet Bowl, and jig it right along the bottom," says Rowell.

But when that deeper water opens up

Fryingpan River

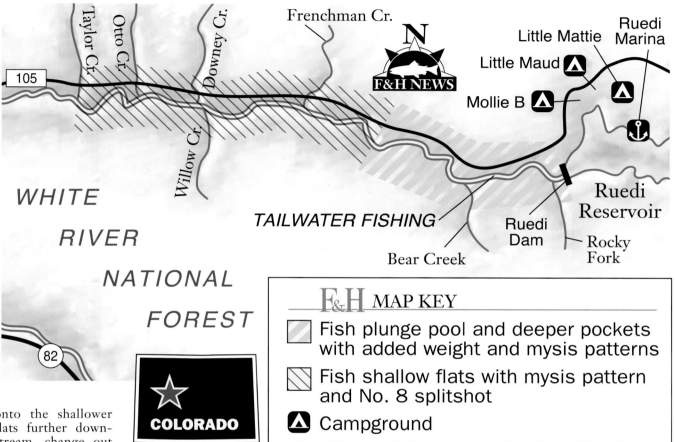

WHITE RIVER NATIONAL FOREST

COLORADO

F&H MAP KEY

▨ Fish plunge pool and deeper pockets with added weight and mysis patterns

▨ Fish shallow flats with mysis pattern and No. 8 splitshot

⛺ Campground

onto the shallower flats further downstream, change out your weights. "When it opens up on the flats, you want very little weight," Rowell says. "Your best bet is a little No. 8 splitshot. Rainbows will be holding right on the flats."

Natural mysis shrimp can be anywhere from ¼-inch long to almost an inch, so pattern sizes need to match up with that. "The average size on the Fryingpan is a No. 16," says Rowell. "You can't go wrong with that. But you can go down smaller, to 18s and 20s, and some guys like the smaller patterns."

This is all floating line fishing, using a 9-foot fluorocarbon leader with 2 feet of 6x or 7x tippet. "The 'Pan fish are extremely leader-shy," Rowell says. "They'll follow you around like a dog, picking bugs off your heels, but if they see a leader, it's all over."

Rowell says he's looking forward to fishing the 'Pan in January. "We need some more snow," he says, "and we want it to warm up. Snow means water, and fish like water."

Directions: Getting to the Fryingpan River should be easy for most readers. From Denver, take I-70 west to Glenwood Springs, then turn south on Highway 82 to Basalt. The tailwater fishery is 15 miles east of Basalt. Fryingpan Road follows the river east to the reservoir.

Contact info: The Fryingpan Angler (970-927-3441) in Basalt is your best source of information on river conditions, fly selections and gear. Information on Ruedi Reservoir is available through the US Forest Service/ Bureau of Reclamation in Glenwood Springs at (970) 945-2521. **F&H**

AT a GLANCE

What: Winter fishing for rainbows and browns in the tailwaters of the Fryingpan River below Ruedi Reservoir.

When: January can be an excellent month, particularly if warmer daytime temps set in around midmonth.

How: Fish mysis patterns in sizes ranging from as big as No. 16s down to No. 18s and 20s. Use splitshot to keep your fly along the bottom.

Where: Fish the plunge pool (aka The Toilet Bowl) right below the dam, and on the flats just down from the dam.

Who: The Fryingpan Angler in Basalt (970-927-3441); US Forest Service/Bureau of Reclamation in Glenwood Springs (970-945-2521).

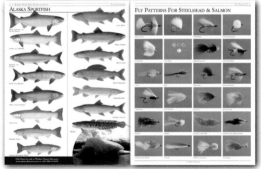
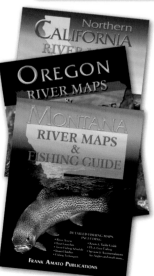

Target shallow inlets for Granby Mackinaw

GRANBY

by Mike Kennedy

Mackinaw are up shallow and on the bite according to Richard Crager, owner and operator of Budget Tackle (970-887-9344) in Granby.

Fish the inlets with tubes, spoons, crankbaits ... most anything, really. The key is water flow. If they're pumping water from Willow Creek Reservoir into Granby's Rainbow Bay, it's the place to be. The inlet is at the far southwest end of the lake. Arapaho Bay is also a good place to fish. The lake is about a month ahead of schedule, but as long as the cool water keeps rolling in, lakers should be up shallow and the fishing should be good. This is the time that bank fishermen can really have a ball.

Recently an angler caught a 33½-inch, 15½-pound Mack in Arapaho Bay. He had a livewell in his boat and kept the fish alive, brought it into Crager's for pictures, weight and measurement, then took the fish back to the lake and released it. Now that's the way to maintain outstanding fishing at Granby!

Other good locations for Macks, rainbows and browns are Quinette Point between Dike 1 and Dike 2 and where Stillwater Creek comes into Granby by Stillwater Campground. All three species are being caught in 23 feet of water or less.

One of the most tried-and-true baits for lakers is sucker meat, either tipping on a tube, spoon or other lure, or on a hook by itself. Once Granby stops filling and the snowmelt is over, Macks will go deep and you'll need a boat to get to them.

You can also get Macks and 'bows trolling crankbaits or worm harnesses. I've had good luck trolling rainbow pop gear with either an Arnie's lure or Mack's Wedding Ring tipped with a half-'crawler. You don't need to be too deep right now, but as the water warms you'll need to go to leadcore line, downriggers, or weights on your line. I seem to get more Macks on the larger size 508 Arnie's Lures in gold and red ruby color, and I got the rainbows on the Wedding Ring harnesses.

If action is slow at the inlets or trolling, drop a white or chartreuse tube tipped with sucker meat on the bottom along the flats on the north side between Twin Pines Point and Arapaho Bay, off of Rocky Point or around Harvey Island.

There's not a lot of kokanee action right now, but it shouldn't be long. Locate fish out over the channel and troll or drift through schools with spoons or Mack's Kokanee Killers tipped with worm.

There's been other large fish weighed recently, including a 25-pounder. Unfortunately, most fish are harvested. A Mackinaw more than about 6 or 8 pounds isn't very good to eat, so Crager suggests you get a good picture and then release the fish. If you think you have a record fish (over 46 pounds), then you'll want to at least keep the fish — preferably alive — for official measurements.

Even with a trophy fish you should try your best to keep the fish alive and eventually release it. If you get a good side picture and length and girth measurements, a taxidermist can make you an amazing replica and you can have your trophy without killing the fish.

Editor's note: For more information, be sure to visit Mike Kennedy's Web site (www.coloradowarmwaterfishing.com)

F&H

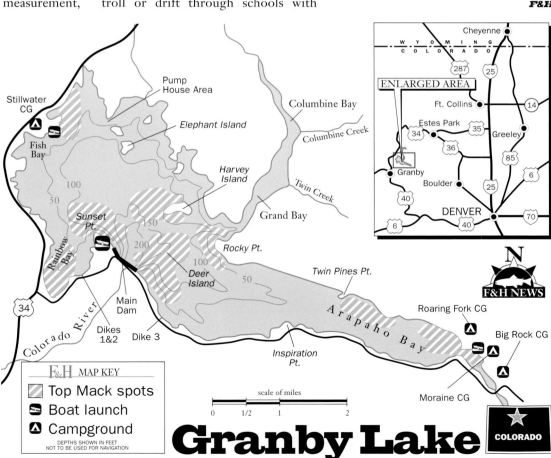

F&H MAP KEY
- Top Mack spots
- Boat launch
- Campground

DEPTHS SHOWN IN FEET
NOT TO BE USED FOR NAVIGATION

Granby Lake

COLORADO

Macks the big attraction on Jefferson's early ice

JEFFERSON

by Mike Kennedy

Jefferson Lake is a good place to start the ice fishing season for those of us who can't wait to get after 'bows, brookies or Mackinaw under solid water. At 10,687 feet in elevation, Jefferson is one of the first lakes to freeze up in the state and should have an ice lid by the time this article hits the stands. The lake almost always has a tight lid by the second week of December, according to Deedee Giesinger of the Jefferson Market (719-836-2389) on Highway 285 just across the street from County Road 35 (the road leading to the lake). Jefferson Market, the closest retailer to the lake, has mealworms and fishing supplies.

The South Park area around Jefferson Lake can receive a lot of snow, and the relatively steep road up to the lake is frequently closed to vehicular traffic. When the road is closed due to snow, you're allowed to make the trip from the main gate to the lake in a snowmobile, but ATVs are NOT allowed according to Diana Bonny of the US Forest Service South Park Office. It's a good idea to call the USFS South Park Office (719-836-2031) to check on road conditions to the lake before you make the trip.

Mackinaw are the big draw at Jefferson Lake, with fish exceeding 40 inches possible. As first ice sets up on the lake, Macks will be on relatively shallow flats or rocky points in 20 to 50 feet of water, but near deep-water drop-offs. Mackinaw spawn in the fall and usually stay in shallow water until the water starts to warm up in the spring.

When Macks are in water of 50 feet or less, they're almost always within 3 feet of the bottom. Their dependable location makes targeting fish much easier. Find the channel or other deep water, then find a relatively flat rocky bottom 50 feet deep or less and put your lure or bait within 3 feet of the bottom. Presto — you get bit.

Fish will tend to be in shallower in the morning and the evening, and venture a little deeper during the day. Start fishing at about 20 feet deep and work

LAKE TROUT like this 28-incher caught by Sam Benson last year are the top draw at Jefferson Lake. You'll also find rainbow and brook trout here.

your way out to 50 feet or so as the day goes on or action slows.

The all-time best go-to bait for Mackinaw is sucker meat. Use either a small whole sucker or a cut slab of sucker meat. You can put the sucker meat on a plain hook, size 2 or larger, rig it up on a quick strike rig (which is usually used for a small whole sucker) or tip your tube, Air Plane Jig or spoon with sucker meat. Some days you need to work your bait more, and other days just letting it sit there seems to work best. The southwest corner of the lake is one of the best areas to try.

I like to fish a two-tube setup with a 4-inch tube at the bottom and a smaller 2-inch tube about 2 feet up on the line. On some days I get more hits on the smaller tube than I do the larger tube. You can also pick up rainbows and smaller Macks on the 2-inch tube. It gives you more options in the water.

To have a good feel for your 4-inch tube when it's down 30 or 50 feet, use a ½- to 1-ounce tube jig. Use a jighead

that fits inside of the tube. Don't push the jighead all the way up to the end of the tube; leave about a ½-inch pocket at the tip of the tube. This air pocket will cause the tube to spiral, like a dying sucker, as you lower it in the water. To keep the line from tangling as your lure spirals, put a high quality barrel swivel up about 4 feet on the line.

Use a multi-colored tube for the smaller tube; red-and-white usually works well for me but other colors can also work. Be sure to tip the smaller tube with a mealworm, wax worm or piece of nightcrawler to give your presentation variety.

On the 4-inch white or chartreuse tube at the bottom of your rig, add an Owner, Eagle Claw Laser or other quality stinger hook to the back of the primary hook. To keep the stinger hook straight behind the tube and not hanging down underneath the jig hook, place a small piece of surgical tubing over the eye of the stinger hook, then run the tube and eye over the tip (point) of the tube jig.

Next tip the tube with a 2-inch by 4-inch slab of filleted sucker meat, turning it skin-side down and putting the jig hook and one tine of the stinger through the sucker skin. With the open meat up it's more apt to attract fish. I usually catch at least half of the fish I get on the stinger hook. The stinger hook is especially important if you're getting short strikes and are missing fish.

Some anglers like to set two poles in the water, then drift off to thoughts of warmer days or other fishing adventures waiting for the big Mack to come by. I'm convinced that you'll catch more fish if you keep your pole in your hand so you can feel the slightest hit and can immediately set the hook. If you have a second rod stamp and feel you're being cheated if you're not fishing with two rods, use a tip-up with a slab or small whole sucker on a quick-strike rig. A quick-strike rig is two sharp treble hooks on wire, Dacron line or heavy mono, 3 to 6 inches apart. If a fish picks up this rig, the tip-up flag goes up, notifying you of a bite. You go to the hole, pull in the line by hand until you feel resistance, set the hook and manually bring the fish to the hole. Be ready to feed the fish line if they make a run.

Roger Biri and fishing buddy Sam Benson like to fish Jefferson. They take their snowmobile to the lake for Mack and trout action all season. In addition to the Macks, there are some nice rainbow and brook trout in the lake, and brown trout downstream. If 'bows or brookies are your delight, move in a little closer to shore in water 20 feet or less. Small tubes, teardrop spoons or ice jigs tipped with a mealworm, wax worm or piece of 'crawler are your best bet.

Always use caution when ice fishing, especially on early or late ice. Take an ice chisel with long handle and strike the ice testing it before you step on the ice. I like to have at least 4 inches of ice under me. Also it's a good idea to have Ice-Scapees (interlocking ice picks on a tether) hanging around your neck just in case.

To get to Jefferson Lake, located 25 miles northeast of Fairplay on Highway 285, from Denver take C-470 west to US 285 south toward Fairplay and go 51 miles to the town of Jefferson. At Jefferson turn west on County Road 35 for approximately 2 miles to Forrest Road 37. Travel northwest on 37 for 6 miles. For more information call the USFS South Park Office (719-836-2031). Be safe, have fun, and let me know of your fishing adventures through my Web site.

Editor's note: For more information, be sure to visit Mike Kennedy's Web site (www.coloradowarmwaterfishing.com).

F&H

AT a GLANCE

What: Trout and big Mackinaw at Jefferson Lake.

When: Now until ice-out.

Where: To get to Jefferson Lake, located 25 miles northeast of Fairplay on Highway 285, from Denver take C-470 west to US 285 south toward Fairplay and go 51 miles to the town of Jefferson. At Jefferson turn west on County Road 35 for approximately 2 miles to Forrest Road 37. Travel northwest on 37 for 6 miles

Who: Jefferson Market (719-836-2389; USFS South Park Office (719-836-2031).

Jefferson Lake

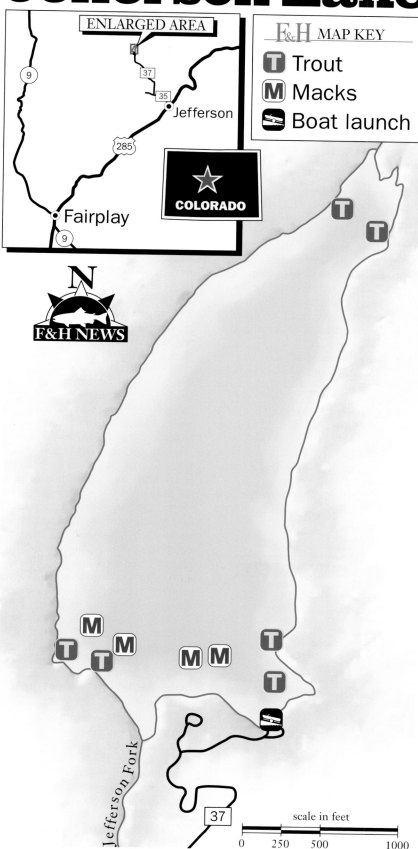

ENLARGED AREA

9

37

35

Jefferson

285

COLORADO

Fairplay

9

F&H MAP KEY

T Trout
M Macks
⛵ Boat launch

N

F&H NEWS

Jefferson Fork

37

scale in feet

0   250   500   1000

Cold weather, hot fishing at North Park lakes

WALDEN

by Mike Kennedy

Lyle Jess, from Fort Morgan, won the Jan. 8–9 North Park Ice Fishing Contest with a beautiful 24.5-inch cuttbow, with a 13.6-inch girth, total size 38.1 inches. The contest covered both Lake John and Cowdrey. The cuttbow won Jess a total of $700 — $500 for the big fish of the contest; an additional $150 for being the biggest fish from Cowdrey; and $50 for being the hourly winner when the fish was turned in.

Jess told me he caught the fish vertically jigging a Kastmaster spoon. Cowdrey is much shallower than Lake John and very weedy, so the key is to find the open spots just off the weeds. Many of us who bypassed Cowdrey for Lake John might have to rethink that next time around.

Other cash winners include:

Harry Ellis, 20.2 inch rainbow, 12.5 inch girth, total size 32.7 inch, Lake John $400

Dave Schissler, 19 inch rainbow, 12.4 in girth, total size 31.4 inch, Lake John $300

Donald Diltz, 19.4 inch rainbow, 11.9 inch girth, total size 31.3 inch, Lake John $200

There also were winners for the largest fish each hour of the contest that won $50 each.

AT a GLANCE

What: Ice fishing in North Park Lakes.

When: Now through ice out.

Where: The best route to Lake John during the winter is through Kremmling. The road is straighter and normally clearer. Take I-70 west to Hwy. 9 Exit 205-Silverthorn, follow Hwy. 9 north 37 miles to Kremmling, then turn northwest for 27 miles to Hwy. 14. Go east on Hwy. 14 for 33 miles to Hwy 125, then 1/2-mile north on 125 to CR 12W. Follow 12W for 8 miles to CR7, then 5 miles NW to CR 7A. Continue 2 miles west on 7A to Lake John.

Who: North Park Resort (970-723-3226).

Yours truly came in fourteenth — out of the money — with an 18.5-inch, 11.5-inch girth, Lake John rainbow that had a total size of 30 inches. I could have won one of the hourly big fish prizes, but happened to bring in my fish the same hour as one of the top money winners. I actually caught and released a slightly larger fish on Friday before the contest began, but believing in playing by the rules, I took his picture and let him go. As this was the first time I'd ever fished the tournament, I was very pleased that I even caught a measurable fish. This year's tournament required that your fish be at least 16 inches to be measurable.

The weather was cold and windy in North Park the weekend of the contest and can be on any given day during the ice fishing season. There were periods of whiteout conditions and winds that blew down many of our portable ice-huts, including mine. However, the fishing was hot if you were in the right place. Rick White and Andy Anderson, from the Sportsman's Warehouse in Thornton, and Tony Hampton and myself from the Aurora Sportsman's Warehouse all caught nice fish though we didn't place in the money.

I caught many fish during the day-and-a-half tournament, most in the 13- to 16-inch range but I did manage to catch the rainbow that put me in fourteenth place on Sunday, in almost blizzard-type conditions, just before the contest was over. This was my first ice-fishing tournament at North Park and I really enjoyed it. Bill and Tish Willcox, owners and operators of the Lake John Resort, their staff, and the North Park Chamber of Commerce, have really organized a nice event. I look forward to fishing the contest again next year.

Many of the things learned during the contest can help you the next time you fish Lake John or other North Park lakes. Prior to the contest, Hampton and I were talking about the different conditions that would probably exist during a tournament that are not there on a normal weekday. On most weekdays you can catch fish right

LOOK FOR AREAS just off ramps, points and the dam along Lake John for a chance at trout through the ice.

off the north boat ramp. On busy weekends or especially during a tournament you might have better luck in a more secluded location. During busy periods, trucks, snowmobiles and ATV's are zooming down off the ramp onto the lake every few minutes and can make that section like trying to fish in the intersection of I-25 and I-70.

Another consideration is getting around on the ice. Willcox told me that in the past few weeks more than a few anglers who thought their 4-wheel drive trucks and SUVs could go anywhere have been humbled as their vehicles got stuck on lake side roads or on the ice.

Since the tournament, another 2 feet of snow has fallen and there is about 3 inches of slush under the snow. There is still a solid 18 to 20 inches of ice under the snow and slush, but Willcox warns that you'd better have chains if you want to venture out on the ice with your vehicle. Also beware of the ice near the shore, especially the eastern shore, as snow and slush can be thicker, and ice thinner there. If you don't have chains, it's better to park at the north end of the lake and take your gear out on foot. If you do decide to drive out on the ice, it's best to enter the lake at the boat ramps. Some anglers attempted to drive down over the bank at other locations on the lake and got hung up in unseen holes.

While you're allowed to leave huts up on the ice overnight at Lake John, unless your hut is a solid unit, I'd recommend against it. I learned the hard way what gusts up to 80 mph can do to a portable hut. I put my hut up on Friday nigh,t planning to have it ready to go for the tournament first thing on Saturday morning, but when I found my hut the next morning it was flat as a pancake with a foot or two of snow blown on to it.

I was one of the fortunate ones because my ice anchors held my hut in place. The hut just blew over but didn't move from the spot where I left it. The wind broke one pole, bent one pole and broke off a clamp at the end of another pole. I was able to buy new conduit and repair the damage for around $10. Next time I'll either not put the tent up until the day I plan to use it, or I'll lower the tent and put a flag of some kind up so I can locate the hut. There were some anglers who found their huts ½-mile or further away and some that never found theirs. Presumably the missing huts were either on their way to Wyoming or buried under lots of snow.

As far as where and how to fish, the keys are depth, structure and presentation. For depth, find water 12 to 14 feet deep. On Lake John look for areas just off the ramps, points, and the dam, or fish the inlet or east shore weed lines where there is 12 to 14 feet of water. On Cowdrey fish along the edges of weed lines or in spots with sandy bottoms. The coves along the west side, the northwest portion of the southern cove and the west and southwest portion of the northern cove generally produce the best.

You need a subtle presentation. I can't overemphasize this. A white, red/white, or pink and white tube or curly tail grub about 1½ inches long tipped with a mealworm is very effective. Processed dead minnows or minnow imitations also work well. Remember that no live minnows are allowed over 7,000 feet.

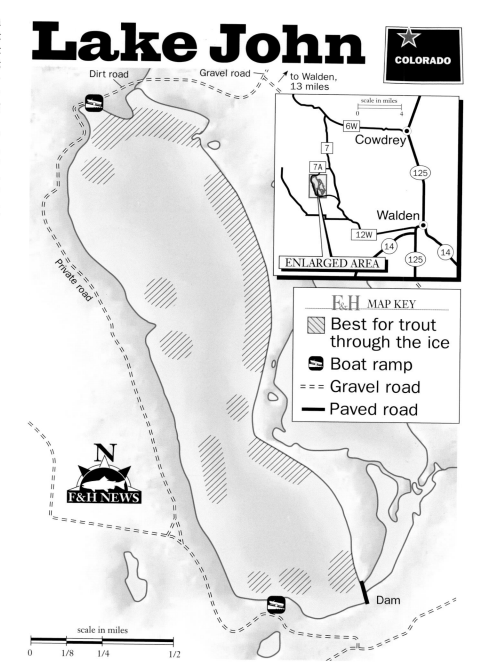

Lake John

For more information on fishing North Park lakes, contact Bill Willcox of the North Park Resort at 970-723-3226. Bill is a wealth of knowledge and very willing to share his knowledge with visiting anglers. The North Park resort has a tackle shop, restaurant, cabins, camping, and rental ice huts and augers. The best route to Lake John during the winter is through Kremmling. The road is straighter and normally clearer. Take I-70 west to Hwy. 9 exit 205-Silverthorn, follow Hwy. 9 north 37 miles to Kremmling then turn northwest for 27 miles to Hwy. 14. Go east on Hwy. 14 for 33 miles to Hwy 125, then ½-mile north on 125 to CR 12W. Follow 12W for 8 miles to CR7 then 5 miles NW to CR 7A. Continue 2 miles west on 7A to Lake John.   *F&H*

I've developed a new Web site and have changed the name to Mike's Colorado Fishing. Visit my new site at mikescoloradofishing.com.

Toss flies to weeds for big Spinney trout

by Jeremy Thurston

 Trout anglers at Spinney Mountain Reservoir have received some low blows during the last few years.

First came pike, which decimated the fingerlings stocked in the reservoir. Liberal limits and encouragement from Colorado Division of Wildlife to catch and keep the pike were of no use. Pike have become as much of a part of the reservoir's biota as the trout.

Then came several years of drought, which reduced the water level significantly. Suddenly, you needed the legs of an Olympic swimmer to kick your way to the far shore.

Despite these setbacks, anglers are catching plenty of large trout. "The fishing has been really good even though the access is limited," says Bob Hix at All Pro Fish-N-Sport (303-795-3474).

The reservoir is approximately 20 feet below its normal fill level. This means the boat launch is high and dry. The normal snowpack this year will not improve the situation significantly.

Hix believes it will take several years of average snowpack before anglers are able to launch trailered boats. So for now, anglers are limited to whatever they can carry to the water's edge. Luckily, not all of the trout live on the other side of the reservoir.

The reservoir carries a mish-mosh of trout species. Brown, cutthroat and rainbow all ply the waters. One thing they all have in common is a fast growth rate.

"The trout that were stocked there last year that were about 14 to 16 inch-

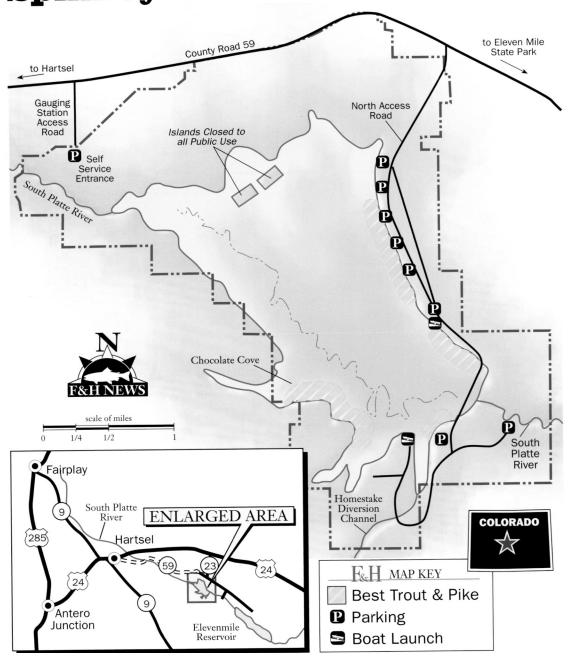

Spinney Mountain Reservoir

to Hartsel
County Road 59
to Eleven Mile State Park
Gauging Station Access Road
North Access Road
Self Service Entrance
Islands Closed to all Public Use
South Platte River
Chocolate Cove
South Platte River
Homestake Diversion Channel
COLORADO

Fairplay
South Platte River
ENLARGED AREA
Hartsel
Antero Junction
Elevenmile Reservoir

scale of miles
0   1/4   1/2   1

F&H MAP KEY
Best Trout & Pike
P Parking
Boat Launch

es are now 16 to 18 inches, and the trout stocked the year before should be between 20 and 22 inches," Hix says. "Most of the browns will be over 20 inches."

Bugs: These trout enjoy a big meal and right now they're feasting on an insect that usually only comes in a size tiny.

Mention the word "chironomid" around novice fly anglers and you'll likely elicit a convulsive shiver. Their eyes will fog over as they remember the time they went to a lake and were forced to fish with flies they needed a monocle to see. The memory will involve inclement weather of some kind and, worst of all, no fish.

Thankfully, Spinney Mountain can provide a cure to all of those down-trodden flyfishers suffering from midge-phobia.

The midges hatching right now at Spinney have grown to the gigantic size of 12 to 14. "These are huge for midges," says Hix.

The hatch will only last for about three weeks, so anglers who want to catch some of this action should get out on the water. Toward the end of the hatch, the midges will have dropped to a size 16.

If for some reason you're unable to make it for the midges, the Spinney Mountain Insect Factory will be churning out another major hatch soon enough. The lovely Callibaetis mayfly will soon be turning the heads of all the trout.

Those who venture to Spinney looking for a dry fly frenzy will be disappointed. "I can only remember consistent dry fly fishing for the Callibaetis happening once in the last 10 years," Hix says.

The most likely time to stumble upon one of these rare events is during the morning hours. A few parachute Adams in a size 14 to 16 thrown in the fly box just in case won't hurt anything. Pheasant Tails and Hare's Ears in a size 14 will imitate the nymphal stage.

The rule for fishing all of these various bugs is diversify, diversify, diversify. Hix recommends fishing a Pheasant Tail with a chironomid trailer, a Hare's Ear with a scud or a chironomid with a scud. You get the idea. If fishing strictly with chironomid patterns, suspend them under a strike indicator or a buoyant dry fly.

Damsel nymphs can also be a major food item. An olive leech pattern in a size 10 or 12 will suffice. Black, purple and brown leech patterns can also be good additions to the above combinations.

Use a moderate sink line and focus in on the weedbeds and water 8 to 12 feet deep. "With the lake so low you don't want a rocket sinking line," Hix says.

The low water has most anglers confined to the north side of the reservoir. Consequently, that's where most of the trout are being caught. Anglers adventurous enough to row or kick their way into the inlets and Buffalo Bay will find both solitude and trout.

Other tactics: Gear slingers shouldn't feel left out by all the fly flinging going on around them. Hix recommends fishing with a bubble-and-fly, Kastmasters or Rapalas. Try rainbow and brown trout colors on the lures.

One of the advantages gear fishers have is a higher chance of hooking into one of the bruiser pike that stalk the weedbeds.

Hix believes the pike are now established and as long as the fish planted in Spinney are of catchable size, trout populations should not suffer greatly from predation.

Anglers who want to focus on the big pike should use big spinnerbaits, stickbaits and rattling baits to get the cruising northerns' sharp-toothed attention. Use a fast retrieve to trigger the predator instinct.

Steel leaders aren't essential for catching pike. "When I'm fishing for pike I get a lot more strikes when I use monofilament," Hix says. "The bigger fish see too much to get fooled by the steel leaders."

Instead, carry a few with you in case of a feeding frenzy. Anglers have a pretty good chance of avoiding the teeth altogether when using 6-inch stickbaits. Hix says he usually lands two out of three pike hooked when fishing with monofilament.

Successful pike anglers rarely need to venture into water deeper than what their waders can handle and luckily, plenty of pike cruise along the north shore.

The fishing at Spinney should remain productive until August, Hix says. The callibaetis will trickle out in late July and the water will be too warm for good fishing.

Spinney Mountain is managed as a trophy trout fishery, and for good rea-

YOU CAN CATCH plenty of pike at Spinney Mountain Reservoir. You'll also find trophy size rainbow, brown and cutthroat trout.

son. "It's the most fertile lake in Colorado," Hix says. Anglers are limited to one trout and it must be over 20 inches long. Anglers are free to keep as many pike as they wish. Only flies and artificial lures are allowed.

AT a GLANCE

What: Trophy size rainbow, brown and cutthroat trout; northern pike.

Where: From Colorado Springs, take Highway 24 west for 55 miles, turn left on County Road 23, go 2.8 miles, turn right on County Road 59 and go 1.1 miles to the park entrance. Most of the action comes on the north shore. Mostly that's because it provides the best access. If you can get yourself to more secluded areas, the fishing will be even better.

Limits: One trout over 20 inches, no limit on pike.

Regs: Flies and artificial lures only.

Who: All Pro Fish-N-Sport (303) 795-3474)

Find deeper water structure to for trophy lake trout

LEADVILLE

by Chris Shaffer

No matter what state, country or county you live in, every single lake, river, stream and pond has issues that keep the fishery from being perfect. Water quality, stunted fish, not enough food, too much food or non-native species can alter the productivity of the lake. In other cases it can make the fishery better.

At Turquoise Lake the yo-yo effect dictates how the fishery will be each year and how anglers can fish it. Sometimes you can get boats on the lake. Other times the ramp is 50 feet out of the water and bone-dry.

Turquoise is a water storage reservoir. Its purpose is to provide drinking water for Denver, Pueblo and the Arroyo area, not to provide great fishing. Nonetheless, the lake's Mackinaw population has lived through high and low water and are obviously reproduc-

VICTOR COLALEO proudly shows off a dandy laker. You can duplicate his catch by jigging the fluctuating waters of Turquoise Lake this summer.

ing like rabbits. While nearly two decades ago Turquoise was known to yield monster Mackinaw, anglers have been somewhat disappointed in recent years. The Macks are still there, just much smaller.

"It started many years ago; I'd say we started seeing it 10 to 15 years ago. I think the Mackinaw are overpopulating the lake," says Mike Cerise of Buckhorn Sporting Goods (719-486-3944). "You'd think they (the Colorado Division of Wildlife) would come up here and do something about it, but they don't."

Management issues are of concern at Turquoise. There's no mystery on how to catch Macks. However, catching bigger fish requires tossing dozens of 18- to 24-inch Macks back. The lake's most sought-after fish are beginning to grow to the size of rainbow trout.

"There are a ton of the Macks in there. Almost too many in my opinion," Cerise says. "There are some big ones in there if a guy can just find them."

Mackinaw to 40 pounds are available, just rare. Many anglers say the limit on Mackinaw should be increased to crop the population and increase the size of the fish.

"They must reproduce really well. You can keep two fish of any size and there are still too many," Cerise says. "They could put a limit of four fish to get rid of all the damn little ones, and they need to put more fish in there so they can eat. They used to stock tons of rainbows and cutthroat in here. Not stocking rainbows is taking away from the food source."

Cerise says that five years ago the DOW stocked many cutthroat and rainbow trout. Unfortunately, now they don't plant the same load that they did in the past.

"They say Turquoise is whirling disease free and they aren't going to stock any fish unless they find fish that are whiling disease free," says Cerise. "I

think its all crap. It's all propaganda."

Propaganda, or not, there are other needs that need to be addressed. Like water levels. Anglers are aware of the abundance of Macks. The mystery is where the water will be.

"Who knows where to tell people to fish? We never know where the lake levels are going to be. I wish I knew," Cerise says. "Heck, I don't even know who to call up there to find out. Too many people take water from this lake. I've never seen it this low before. There was a drought last year which hurt us. We got a lot of snow this year, but it depends on if they keep it stored here or if they send it down south. It all depends on what the water companies do."

In mid-June the lake was down 30 to 40 vertical feet. There was no way to get a boat on the water, no telling where the water would be next.

Finding fish: Ah-ha. So we've learned quickly that Turquoise Lake can be a challenge to fish. With water yo-yoing up and down the fishery can change daily. The fish are constantly on the move.

How can you be successful in following the curve? The secret in this lake is keying in on structure. When the lake is full, finding the structure is easier because many anglers have pinpointed all the structure through years of practice. However, with recent low levels, locating the best spots is more difficult.

"You fish the reservoir the same way you do when it's full. You just have to find the structure," Cerise says. "When the lake is up we know where the structure is. It just makes it easier. There are some good fish in there. If anglers find good structure they're going to find fish."

Structure is available all over the lake. However, the north and south side tend to harbor more fish, and better structure. In July, typically, look for deep water. Water containing Mackinaw can be found on either end of the dam, with most fish coming out of 20 to 50 feet of water. Most Macks can be found wherever you locate steep drop-offs.

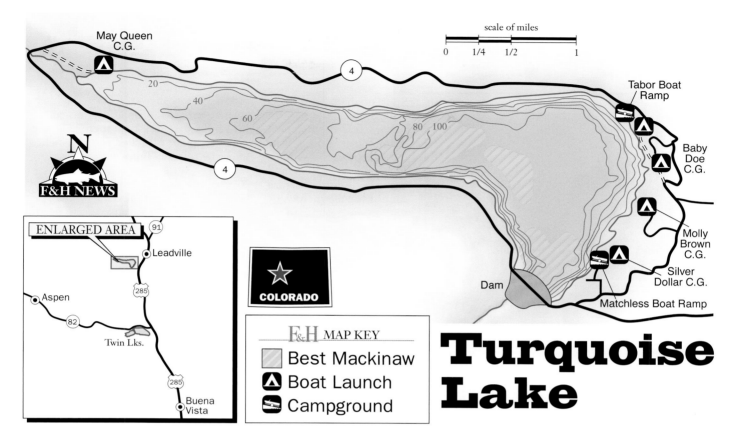

F&H MAP KEY

▨	Best Mackinaw
⛺	Boat Launch
⛴	Campground

Turquoise Lake

Techniques range from bait fishing to trolling to jigging. Macks can be attained from shore or boat.

When fishing lures, drag the bottom. While you will lose some rigs, your chances of catching more fish are greater if you pull your lures as close to the lake bottom as possible.

Want to really increase your catch rates? Plan on getting hung up on rocks and stumps. Dragging your lure right on the bottom and stirring up silt, mud and sand can stimulate a feeding frenzy. The movement on the bottom of the lake calls in curious Mackinaw who think baitfish are swimming through.

Turquoise's contour is composed of tree stumps, rocks, sand and silt. Flatfish and Rapalas are your best bet for dragging the bottom. Rainbows, browns and perch pattern Rapalas take the most fish.

From shore, most anglers experience success casting Kastmasters, Rapalas and Dardevles. Live bait is also an option. Dead sucker meat, night-crawlers and waterdogs will pull Macks if you fish these baits on the bottom. "Let it sit on the bottom just like you're catfishing," Cerise says.

Jigging can also be productive. Gitzits with sucker meat tipped on the hook or ¼- to ¾-ounce jigs in pearl, white, glow and chartreuse all work well. In the deepest water, some anglers use 2-ounce jigs.

Jigging tends to be most productive if you let your jig sink to the bottom and then reel up two or three cranks before jigging. However, use your fish finder to your advantage. If you see fish suspended, jig at the depths that correspond to where the fish are on your finder.

At Turquoise, catching larger Macks can take patience and a lot of work. Rather than using smaller lures, many anglers drag much larger plugs and throw out entire suckers to try and discourage the dinks from grabbing them. A T-60 Flatfish works great.

"To get a big one it takes hours of fishing," Cerise says. "I'm talking 200 to 300 hours of fishing, and then you may get a bigger one. It just takes a lot of time and a lot of luck. This year I haven't heard of any big ones. We used to get a lot of big ones; it just doesn't happen as much anymore." **F&H**

AT a GLANCE

What: Battling water levels and weeding through abundant smaller fish to find trophy Mackinaw on Turquoise Lake.

Where: Turquoise Lake is just west of Leadville, along the upper stretches of the Arkansas River.

When: You can catch Macks year-round. It can be a battle when waters are low. In July, head for either end of the dam or the deeper water on either end of the lake.

How: Trolling or jigging will produce most. Pull banana plugs or stickbaits right on the bottom. You can also jig light colored jigs and twisters or tube baits. Bait works fabulously too.

Who: Buckhorn Sporting Goods (719-486-3944).

Head to Williams Fork for pike, Macks, more

PARSHALL

by Mike Kennedy

40-INCH pike like this one caught by Andres Barraza in January of 2003 await you under the ice at Williams Fork Reservoir. You can also catch Macks, trout and kokanee here.

Department of Wildlife biologist Bill Atkinson told me that the water level at Williams Fork Reservoir was at 7,775 feet in elevation in early December, which is down 36 feet from normal pool. Being down 36 feet may sound like a lot, but when you consider that the reservoir was down 110 feet back in 2002, 36 feet is not a major drop for this deep lake. This is good news for ice fishermen.

Williams Fork has Mackinaw, rainbow, cutthroat, brown trout and kokanee salmon, but it's probably best known for its huge northern pike. The state record pike — weighing 30 pounds, 6 ounces and measuring at 43½ inches — was caught at Williams Fork in 1996 by Dave Van Cleave.

Sportsman's Warehouse (303-858-1800) in Aurora had their annual customer/employee fishing derby at Williams Fork on Jan. 1, 2004, and customer Andres Barraza caught a 40-inch, 20-plus-pound northern pike through the ice. Barraza caught his trophy on 6-pound test without a steal leader, but that's not the recommended way to go after pike.

Don't go to Williams Fork (or any lake, for that matter) with one fishing rod and expect it to be adequate for all species. The trick for catching multiple species through the ice is to adapt your gear, lures and bait to the target species. For pike or lake trout, you generally need tougher equipment than you do for rainbows. Barraza was able to land his giant fish with light gear, but more fishermen will lose good fish using light equipment than will catch them. For larger fish it's best to use at least a medium action 30- to 45-inch rod and use at least 8-pound test line. I like to use 12-pound fluorocarbon or fluorocarbon coated line.

You can catch pike by jigging spoons or swimming lures like the Northland Air-Plane jigs, Rapalas or Nil's Master jigging minnows, but fish normally have to be in an aggressive mood. When fish are not hitting aggressively, use a 2- to 4-inch tube tipped with sucker meat. You can also use a whole sucker or piece of sucker on a quick-strike rig. If you have a two rod stamp, it's a good idea to set up a tip-up in close to shore (6 to 10 feet deep) with sucker meat laying on or near the bottom, then jig a tube tipped with sucker meat on a rod in slightly deeper water. Fish off the east boat ramp, near the inlet or in the west side finger coves.

Mike Crosby, DOW Wildlife Manager for Williams Fork, asked me to remind anglers that there is a slot limit on pike. All pike 26 to 34 inches must be released immediately.

If you're after lake trout, you can use the same equipment you would for pike, but you might move out to deeper water. Flats or humps in 20 to 50 feet of water with rocky bottoms seem to attract winter Macks. You might start the day fishing at 10 or 15 feet in early morning, then continue to work your way out toward 50 feet of water as the day goes on or until you find fish. A flat near a sharp drop-off is a good location to try.

I like to use white or chartreuse tubes for lake trout. White is the most popular color because it resembles a sucker, but chartreuse works better at certain times. When you place the tube jig inside the tube, don't push it all the way to the end of the tube. If you leave about ½-inch of hollow space at the tip of the tube, it will cause the tube to circle as it falls through the water, much like a dying sucker. You'll want to add a high quality barrel swivel up about 4 feet on your line to reduce line twist.

If you're fishing tubes and getting bites but missing fish, you might need to add a stinger hook. Missed fish usually mean short strikes. Fish are nipping at the tail of the tube. Adding a stinger hook will catch those tail biters. I almost always use a stinger hook and probably catch at least 50 percent of the Macks I get on the stinger. A stinger hook is an ultra sharp No. 4 or 6 treble hook attached to the back of the tube hook. Use a ¼-inch piece of surgical tubing, place it over the eye of the stinger hook, then push the point of the tube hook through the tubing and stinger hook eye. The tubing keeps the stinger hook pointing straight behind the tube and doesn't allow it to hang down below the tube. Cut a piece of sucker meat 2 by 4 inches, turn it skin down (toward the hooks) and place the tip of the tube hook and one tine of the stinger hook into the sucker skin. If you're not sure how to do this, come into the Aurora Sportsman's Warehouse any Friday or Saturday and I'll show you how.

You'll want to use much lighter and more sensitive equipment when fishing for rainbow, browns, cutts or kokanee. You won't even notice most of the bites if you're using medium-action gear and heavy line for these smaller fish. While trout might show periods of aggressive behavior, they'll more frequently be in a neutral or negative mood, and if you don't have light and very sensitive gear they may mouth your offering and you'll never know it. Work your lure too aggressively and you won't get a bite.

When fishing any trout lake through the ice, a good technique is to slowly jig a slab spoon or ice jig tipped with Power Bait or worm in one hole and have a stationary rod in another hole trying for inactive trout. On the stationary rig try a size ten Ratfinkee, or even No. 8 or 10 plain gold hook tipped with Power Bait or a piece of mealworm or wax worm. Small 1- to 1 1/2-inch tubes tipped with Power Bait or worm also can be effective.

For very subtle bites, lower your bait or lure into the water with your stationary rod to the level you want to try, then lift the line a few inches and put a small slice of cork on the line as a strike indicator. Don't wait for the cork to go under like a bobber, but watch for a subtle wiggle. When you see the wiggle, pick up the rod and slowly lift. If you feel any tension, gently set the hook. A small piece of cork works better than a small float because the float will freeze unless you're inside of a hut. The piece of cork will just pop off your line as you reel in the fish.

Jig the lure an inch or 2 every few minutes, but mostly leave it alone. Trout will be near shore in 20 feet of water or less. The kokanee spawn at Williams Fork is over, so look for non-spawning kokanee suspended out over the channel.

Use caution on ice at Williams Fork. Water fluctuation can cause water to drop below the ice cap, creating an air pocket and unsafe conditions. Always test ice before going out on it, don't fish alone and carry safety equipment. In addition, remember that no snowmobiles are allowed at Williams Fork.

To get to Williams Fork take I-70 west to Silverthorne and go north 36½

Williams Fork Reservoir

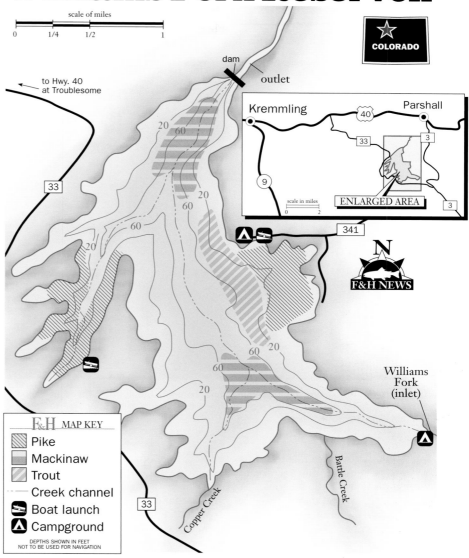

miles on Highway 9 to Highway 40 at Kremmling. Turn east on Highway 40 and go 13 miles to CR 3 just east of Parshall. Follow CR 3 2 miles south to the entrance to the east boat ramp. For more information contact Dan

Murphy at The Fishing Hole (970-724-9407) in Kremmling.

Editor's note: For more information, be sure to visit Mike Kennedy's Web site (www.coloradowarmwaterfishing.com)

F&H

AT a GLANCE

What: Ice fishing for trout, kokanee and huge pike at Williams Fork Reservoir.

When: From now until ice-out.

Where: To get to Williams Fork take I-70 west to Silverthorne and go north 36 1/2 miles on Highway 9 to Highway 40 at Kremmling. Turn east on Highway 40 and go 13 miles to CR 3 just east of Parshall. Follow CR 3 2 miles south to the entrance to the east boat ramp.

Who: The Fishing Hole (970-724-9407) in Kremmling.

Find brookies, songdogs at Willow Creek

RAND

by Giles Alkire

HEAVING FLIES on Willow Creek can produce some beautiful brook trout. There are some big browns in the heavy cover too. You'll also do well fishing beaver huts. And on top of all that, you can drop a coyote or two.

How'd ya like to find a place that's a dream for all seasons? A place that'll provide a parade of splendid colors in September, big game galore in October and plenty of snowshoein' or X-country ski ventures in Old Man Winter's snowy wonderland? What if it included a stream for a brookie bash that'll last 'most all summer and also has prime opportunities for songdog shootin' all year 'round?

Well, as a matter of fact, I know of many that'd fill that bill, but there's a few of 'em that stand out like sore thumbs. If you'd like to visit one of my own all time favorites, follow me and we'll take a trek to upper Willow Creek.

Willow Creek? Good gosh! How in Billy Heck are you supposed to know which one I'm talkin' about?

Sometimes I think the early scouts were sorely lackin' in imagination when it came to namin' things. As the Colorado Water Code Book lists 'em, we've got *102* Willow Creeks! Every stream with a copse of nearby willows got tagged with the name.

(There are 35 Muddy Creeks, an appellation intended to attest to the roily nature of the water. It seems some of 'em were a shade on the careless side, too, because they apparently found — and Lost — 37 lakes that bear that name. To top it off, when all other options were exhausted, they named 15 li'l streams "No Name Creek.")

So you see, we have Willow Creeks and Willow Creeks, but *this* one is special! To get there, go 5 miles south of Rand on Highway 125 and turn west on FSRD 106. The road is a good one, gravel surfaced and usually well maintained. Five miles after leaving the pavement, you'll punch out of the timber and cross the stream on a bridge.

The stream's thin and wispy near the bridge, but deeper downstream if fishin's your bag. Upstream, a series of densely willowed beaver dams are on the road's south side. Meandering, gravel-bottomed open-water runs squirm their way through the meadow between the dams.

Those beaver dams are great summer fishin', if you don't mind a close encounter of the moose kind from time to time! And it will cost you some tackle; there are dozens of my flies and lures lodged somewhere down there. But all in all, it's been one heck of a good trade-off through the years. I've brought hundreds of fish to hand. Put most of 'em back, but filled many a sizzlin' streamside skillet too.

About 2½ miles after crossing the first bridge, you'll come to another one. I've hung the wheels in the li'l pocket just across the bridge on the south side of the river more times than I can count. It's a beaut of a spot to spend a day or a weekend.

Few beaver works are above this point. many were once there, but most have failed. The stream is pocketed, twisting, and even though it's not impressive at first sight, actually has

AT a GLANCE

What: Heading for the high country south of Rand to ply the pools and beaver water of Willow Creek.

Where: You can fish just about any of the water you find. Head south of Rand on Highway 125. Head west FSRD 106 and proceed to the bridges. They'll provide access.

When: Now that things are warming up, you can't miss the timing. The fish are there and will fall to a simple box of tackle.

How: It's simple game. Your most basic baits will work. Try taking a simple fly box for a great time haulin' flies.

Who: Give Giles Alkire a ring at (970) 352-9501 or stop by and see him at his shop at 1211 9th St. in Greeley between 10 a.m. and 4:30 p.m. any weekday.

Willow Creek

quite a few really fine trout in it. They're easy to nail on Fireballs, Garden Worms or Cheese Baits. Wanna toss a few flies? Well, that's actually about all it'll take; you won't need a box full of patterns.

Take Hornbergs, Black Halfbacks, Parachute Royal Coachmen, Bead Head Hare's Ears and Float-N-Fools and you'll come home happy. Tuck the Hare's Ears and Halfbacks as tight to cover as your ability to cast will allow and throw the rest of 'em at the still pools. Cast 'em upstream, keep a pretty taut line, but let 'em run the current.

Coyote gunnin': From that second bridge all the way to Troublesome Pass lies a long stretch of excellent coyote-callin' country. The terrain of the whole area changes in a matter of a few hundred yards from the deep, narrow valley with heavily timbered hills to a series of wide-open, rolling slopes strewn with low brush, thin timber pockets, sagebrush and potentilla clumps.

Game is abundant, both large and small, and the 'yotes are well fed, creating quite a paradox. They're quick to pounce on a potential meal.

The stream pretty well hugs the north side of the meadows. it's often hidden in willow patches, but much of it is open to the sky. A number of marmots as well as rabbits inhabit the grassy slopes. For a different kind of play, you just might wanna try snooker-in' in a sassy songdog or two with a whistle instead of a scream. I'm sure you've heard woodchucks whistlin' in the woods. If so, you know the sound.

Here's a new way to play the coyote callin' game. Remember that old playground attention getter when you were a kid? Two fingers in yer mouth between yer teeth and one mighty big lungful of air was all it took to get people lookin' at you. Shucks, in *those* days we even whistled at *girls!* Well, that's the groundhog whistle coyote callin' caper. With a bit of practice, it'll work!

Give a couple of quick chirps, a 10- to 20-second pause, a couple more spaced closer together, a pause and one long "Wheeeooo;" then pipe down and wait. It won't always work, but when it does it's quite a satisfaction to know you did it all yourself.

A soft-voiced rabbit distress call is always a reliable standby to fall back on. Don't call too loud; your call is likely to travel farther than your rifle can shoot. If you give an old 'yote too much time to think things over he'll bolt and be off to far places faster than you can say "Dadgummit," or sumpin' similar.

In the summer when it's dry, this road can be run in the family sedan. But if we've had a rainy spell, plan on takin' a 4X4 and headin' for the car wash when you get home. I can almost guarantee you're gonna be driving a mighty muddy buggy!

F&H

F&H MAP KEY

(diagonal hatch)	Top trout fishing
✳	Good beaver dam fishing
(horizontal lines)	Excellent coyote shootin'

Get buggy for Yampa's August trout

by Dusty Routh

Just about everyone in Colorado will be swearing at the sweltering dog days of August as summertime weather comes on with a vengeance. Just about everyone, that is, except practitioners of the *coup de grâce* of fly fishing, and that's dry fly fishermen. Hot summer days mean strong hatches, big numbers of terrestrials and active fish. If there's one month out of the year when you need to be on the water, it's now.

Fishing this time of year is spurred by early morning and evening insect activity, midday terrestrials like 'hoppers hitting the water and insatiable trout appetites. So put your cold weather nymphs and streamers away, get out your micro-sized tippets, line out your featherlight 3- and 4-weights and let's go fish some dries!

Yank 'em out on the Yampa: One of the best and most accessible rivers in the state for dry fly action is the productive Yampa River. This is one of the most versatile and fun rivers to fish in Colorado. From snowshoe and parka fishing in February to shirtsleeves and shorts in August, the Yampa offers a wide variety of gamefish and an excellent setting in which to pursue them.

Tom Cox at Bucking Rainbow Outfitters in Steamboat Springs (888-810-8747) recommends hitting the Yampa right in town this time of year. Fly anglers will find excellent opportunities for rising fish that are coming after 'hoppers, particularly at midday.

"The 'hopper/dropper combo can be deadly," Cox says. That's a foam 'hopper imitation up top, trailing a small beadhead dropper. The dropper should be a size 18, and can be your choice of a Pheasant Tail, Prince nymph, or a Copper John (so don't put your winter nymphs completely away). "That's really a midday thing," Cox says.

Early and late in the day, you can opt to go with Yellow Sally stoneflies or any caddis imitation. Parachute Adams are also very, very effective on the Yampa.

"There's really good 'hopper activity on the Yampa," Cox says of recent days on the river. "If you fish a foam 'hopper

IF IT'S AUGUST, it's time to chase trout on the Yampa River. This is the time of year when dry fly anglers shine. Natalee Faupel and her fishing buddy Sean caught this brownie in 2003.

this time of year, the water is low enough you can fish it just about anywhere."

Cox recommends floating the 'hopper/dropper combination on a dead drift. "Fish it right over the holes," he says, "and in all the side pockets."

Cox says he hasn't heard of really big trout being taken, but the numbers of trout you'll hit will be impressive because the 'hopper/dropper combo fished correctly can be irresistible to trout in August. The Yampa offers browns, rainbows, Snake River cutts and a few brookies. On the lower river over near Craig, you'll find smallmouth bass and even northern pike. The trout average 12 to 16 inches, which isn't bad, while the browns can get considerably larger.

Where-to on the Yampa: Between Stagecoach Reservoir and Lake Catamount, fly anglers will find good

tailwater fishing access just below Stagecoach (mile 13) and excellent access at the Service Creek State Wildlife Area (mile 15) and again on BLM land (at mile 16).

Once you're below Lake Catamount, Bucking Rainbow Outfitters guides on a private lease at the tailwaters below Catamount in the Pleasant Valley area. Fly anglers can also approach the river between Catamount and Steamboat Springs. The creek mouths along this stretch of river can offer great fishing, including Fish, Watson, Agate, Oak and McKinnis creeks.

Even better, catch-and-release fishing right in Steamboat Springs can be awesome. This is restricted water (flies and lures only, catch-and-release only) and it's stuffed with lots of eager rainbows. There's tons of public access in town.

Once you're down past Steamboat Springs, there's great fishing all the way to Hayden, Yampa and Craig, with the warmwater fish picking up in numbers.

Guide picks: Most Bucking Rainbow guides are working private ranchland sections on the lower Elk River near the confluence with the Yampa, on the White River near Meeker and in the tailwaters of Lake Catamount. As usual for this time of year, the White is producing some big browns. The 'hopper/dropper works well on the White, and so does a beadhead mini-leech in black or olive.

"I think two of the best places around for dry fly fishing are the Yampa right here in town, and the Elk or Bear rivers," Cox says. "On the upper Elk and the upper Yampa, I'd fish Red Humpies and other attractor flies like a Renegade or a Royal Wulff. You can fish those almost all day on the upper Elk and throughout the Yampa."

Yampa River

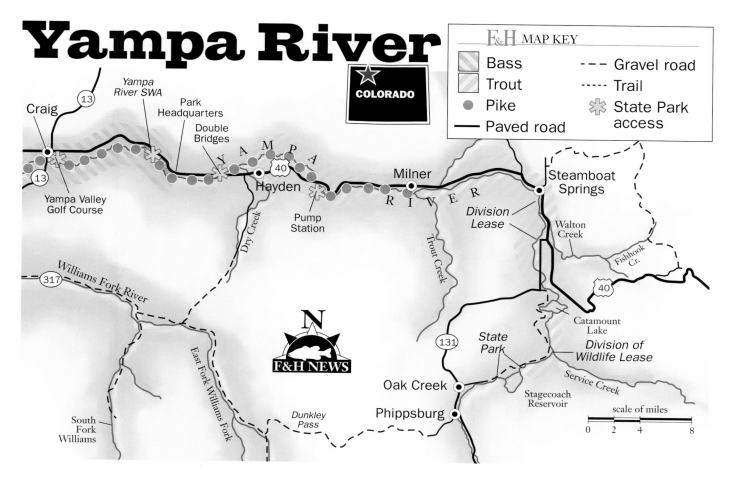

F&H MAP KEY

Map Key:
- Bass
- Trout
- Pike
- Paved road
- Gravel road
- Trail
- State Park access

COLORADO

(Map labels: Craig, 13, Yampa River SWA, Park Headquarters, Double Bridges, Yampa Valley Golf Course, Dry Creek, Pump Station, Hayden, 40, Milner, YAMPA RIVER, Trout Creek, Steamboat Springs, Division Lease, Walton Creek, Fishhook Cr., 40, Catamount Lake, Division of Wildlife Lease, Service Creek, Stagecoach Reservoir, State Park, 131, Oak Creek, Phippsburg, Dunkley Pass, East Fork Williams Fork, South Fork Williams, Williams Fork River, 317, N F&H NEWS, scale of miles 0 2 4 8)

Don't forget smallmouth: Yeah, yeah, we know, smallmouth bass aren't trout. But they can be just about as scrappy as any freshwater fish that will hit a fly, and if you haven't tangled with some redeyes on a flyrod before, you should give it a try.

Smallmouth are amazingly active in August, being warmwater fish, and you'll find them a lot less prone to warmwater lethargy than their cold-water cousins. The Yampa over near the Craig area can be awesome for smallmouth from early August until early September.

Cox recommends going after these river bronzebacks with crawdad imitations and leech patterns. Woolly Buggers will do the trick in blacks and olives and even maroon colors. But if you want some real heart-pounding action, try fishing in flat side pockets and back eddies early in the morning and late in the evening with topwater poppers. These can be the small wood variety like you'd use for bluegill, all the way up to the larger Mylar and tinsel varieties that saltwater fly fishermen favor.

The biggest mistake that most anglers make when they're fishing topwater patterns for smallmouth is to move the fly too often and too fast. Smallmouth have admirable sight and sound senses, and they can key on topwater offerings from a distance. But they can be maddeningly cautious.

To catch these tricky fish, make your cast, pop it once or twice and let it sit. And let it sit. And let it sit. Then pop it again. This slow, deliberate pop-and-pause retrieval works like a charm on bass.

The Juniper Springs and Duffy Canyon areas are perfect if you want to get some fight time with these bronzebacks. You might also hit a pike while you're there. ***F&H***

AT a GLANCE

What: Outstanding summertime dry fly action on the Yampa River.

How: A 'hopper/dropper combination works wonders for the Yampa's browns, cutts and rainbows. Go with leech patterns like Woolly Buggers and topwater fly poppers for smallmouth.

Where: Dry fly action is good this time of year throughout the river. For some of the best water, fish the CNR section right in Steamboat Springs. Fish near Craig for smallies.

When: August is awesome for terrestrials ('hoppers, Chernobyl ants, etc.), and classic dries (Royal Wulffs, Stimulators). Expect excellent dry fly action on smallmouth until early September.

Who: Contact Tom Cox at Bucking Rainbow Outfitters in Steamboat Springs (888-810-8747). Bucking Rainbow has access to private land in the area.

SOUTHWEST FISHING

Blue Mesa offers hot summer fishing for kokes, 'bows

GUNNISON

by Steve Nelson

JOHNATHAN BERCKETELDT with a 5½-pound Blue Mesa brown trout.

Juue means fireworks and summer vacations, for most people. For fishermen at Blue Mesa Reservoir, it means all of the above and kokanee salmon. "They are the leading species for summer fishing," says Colorado Division of

Wildlife biologist Dan Brauch (970-641-7060). "This year I believe anglers are doing pretty good. Our kokanee fishing rebounded last year after a 7-year decline. Things look good; the fish I'm seeing are running in the 12- to 14-inch range, with some 16- to 17-inchers."

That's not huge by some standards, but it is respectable, and anglers are catching enough to keep them interested. Expect the bite to stay strong through the end of the month and then slow in August as the salmon begin their annual spawning run up the Gunnison River.

Where and how: Blue Mesa is a huge reservoir, but there are several places that consistently produce kokanee: Iola Basin, the mouth of Cebolla Creek, the mouth of West Elk Creek, and the area around Middle Bridge. Most are caught on small, bright-colored lures. Blue Mesa fishing guide Randy Wiig works out of the Elk Creek Marina (970-641-0707) and has some suggestions for anglers. "We fish for kokanee with 12- to 15-pound test leadcore line, and in July we'll be running about 4 or 5 colors out," he says. "I use 15 to 20 feet of 6- or 8-pound test leader and run a Dick Nite, Needlefish or an Arnie's

lure. Good colors are pink, red and chartreuse.

"Some people like to use a small stringer of flashers like Pop Geer. And they do work — especially when the bite is slow. They'll also tip the hook with a kernel of white corn, and I think that can help too."

When you hook a kokanee, remember that they have very soft mouths and it's easy to pull the hook out. Bring them to the boat quickly, but don't try horsing them in or you may lose the fish.

Wiig adds that the best time to fish for kokanee is early in the morning. "Definitely, it's by far the best time," he says.

Other species: Next to the salmon, rainbow and cutthroat trout are the most popular fish in the summer. "We stocked the reservoir with 850,000 sub-catchables (150,000 were Snake River cutthroat) this year," says Brauch. "We don't put catchables in, so the larger fish people are catching this summer were stocked the previous year. Last year the average for rainbows and cutthroat was around 14 inches, and that was a little better than we see during most years.

"There are also brown trout in the lake. They reproduce naturally, and we think many of them come into the lake from the tributary streams. This spring we saw a lot of nice-sized browns landed."

Where and how: "Trout fishing can be very good using the same tackle we use for kokanee," says Wiig. "You just have to fish them shallower. A lot of people fish a flasher or Pop Geer trailing a worm, and that's very effective on the trout. It's real popular. And for the browns, the best fishing is trolling the shoreline with a Rapala."

An average brown trout is usually solidly in the 14- to 18-inch range. They can be caught during the summer, but the best fishing is in the spring and fall — that's when the really big browns are landed. If you're hoping for a brown trout during the summer, the best fishing is very early in the morning or late in the evening. Troll the points

AT A GLANCE

Location: Just west of Gunnison accessed via Highway 50.

Species: Rainbow trout, cutthroat trout, brown trout, lake trout, kokanee salmon.

Bag limit: Trout is four fish, lake trout is eight fish, kokanee salmon is 10 fish.

Fees: There is a fee to launch your boat. A 2-day launch permit is $4, a 14-day is $10, and an annual permit is $30.

Camping/Facilities: There are numerous private and public campgrounds at the reservoir. Groceries, gas and motels are available in nearby Gunnison. The lake has two full-service marinas: the Elk Creek Marina (970-641-0707) and the Lake Fork Marina (970-641-3048).

For more information: Contact Gunnison Sporting Goods (970-641-5022), the Colorado Division of Wildlife (970-641-7060), or the Curecanti National Recreation Area (970-641-2337). You can also access them at <www.nps.gov/cure/>.

and rocky outcrops. Fish baits around the inlet areas.

For those of you who don't have a boat or aren't willing to rent one, the shoreline can be quite productive. "They catch a lot of trout around the inlets with Power Bait and worms," says Wiig.

Rigging up is simple. Run a good quality 4- or 6-pound test line, use a sliding sinker above a swivel, and run 12 to 18 inches of leader to a single-egg hook or small bait-holder hook. Power Bait will take both cutthroats and rainbows. If you're hoping for one of Blue Mesa's bigger brown trout, stick with nightcrawlers or salmon eggs. Natural baits are more effective for the browns, and there's nothing a brown trout likes more than a nightcrawler.

You should also be able to catch plenty of trout on lures cast from the shoreline. Almost any kind of flashy spoon should work, so use your favorite and change lures often if you're not getting bites. Run at least 6-pound test line, as there are quality fish in the lake and you don't want to lose a big brown or rainbow because you fished with too light a line.

A more active lure is more effective than a passive one, so cast out, let it sink, and then bring it back slowly, jigging the rod tip occasionally to add some action. Move often if you aren't getting bites. Spending more than 15 minutes in one spot isn't good strategy.

Popular areas for bait dunkers include the Lake City Bridge, Red Creek, Cebolla Creek, West Elk, Lake Fork and Soap Creek.

Lake trout: Blue Mesa holds some of the largest lake trout in the state, but the middle of summer is not the time to fish for them. "There's not much effort on the lake trout during the summer," says Wiig. "They go into the deeper water and scatter. They are hard to find. Fishing picks back up again in the fall when the lake begins to cool down, but it's still not as good as the spring after ice-out. That's the best time of the year to fish for them."

Should you want to try for lake trout, you'll need a boat with a depth finder. Jigging the bottom with tube jigs tipped with sucker meat should be effective. Find the deep-water structure: a hump, shelf, dropoff, contour change. Lake trout tend to associate themselves with structure.

Brauch says that the lake didn't fill this year, but there is plenty of water. No problems launching a boat are expected.

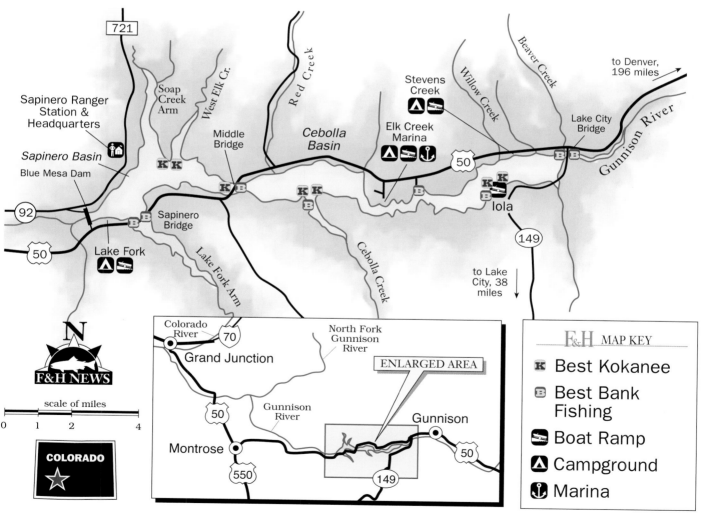

BLUE MESA RESERVOIR

Blue Mesa: Colorado's best big Mack fishery

GUNNISON

by Dusty Routh

MONSTER MACKS: Jig for big Mackinaw like this one at Blue Mesa Reservoir. Anglers have broken the Colorado Mack record at Blue Mesa on multiple occasions.

From his front porch overlooking big Blue Mesa Reservoir near Gunnison, John Ferro with Ferro's Blue Mesa Guide Service and Blue Mesa Ranch (800-617-4671) can plainly see the day-to-day developments and fishing activities on this sprawling impoundment of the Gunnison River. He knows better than just about anyone else when it's time to hit the lake for the best springtime laker bite.

In late April, Ferro said it wasn't time just yet. But May is usually one of the top times to get on the lake to fish for lakers the size of your leg as they come up from the depths on their springtime feeding binges.

From hayfields to lake trout troughs: Way, way back before Blue Mesa was one of Colorado's most beautiful and most productive reservoirs, this area around the Gunnison River was a series of high plateau hayfields. When the reservoir went in, those hayfields were transformed from their dry land crop-growing capacity to shallow,

underwater plateaus that draw lake trout in the spring like John Elway draws autograph seekers.

Ferro says Blue Mesa had a nice, early ice-off this year, and conditions are right for the month of May for hitting these monster lake trout. "Most of the anglers fishing this time of year will be targeting those oversized mackinaw," he says. "That's because in early spring the Macks come up close to the surface. You can catch them in fairly shallow water. They'll come up and feed pretty hard."

Ferro advises that anglers who want a shot at these fish not waste time. May is the hottest month for producing big fish. "Once June comes around, those fish will go back down into the depths of the lake, and their appetites can become dormant," he says. "So that's why I watch from my front porch, to see the boats. Once there's 10 or 15 boats in a spot, I know the lakers have shown up."

Ferro says it can be a real bonanza. "May is just such a good month. There will be tons of people out there, all trying to knock them dead. And they'll do pretty good. A lot of state records have come from Blue Mesa."

Ferro says that the 46.16-pound state record caught last season would have come closer to 50 pounds except that it had nothing in its stomach. "The big fish before that one, another 46-pounder, had something like 8 pounds of food in it. Imagine if this latest fish had had something in its stomach when it was caught. It would have topped 50 pounds easy."

What and where: Ferro says the most productive way to get on these shallow feeding lakers is to jig with sucker meat. You can catch them trolling too, but jigging is absolutely, hands-down the most preferred and most effective way to trigger a strike.

"Bounce that jig right off the bottom," Ferro says. "In May you're looking for fish in only about 20 to 30 feet of water. Go with black or green jigs and use plenty of sucker meat."

Blue Mesa hot spots are pretty easy to find. If you're new to the lake, hire a guide or watch for where the other boats are fishing. "It will be good all around the islands," Ferro says. "And look for where the bottom flattens out on the lake, like in the Sapinero Basin. That's where the river went through those fields, at the upper end, those hayfields and little plateaus. The lake trout stay down low in the river channel trough, then come up on those old hayfields going towards the middle of the lake, near the Middle Bridge, and over by the Lake City bridge at the deep end, and all around Mack Island."

Kokanee kamp: While lake trout might hold his interest, Ferro's heart is more firmly planted in the outstanding kokanee fishing that Blue Mesa offers. Fishing from his pontoon boat kokanee platform, Ferro loves chasing down these fine-eating fish.

"The real game fish in my opinion in Blue Mesa is kokanee," he says. "They just eat so well. That's what most of the people are after, good eating fish. Now, there are a lot of people who fish for the big lakers, no doubt about it. But about 99 percent of them throw the lakers back even though the government would like those lakers to be taken out. The lakers just aren't very good to eat."

Ferro says the fact that Blue Mesa grows such huge lakers is both a blessing and a curse. "Oh, they're fun to catch, those big lakers. But after they reach about 9 pounds or so, they just get too big and too fatty. They get oily. Needless to say, by that point they're just not a good eating fish."

Ferro also guides for big rainbows, the lake's resident brown trout and splake (a cross between a brook and a lake trout).

Blue Mesa has been plagued by low water, of course, like practically every other reservoir in the state. But it looks to be a little better this year than last year. "It was down something like 94 feet last year," Ferro says. "So far this year I think it's only down 74 to 80 feet. So that's a little better. But there are some real low spots in the lake, so you have to be careful when you're out there in a boat."

Ferro says the low water doesn't seem to be affecting the mood of the Mackinaw. "The way I look at it, when the water's low you have a smaller body of water, but the same amount of fish," he says. "I think it makes it easier to fish."

Ferro says that the DOW is continuing to stock Blue Mesa with a very aggressive stocking schedule. "They just continue to stock it like always," he says. "They put 3.5 million kokanee in there, and rainbows in the 300,000 to 400,000 range. A lot of those rainbows naturally reproduce on top of all that stocking. So you have a lot of fish in the water."

All that stocking is good if you're a Mackinaw nut, too. Those granddaddy Macks have plenty to munch on. "That's another reason the Macks come up on those flats," Ferro says. "They come up for those fingerlings that are being stocked. Those Macks really hone in on those areas."

Other goodies: Ferro's operation also offers horseback riding, stream fishing for cutthroat in all the surrounding trib-

utaries to Blue Mesa and overnight trips. He also offers cabins and a store. You can also stay at Lake Fork Cabins and RV Park (800-368-9421). Nearby Lake Fork Marina (970-641-3048) opens Memorial Day weekend. **F&H**

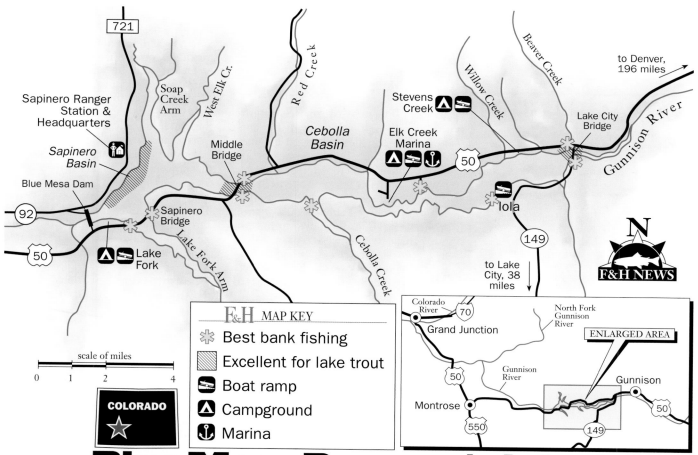

Blue Mesa Reservoir lake trout

The Gunnison: A hatch to beat all hatches

ALMONT

by Holger Jensen

The Gunnison River begins at the confluence of the East and Taylor rivers near the little town of Almont on the western side of the Continental Divide. There are no headwaters as such; being a combination of two others rivers, it's big to start with and gets bigger, draining nearly 4,000 square miles of Western Slope before it empties into the Colorado River near Grand Junction.

There are two distinct sections of the Gunnison above and below Blue Mesa Reservoir, which itself stretches 23 miles long with 75 miles of shoreline and offers superb fishing for lake trout, big browns and kokanee salmon. A record Mackinaw weighing more than 45 pounds was caught there April 11.

But the Gunnison is a flycaster's dream, offering a variety of wet and dry fishing capped by the world-renowned salmonfly hatch. And that hatch will start soon.

SALMONFLIES are the key to fish like this brown trout on the Gunnison River in the next few weeks. Big horkin' ugly bugs will be your best bet, and don't worry about making subtle presentations.

AT a GLANCE

What: Fishing an amazing salmonfly hatch on the Gunnison River from Crystal Reservoir to the confluence with the Colorado River.

Where: The entire Gunnison River provides some excellent fishing this time of year. But the salmonfly hatch is something to behold. They begin hatching about 5 miles below the confluence of the North Fork near Highway 92 and move steadily upriver through the Black Canyon of the Gunnison National Monument until they run out of aerated water at Crystal Reservoir.

When: Things should start picking up as runoff starts to taper. Look for things to pick up in the next couple weeks.

How: Fishing salmonflies from sizes 2 through 8. You may do well with an assortment of dries.

Who: Three Rivers Resort (970-641-1303); Gunnison River Pleasure Park (970-872-2525).

Of course, a lot depends on weather and ambient temperatures. The hatch occurs when the water reaches 50 degrees, and it's not as if you can climb down 2,000 feet into the Black Canyon every day with a thermometer. The best bet is to keep in touch with Leroy Jagodinsky at the Gunnison River Pleasure Park (970-872-2525). He has lived on the river for 29 years and and racked up an enviable record for predicting the arrival of old "Ptero," the prehistoric monster of the aquatic insect world.

Bugs: The Western Salmonfly (*Pteronarcys*) is the biggest of the dark stoneflies, 2 inches long with a 4-inch wing span. The body and wings are dark gray or brown ranging to black, but the soft parts between the head and thoracic segments are a bright smoked salmon orange, hence its name. Although salmonflies are found on both the east and west coasts, only a few large western rivers see such a profusion of the awkwardly flying insects that they actually create a traffic hazard on nearby highways.

The Gunnison is one of those rivers. Salmonflies are found only on the lower section downriver of Blue Mesa. They begin hatching about 5 miles below the confluence of the North Fork, near Highway 92, and move steadily upriver through the Black Canyon of the Gunnison National Monument until they run out of aerated water at Crystal Reservoir. Large trout follow the hatch, gorging themselves on both mature nymphs and flying adults while providing fantastic

fishing for a week to 10 days.

Last year Jagodinsky predicted the hatch would start May 23. It did precisely that, moving upriver through mid-June. Between June 10 and June 19, salmonflies were concentrated in a 14-mile stretch of river from the North Fork confluence to the Chukar Trail, providing what Jagodinsky called "the best nine days of fishing in our lives."

This year he predicts an earlier start for the salmonfly hatch, May 20, which means it should end in the Black Canyon around June 15.

The best way to fish that part of the Gunnison is by raft or jetboat. Much of the water is only Class I and II, the worst rapids are Class III, and any experienced oarsman who signs in at the bottom of Chukar Trail can float the gorge to takeout at the North Fork. Not so the upriver Monument section. There the rapids are Class V and VI, and the only way to fish the upper canyon is to hike down one of the steep — *very* steep — Monument trails.

Presentations: Salmonfly anglers try to nymph with emergers in the morning and switch to dries in late afternoon, when flying females return to the water to lay their eggs. Many fall exhausted into the water or are blown off willow branches by wind to be devoured by waiting trout beneath. Because the insects are so large, no delicacy is required in presenting imitations. Jeff Butler of the Colorado Division of Wildlife says he does quite well simply slamming a fly into the canyon wall and then letting it drop into the water.

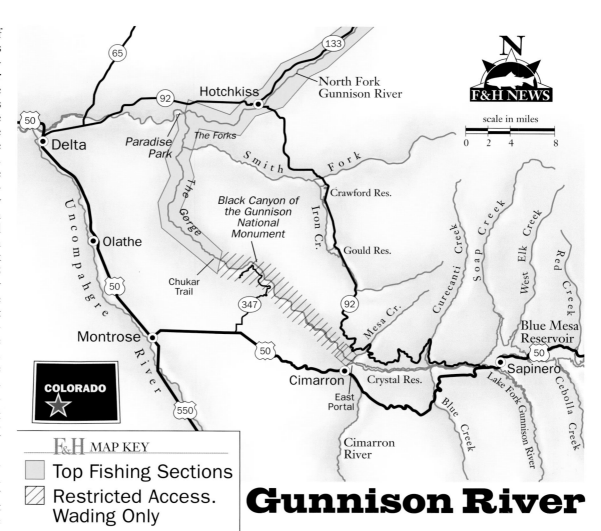

A variety of salmonflies in sizes 2 to 8 are recommended. Popular dries include the Sofa Pillow, Bird's Stonefly, Double Humpy and large yellow or orange stimulators. Nymphs include the Halfback, 20-Incher, Woolly Bugger, Montana Stone and Red Bitch (a variation of the Bitch Creek nymph). Size 8 flies are actually smaller than the real thing, but some anglers prefer them because they float better. Others solve the floatation problem by tying a small piece of styrofoam to the fly — as I said, no delicacy required.

In some stretches, the Canyon walls drop nearly 2,000 feet almost vertically into the river, providing some of the most spectacular scenery in the country. Caddis provide excellent fishing before the salmonfly hatch, but after that the lower canyon is best fished with streamers and deeply drifted nymphs, usually in tandem.

One popular "bounce rig" features a tippet with three blood knots, leaving the tags tied long. Two flies are attached to the top two blood knots and a weight to the last one. This rig enables the weight to tickle the bottom without catching the flies in the ever-present moss on the river bottom. Another double streamer rig has a large conehead Muddler Minnow or Maratuka Minnow tied directly to the end of the leader with a smaller black or brown Woolly Bugger tied 6 inches behind the first streamer off the hook.

Fishing the Gunnison from a raft or boat is physically demanding and requires very accurate casts. Most of the fish hold in riffles and pockets, and since you're floating over these very rapidly you must always look 10 to 20 yards ahead for your next cast. Big browns and the occasional rainbow will chase the flies, often hammering them right next to the boat.

There are excellent spots to take out of the river and wade fish these riffles more thoroughly. But use caution wading as the river bottom is slippery, and the current strong.

Rules & regs: Only flies and lures are allowed on the Gunnison from the upstream boundary of the Black Canyon National Park, through the Gunnison Gorge Wilderness and downstream to the confluence with the North Fork. All brown trout between 12 and 16 inches in length must be returned to the water immediately. The bag, possession and size limit for brown trout is four fish, 12 inches in length or less OR three fish less than 12 inches in length and one fish 16 inches in length or longer. All rainbow trout must be returned to the water immediately.

The upper Gunnison, which runs 20 miles from Almont to Blue Mesa, is a little murky right now because of spring runoff. The Taylor River is running clear, but the East River tends to become a muddy mess, discoloring the Gunnison. However, the water should clear up by the latter half of June, just in time for great hatches of Willowflies (*Leuctra*), Yellow Sallies (*Alloperla*) and Golden Stones (*Acroneuria*), a smaller and brighter version of the Western Salmonfly also known as the California Salmonfly.

Mark Schumacher at the Three Rivers Resort (970-641-1303) is the man to call for conditions at the top end of the Gunnison. He says the best dry fly fishing doesn't really kick off up there until the beginning of July.

F&H

Gunnison River

F&H MAP KEY
- ☐ Top Fishing Sections
- ▨ Restricted Access. Wading Only

Smallmouth spawn on McPhee may be late

DURANGO

by Tom Behrens

THE SMALLMOUTH SPAWN at McPhee Reservoir may be late this year, but it will happen. Take advantage of the new structure to take bass. Yolanda Haswell caught this smallmouth a few seasons back.

The smallmouth spawn at McPhee Reservoir is probably going to come a little later this year, which is not all that bad when you consider the reason why. The state has been in the grips of a drought for eight or nine years, creating a big drain on available water sources, such as McPhee. Good news is that all the snow this past winter is expected to bring McPhee up to near capacity this year. Capacity is 4,470 surface acres. Maximum water depth at the dam is 270 feet. But back to the delayed spawn; the cold waters from the snowmelt runoff will keep the reservoir waters below the desired temperature for spawning. Fear not, it will happen — maybe not until late May or early June, though.

Another benefit of the combination of drought and high snowmelt runoff is the additional structure created by the natural processes. The dropping lake level left a lot of ground high and dry. Brush and other natural terrestrial plants have staked claim to that land and prospered. All of this growth will soon be flooded, creating new fish hiding structure for a number of species, including smallmouth bass.

Where are you going to find the smallmouth during this time of rising waters? Tom Knopick (970-385-4081), who has guided on McPhee for 22 years, says it's just going to be a matter of getting out and looking for indications of spawning fish. But "finding the fish on the beds is kind of finding a moving target," says Knopick. "All of the canyons would be good places to fish…points, rocky points. For smallmouth any kind of rocky point is going to be a good bet."

Knopick voiced his fishing philosophy in a short sentence.

"Whether it be May or June, it is just a good time to be out fishing, regardless if the bass are spawning or not," Knopick says.

Knopick would be searching for fish around structure, just like any other time.

"Some of the side canyons are probably your best bet to find spawning fish on beds for sight fishing," he says. "If you see the fish, obviously cast to them."

Knopick's first choice as far as fishing method is fly fishing.

"I am typically throwing streamer patterns, and there are a lot of them. On that reservoir I particularly like a White Zonker, a pretty well known streamer, which is a minnow imitation," he says. "At that time of the year, the White Zonker is going to do the trick. If I am not catching them, it is not what I am throwing. I am just not finding the fish."

D.J. Winters, (970-882-3099) owner of Dolores River Outfitters uses a topwater fly presentation at this time of the year.

"I use a foam bodied spider," Winters says. "If that doesn't produce, I will switch off to a deep presentation. The lake is in a natural canyon so there is a lot of cedar and brush. I will go to some streamers, like the Mudder Minnows. A lot of the local people will use live bait such as nightcrawlers or salamanders."

Scot Key, who lives in Durango, is another dedicated bass angler who also uses fly rods to tempt fish. He describes himself as "just a local yokel."

Key is local, but if he is gullible, it's not in terms of absorbing bad fishing information.

"Lately we've been fishing for bass and pike in 10 to 15 foot depth range," Key says. "We are using big streamers. I tie all of my own flies. I don't know the names of them. I just tie it. We try to mimic rainbows or little German Browns within our fly patterns. I know they have names for them. I don't know the names for a lot of flies. I just know how to tie a lot of flies."

Key's favorite fly pattern at this time of the year resembles a big minnow. A couple of the popular spinning and bait casting lures at this time of the year are Rapalas and large Panther Martin spinners.

"I am tying to copy one of these baits," Key says. "But instead of paint on a hard plastic or metal body, my fly consists of layers of different colored yak hair to create the rainbow image."

Instead of fishing on the top as Winters does, Key plumbs the bottom.

"We are using 8-weight rods," Key says. "The line still floats, but we are using longer leaders, and the leaders that we are using are reinforced. They kind of are like a steel leader, mainly because of the pike. With the bass we are just using a bigger leader as far as test strength, but it is still like a monofilament-type leader."

The weight used to sink the fly to the bottom comes either from small split

AT a GLANCE

What: Smallmouth bass on the fly at McPhee Reservoir.

When: May and June is the peak time for the smallmouth spawn.

Where: McPhee Reservoir is next to the town of Dolores in the southwest part of the state.

Who: Guide Tom Knopick (970-385-4081), Dolores River Outfitters (970-882-3099).

shot, or he adds weight to the hook before he ties the fly. He compares the retrieve as similar to what is being done using a casting or spinning reel. "It's what is known as stripping. You come up with patterns, like two, two, one or like some would say, quick, quick, and longer. It depends on the fish and the day. Sometimes you will jerk it 3 or 4 inches and kind of let settle. It is the same thing you are doing with other spin or casting baits — making it dance."

The pattern all depends on what the fish are doing that day. "If they are real lazy and you are in shallow water, you let it sink and kind of fish the fly like you would fish a plastic worm on the Carolina rig, bouncing it off the bottom. We will do the same thing, but instead of having a weight and the bait floating as in the plastic worm 3 feet up, we will let it bounce and by the way we jerk it, it will come off the bottom a couple of feet and then bounce back to the bottom."

Some of Key's favorite places to fish on McPhee are along the dam, House Creek, Sage Hen and Dry Canyon. Another favorite is where the river comes close to the town by Big Ben and right before Dolores.

No matter whether the spawn occurs in early May or in June on McPhee, it will happen. **F&H**

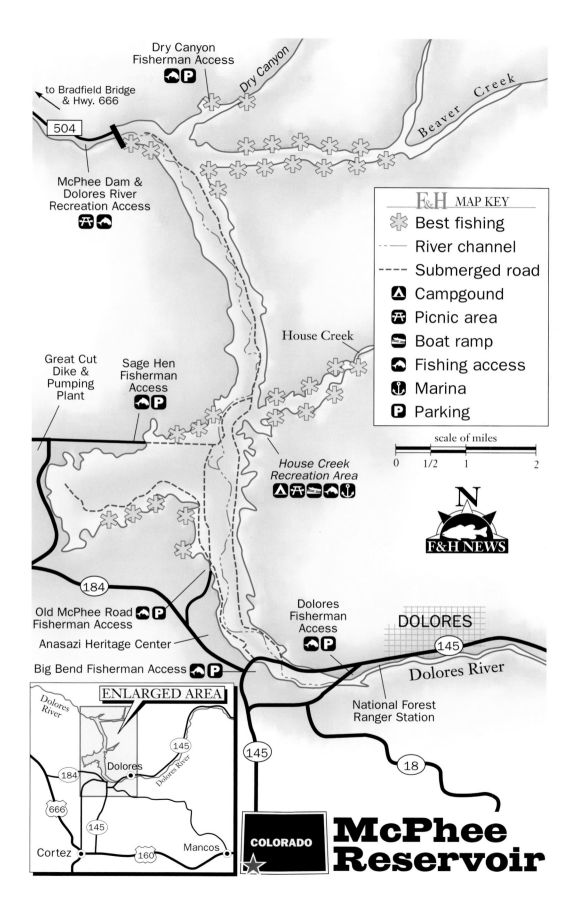

Road Canyon Reservoir holds good rainbow numbers

by Steve Nelson

If you are like most fishermen, you're always looking for a new place to wet a line, and preferably, somewhere where you stand a good chance of hooking a fish. Road Canyon Reservoir near Creede is a such a place. At about 100 acres when full, it is not a large reservoir but it is big enough to accommodate a lot of fishermen and it does receive quite a bit of fishing pressure. It is home to a strong population of rainbow trout, a much smaller number of brookies, and an occasional cutthroat.

"It's one of the better lakes in the region," says Colorado Division of Wildlife biologist John Alves (719-587-6900). "It's a highly productive lake, definitely more than a put-and-take fishery."

Rainbows average 9 to 13 inches, brook trout more like 12 inches and should you happen to catch a cutthroat it will be well over 16 inches. The reservoir is typically stocked with about 14,000 subcatchables, and when fish are available, another 8,000 catchables. It is expected to receive some catchables this spring but the number had not been set

ROAD CANYON RESERVOIR is one of the better trout fisheries in the region. Most will be pansize but fish stretching into the mid-teens are possible.

AT A GLANCE

Location: From Creede go 25 miles west on Highway 149 to USFS 520, then go 4 miles west to the lake.

Species: Primarily rainbow trout, a smaller number of brook trout, and a few cutthroat trout. Average size is 9 to 13 inches for the rainbows, 12 inches for the brookies, and the cutthroat run in the mid-teens. Larger fish are occasionally landed.

Bag limit: Eight trout in the aggregate, brookies 8 inches or less, 10 fish.

Facilities: Camping is available at the upper end of the lake on Forest Service land. There is a boat ramp and restrooms, picnic area at the lake. Wakeless boating only. Motels, restaurants and groceries available in nearby Creede.

For more information: Call the Colorado Division of Wildlife (719-587-6900) or the Ramble House (719-658-2482).

at press time. The subcatchables grow quickly to catchable size, and the lake is big enough and deep enough to sustain some carryover.

The average catch rates have held up pretty well over the past few years, about one fish per hour from boats, one fish every two hours from the bank.

Road Canyon Reservoir is a Colorado State Wildlife Area and offers excellent public access. It is a long and narrow lake and USFS 520 runs along the western shoreline providing access to the lake. "Most people fish along that road side of the lake," says Alves. "The north side of the lake towards the dam are the most popular areas. There are a lot of little points that people like to perch on and fish from. It's also a popular area for float tubers."

Flies and lures are popular in the spring but Road Canyon is primarily a bait fishermen's lake. Many anglers like to sink a worm or salmon egg, or float a dab of Power Bait just off the bottom, and there are plenty of places where the slope is gentle and you can pull up a folding chair, sit back and visit with friends while you wait for a fish to take your bait.

Light tackle is best; don't go any heavier than 6-pound test line — 4-pound is probably better — but set a light drag as there is a chance for a larger trout.

But if you are willing to go to a little more effort, you stand a very good chance getting into fish with hardware. "It's an excellent fishery," says Shane Birdsey at the Ramble House (719-658-2482). "I've seen some very nice fish come out of that lake, fish up to 14 inch-

es are possible and I saw a 5-pounder come in last summer. So there are some nice trout in there.

"Black Woolly Buggers fished deep are good bets after the ice comes off, and nymph patterns work well in the early spring up until about mid-May. After that you will start seeing some midges. In the summer there's a lot of fly fishermen who work the lake in the evenings; quite a few spin fishermen will use a fly and bubble rig and they do pretty well."

Lure fishermen typically do just fine with Kastmasters, Thomas Buoyants, Panther Martins and other small spinners/lures, as long as they keep moving and work the deeper water early in the spring.

As mentioned earlier, most anglers fish the road side of the lake but Birdsey has a better idea. "I do think there is better fishing on the other side of the lake. There are some little pockets with springs that can be very good fishing." he says.

The lake should be ice-free by the time you read this but it depends on the recent weather. Anglers should call for the latest conditions before traveling. The first few weeks after ice-out can provide good fishing but Birdsey says that this is a lake that can fish well all year long. "It's one of those places that produces well all year," he says. "But in July and August when it's very hot, you have to fish it in the early morning or late evening. You're wasting your time if you fish during the heat of the day."

There is a boat ramp about the midpoint of the lake on the west side, but this is not a big trolling lake. It is restricted to wakeless speeds only, so many boaters go elsewhere. Anglers who bring their boats usually do well with the usual gang troll or spinner and worm combinations and they often don't have much in the way of competition.

By midsummer the lake will often have an algae bloom and heavy weed growth that can cause problems, especially at the upper end of the lake. Camping is not permitted on the state wildlife area property, but there is a Forest Service campground at the upper end of the lake.

During the winter months Road Canyon is a popular ice fishing lake.

RITO HONDO AND REGAN LAKE: Alves adds that fishermen coming to this area should plan to check out some of the other reservoirs like Rito Hondo and Regan.

"Rito Hondo has brookies, rainbows and cutthroat and there's typically a lot of fish up there," he says. "Regan Lake is mainly brookies. Both should be good after the ice comes off. Both of them are put-and-grow fisheries and should have a lot of fish in them."

Most of the fish will run pansize but both lakes are productive and can and do grow some decent-sized fish.

And if you like to fish moving water, the Rio Grande River offers excellent fly fishing opportunities after the runoff subsides, usually in early to mid-June, depending on the weather.

There may still be a window of opportunity before the runoff starts, but it's pretty difficult to time. Call for conditions before you go.

Special regulations do apply to portions of this river and there is a lot of private property, check the regulations and obtain up-to-date maps before going. If you are new to the area, stop at a local tackle or fly shop for information.

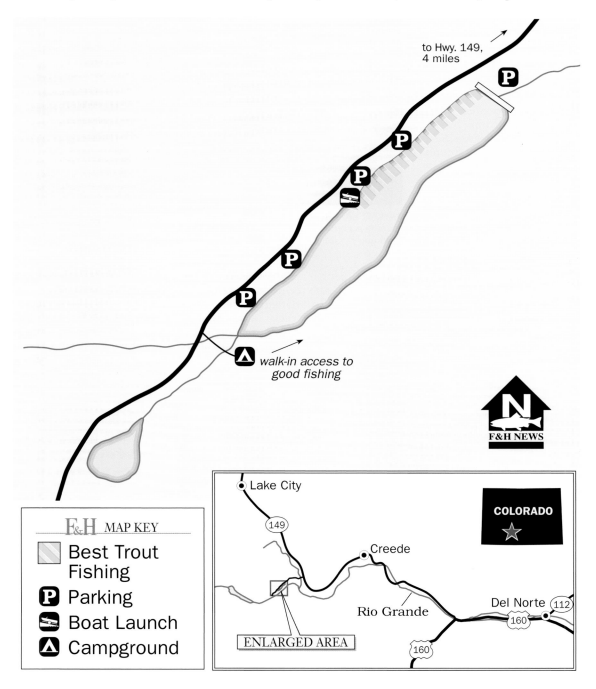

walk-in access to good fishing

F&H MAP KEY

■ Best Trout Fishing
Ⓟ Parking
⛴ Boat Launch
⛺ Campground

Lakers, trout, kokes: Taylor Park worth the trip

GUNNISON

by Dusty Routh

Make no bones about it, it's a haul to get up to Taylor Park Reservoir in the Gunnison National Forest southwest of Denver. You'll want to check your tire pressure, double check your trailer lights, run your overnight packing checklist and throw in an empty cooler for bringing fish home. But all that pre-trip work will be darn well worth it.

"We're definitely a destination lake," says Diane Marriott from Taylor Park Marina (970-641-2922; *www.taylorparkmarina.com*). "People just don't pop up here. We're at 9,500 feet way out here in the Gunnison forest. You need to plan your trip and make reservations."

One thing you should plan on is the plethora of fish you can eliminate from the gene pool while you're there. Taylor Park offers all that is good and decent in the freshwater world, ranging from water-wolf northern pike to cagey rainbow, cutthroat and brown trout to the ever-elusive (and tasty) kokanee salmon. And don't forget the real reason to come to Taylor Park: the magnificent, obstinate, deep-dwelling lake trout, or Mackinaw.

"The lake trout is definitely the

TAYLOR LAKER: This beefy 20-pound, 35-inch Taylor Reservoir laker bit a sucker-meat-tipped hammered brass Cowbell for Bruce Chisnell of Colorado Springs late last May. It won him a Colorado Master Angler Award.

hottest ticket here," says Marriott. "We think a new state record was set on July 5. They're still working it all out to see if it's going to be official or not. Grant Frerich from Crested Butte caught it. It weighed 39¼ pounds. He caught it on a Len Thompson spoon 87 feet down, trolling it with a downrigger."

At normal full pool, Taylor Park covers more than 2,000 surface acres. Marriott estimates the water is down by 35 to 40 feet, but it hardly matters, she says. "We still have depths as much as 112 feet, even with the water all the way down like this. The only problem is, you can't use the new concrete ramp. But you can use the dirt ramp, the original ramp."

For years, the "original" ramp was the only ramp, and the lake's faithful used it year in and year out. Two years ago, Marriott says, a fancier and easier concrete ramp was installed. But at low water it's useless.

"The old clear area ramp was just fine," she says. "We can get 24- to 30-foot pontoon boats in there with no trouble."

Most people who come up have a 4-wheel-drive, she says, and that's helpful but not always necessary. "I wouldn't say you have to have a 4-wheel. I

mean, I don't want to discourage anyone from coming up if they don't have a 4-wheel-drive. But most people who come up do have a 4-wheel-drive, and it's easier to use the launch."

Taylor Park Marina is only a stone's throw from the concrete ramp. There you'll find tackle, bait, fishing licenses, advice, pop, beer, ice and a few snacks.

> **"What you do is set up a slip sinker above a swivel. Then attach a 12-inch leader with a No. 6 or No. 8 hook. You want a hook that's big enough, but not too big."**
> — Dianne Marriot

There's no camping on the lake — that's a big forest service no-no — but you'll find boat storage and car parking at the marina.

Lakeview Campground (877-444-6777; *www.reserveusa.com*) is located nearby, but be sure to get reservations squared away well ahead of your trip.

Taylor Park is a large, clear, cold,

AT A GLANCE

What: One of the best fishing lakes in the Rocky Mountains. Taylor Park is 2,000 acres (full pool), impounding the Taylor River.

Where: Situated at 9,500 feet in the Gunnison National Forest, southwest of Denver.

Who: Contact Diane Marriott at Taylor Park Marina (970-641-2922; *www.taylorparkmarina.com*). For camping, dial in to the Lakeview Campground (877-444-6777; *www.reserveusa.com*).

Why: Fresh air, beautiful surroundings, breathtaking scenery. Oh, and lake trout as long as your leg, three other kinds of trout, succulent kokanee and trophy-class northern pike.

high mountain reservoir damming the rich waters of the Taylor River. This is the land of deep water fishing in cold water temps, so come prepared to do just that. And remember the elevation. It can get cold at night, and hot in the day.

Lakers: You can troll off downriggers, as Grant Frerich did for his potential record Mack, but Marriott points out that most anglers dig their lake trout out by fishing off the bottom with bait rigs.

"The water is very clear and there's plenty of oxygen down there for them," says Marriott. "What you do is set up a slip sinker above a swivel. Then attach a 12-inch leader with a No. 6 or No. 8 hook. You want a hook that's big enough, but not too big. Keep in mind these fish have very large mouths."

Bait that hook with worms or suckermeat, and fish it right off the bottom. You can allow the wind to move you over potential Mackinaw water, but if it's too windy use your kicker motor or electric trolling motor to slow you down.

Trout: Brass or fluorescent Krocodile spoons are immensely popular on Taylor Park, trolled just quickly enough so they waggle, but not so fast that they roll from side to side. You want a tantalizing action.

If you don't like to use spoons, try Rapalas in rainbow, fire tiger, gold/black and brown trout patterns. "Anything that looks like a small minnow or baitfish or small fish will work for the trout," says Marriott.

FlatFish are also good, of course. If you really want to latch into some cutts, rainbows or browns, lash on your Pop Geer lake troll and drag a gob of nightcrawlers, or use a two-hook harness with nightcrawler. "Pop Geer trolling works just great," says Marriott.

Kokanee: Taylor Park isn't famous for its population of kokes. "We don't have them like we'd like to have them," says Marriott. "They keep stocking us with them, but it's just fingerlings and I think those pretty much go to the Mackinaw."

Small 000 flashers and red or green Wedding Rings tipped with maggots or corn are definite kokanee killers. If you find a school, you can also jig with small Nordics or Buzz Bombs or similar metal jigs.

Some people may frown on it, and we aren't proponents of it, but Taylor Park also has a kokanee "snagging season" that opens on Sept. 1. You can purchase "snagging hooks" at the marina. Check your regulations for specifics in terms of locations, season and limits. But if you're like most fishing enthusiasts, you'll pursue these beautiful fish using skill and cunning and a little luck, and hopefully find that imminently more rewarding than snagging a limit of fish.

Water-wolves: "We have a lot of northern pike in the reservoir," says Marriott. "A lot." That's what we like to hear!

In fact, Marriott and a few of her associates in the tackle business believe the next state record northern pike will come from here. Fly fishing for these aggressive, toothy, nasty brutes can be awesome. Also try casting and retrieving around the outside edges of weedbeds with bucktail spinners, spoons and plugs.

"The key is to have a jerky, erratic retrieve," says Marriott. "You have to make that fish think that something in the water is in real distress, you know, like an injured fish."

F&H

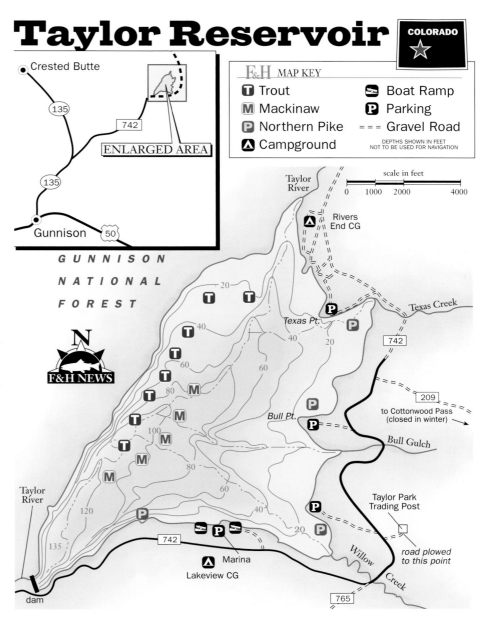

Taylor Reservoir

COLORADO ★

Crested Butte

135

135

Gunnison 50

742

ENLARGED AREA

F&H MAP KEY

T Trout
M Mackinaw
P Northern Pike
▲ Campground

⛴ Boat Ramp
P Parking
= = = Gravel Road

DEPTHS SHOWN IN FEET
NOT TO BE USED FOR NAVIGATION

scale in feet
0 1000 2000 4000

Taylor River

GUNNISON NATIONAL FOREST

N F&H NEWS

Rivers End CG

Texas Pt.
Texas Creek

742

209
to Cottonwood Pass (closed in winter)

Bull Pt.
Bull Gulch

Taylor Park Trading Post

road plowed to this point

Willow Creek

Taylor River

dam

742

765

Marina
Lakeview CG

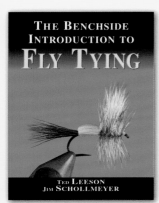

The Benchside Introduction to Fly Tying
by Ted Leeson & Jim Schollmeyer
Following the incredible success of *The Fly Tier's Benchside Reference*, Jim & Ted now offer the first beginner's book of fly tying to allow readers simultaneous access to fly recipes, tying steps, and techniques. The first 50 pages of this oversized, spiral-bound book are filled with impeccably photographed fly-tying techniques. The next 150 pages are cut horizontally across the page. The top pages show tying steps for dozens of fly patterns, including references to tying techniques that are explained step by step in the bottom pages. Over 1500 beautiful color photographs, 9 X 12 inches, 190 all-color pages.
SPIRAL HB: $45.00   ISBN-13: 978-1-57188-369-8
                       UPC: 0-81127-00203-0

The Fly Tier's Benchside Reference To Techniques and Dressing Styles
by Ted Leeson and Jim Schollmeyer
The *Benchside Reference* will astonish you with the number of fly-tying techniques inside, each including step-by-step instructions and photos. Culled from fly-tiers the world over, if it's not in here, you just don't need it! All color, 8 1/2 x 11 inches, 464 pages, over 3,000 color photographs, index, hardbound with dust jacket.
HB: $100.00   ISBN-13: 978-1-57188-126-7
                     UPC: 0-81127-00107-1
CD: $59.95 for PC or Mac   ISBN-13: 978-1-57188-259-2
                     UPC: 0-66066-00448-2

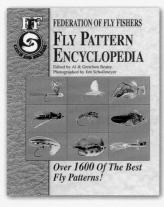

Federation of Fly Fishers Fly Pattern Encyclopedia
Edited by Al & Gretchen Beatty
The flies, ideas, and techniques in this book are from the "best of the best" demonstration fly tiers in North America; the famous and the unknown with one simple characteristic in common, they freely share their vast knowledge. Full color, 8 1/2 x 11 inches, 232 pages.
SB: $39.95   ISBN-13: 978-1-57188-208-0
                    UPC: 0-66066-00422-2

Fly Tying Made Clear and Simple
by Skip Morris
A top-seller for almost 20 years, *Clear and Simple* is still the go-to book for fly-tiers of all skill levels.
8 1/2 x 11 inches, 80 pages.
SPIRAL SB: $19.95   ISBN-13: 978-1-878175-13-7
                     UPC: 0-66066-00103-0
SB: $19.95   ISBN-13: 978-1-57188-231-8
                     UPC: 0-81127-00131-6
DVD: $26.95   ISBN-13: 978-1-57188-365-0
                     UPC: 0-81127-00199-6

Woolly Wisdom
How to Tie and Fish Woolly Worms, Woolly Buggers, and Their Fish-Catching Kin
by Gary Soucie
The Woollys are the most famous and productive fly family of all time. Everything you need to know to tie and fish these effective flies, including hundreds of proven patterns. 8 1/2 x 11 inches, 170 pages, all-color.
SB: $29.95   ISBN-13: 978-1-57188-351-3
                    UPC: 0-81127-00185-9
HB: $39.95   ISBN-13: 978-1-57188-352-0
                    UPC: 0-81127-00186-6
Limited HB: $125.00   ISBN-13: 978-1-57188-355-1
                    UPC: 0-81127-00189-7

Saltwater Flies of the Northeast
by Angelo Peluso
More than 100 fly-tiers, guides and captains—from the southern tip of New Jersey up through the rugged coastline of Maine—share their most productive saltwater flies. The fly photographs and artwork throughout this book are stunning! 11 1/4 x 8 3/4 inches, 191 pages, full-color.
HB: $29.95   ISBN-13: 978-1-57188-394-0
                    UPC: 0-81127-00228-3

Tube Flies Two: Evolution
by Mark Mandell and Bob Kenly
Artistic, durable, effective—this book features 227 tube flies from 35 tiers in 14 countries. Tube flies are used on all fish species in all types of water. 8 1/2 x 11 inches, 170 pages.
SB: $29.95   ISBN-13: 978-1-57188-401-5
                    UPC: 0-81127-00235-1
HB: $35.00   ISBN-13: 978-1-57188-402-2
                    UPC: 0-81127-00236-8

Steelhead Flies
by John Shewey
Shewey's well-written and researched book is rich in history, technique, method, and innovation. Step-by-step photos and instructions are enhanced by exquisite fly plates. A must for all steelhead fly-fishermen. 9 x 12 inches, 216 pages, full-color.
Spiral HB: $29.95   ISBN-13: 978-1-57188-400-8
                     UPC: 0-81127-00234-4
HB: $29.95   ISBN-13: 978-1-57188-404-6
                     UPC: 0-81127-00238-2
HB Limited (125): $135.00   ISBN-13: 978-1-57188-405-3
with fly   UPC: 0-81127-00239-9

Flies of the Northwest
by Inland Empire Fly Fishing Club
The Northwest is known for its great trout, salmon, and steelhead fishing, and these proven patterns will help you catch them. 200 flies, including how to tie and fish them, originators and dressings. Full color, 6 x 9 inches, 136 pages.
SPIRAL: $24.95   ISBN-13: 978-1-57188-065-3
                    UPC: 0-66066-00315-7

Bounce tubes on bottom for pre-ice Twin Lakes Macks

GRANITE

by Mike Kennedy

Just before first ice is the time to try for the big lakers at Twin Lakes. Max Snyder of the Granite General Store (719-486-1679) says to use sucker meat, nightcrawlers, Dardevles or large Rapalas for Twin Lake Mackinaw.

According to Snyder, the lake doesn't normally freeze over until mid-January, so there's still time to get up there and try for one of the big boys. The lake hasn't had too many fishermen recently because of all the hunters in the area and fear of someone mistaking their boat for a deer, or more likely because most of the fishermen have been hunting. But by mid-December deer season will be over and it will be time to try to satisfy that Big Mack craving in the pit of your stomach.

Fish dropoffs, ledges and humps. Since there's so little structure in the lake, any that you find is important. For late fall and winter fishing you can also use Fat Gitzit jigs tipped with a ½-inch by 2- to 3-inch strips of sucker meat. Use at least a 1-ounce leadhead jig to get down to the 30- to 50-foot depths where Macks are coming up to spawn. Lake trout like to hug the bottom, so fish on or just off the bottom. You'll want to use at least 10-pound line you if want any hope of handling a bigger fish.

From the shore, you can fish a plain hook with sucker meat on the bottom, as many bank fishermen do. You might also try heavy spoons, airplane jigs, marabou jigs or large Kastmasters. Fish in front of the boat ramp, Cabin Cove, Flume and Dexter Points and the area around the channel between the two lakes. Working the bottom by the dam is also a good tactic. Fish deep, at least 30 to 50 feet, for your best chance at a large fish. You can fish in these same locations once a solid ice cap is on as well. Call the Granite General Store ahead of time to find out if you'll be taking your boat or ice auger.

Twin Lakes also has rainbow and cutthroat trout. You'll want to fish shallower for these fish, usually probing the top 30 feet of water.

Use a variety of small jigs and lures like Swedish Pimples, Kastmasters, Krocodiles, teardrops, Iceman jigs, Don Cooper Ice Critters and small Nordic jigs. Most fishermen will tip them with a meal worm or wax worm. Most of the action is just off the bottom in water under 30 feet. The best fishing will be in the coves and in the channel that connects the two lakes. Again these locations are hot in open water and after the ice cap is formed.

Once the lake is open to ice fishing, remember that there are always soft spots or open water by the power plant on Lower Lake just north of Dexter Point.

No one can predict what our weather will be like this winter, so before you travel to Twin Lakes call the Granite General Store. The general store has gas, food, drinks and all your fishing supplies. It's located on Highway 24, 2 miles south of Highway 82. **F&H**

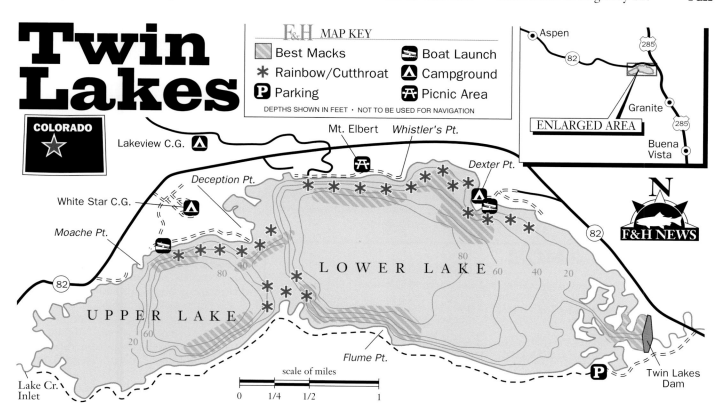

Twin Lakes

COLORADO

F&H MAP KEY

- Best Macks
- ✳ Rainbow/Cutthroat
- P Parking
- Boat Launch
- ⛺ Campground
- Picnic Area

DEPTHS SHOWN IN FEET · NOT TO BE USED FOR NAVIGATION

Lakeview C.G.
Mt. Elbert   Whistler's Pt.
Deception Pt.
Dexter Pt.
White Star C.G.
Moache Pt.
LOWER LAKE
80   60   40   20
80   40
UPPER LAKE
20   60
Flume Pt.
Lake Cr. Inlet
scale of miles
0   1/4   1/2   1
Twin Lakes Dam

Aspen
82   285
ENLARGED AREA
Granite
285
Buena Vista
82
N
F&H NEWS

Vallecito pike move shallow — no, shallower

BAYFIELD

by Dusty Routh

INTERESTED in 40-inch pike? You'll find them at Vallecito Reservoir. Mike Kew caught this 40-plus-incher a few years back.

Vallecito Reservoir was always a pretty place. The scenery was breathtaking, the lake a beautiful gem that offered local anglers outstanding fishing for bragging-size northern pike. The reservoir, which dams up Vallecito Creek (a terrific trout fishery in its own right), as well as the Los Pinos River, also offered a good population of rainbow trout, healthy browns, kokanee, a few crappie and, for the knowledgeable, even good smallmouth bass fishing.

But Vallecito (properly pronounced "Vie-uh-see-toe") was ravaged by the firestorms that hit in 2002, and everyone worried whether or not this outstanding fishery and the land around it would ever recover. This spring, it may be as pretty as ever, and it may be fishing just as good as it always had.

Says Chris Choate with Garden Swartz Sporting Goods in Durango (970-247-2660), "the one thing about it was when the fire went through there, it went through there *hard*. People were panicked about whether or not it would recover. But it's gorgeous up there. Last year the grass was green, the flowers were out. They've really rehabilitated it. The scenery really came back. And the water is probably 10 to 15 percent higher than at any time since I've lived here."

Vallecito doesn't get much press, and for the most part it's a lake where only the locals fish it.

Located a scant 25-minute drive from Durango, it nonetheless offers up some pretty hefty pike, and if you're a fan of the toothy water-wolf northern, this is a lake that you'll want to get to know.

Ice-out pike: There aren't too many anglers who ice fish on Vallecito. Instead, most of the winter fishing in this part of the state tends to be on the local rivers, which include the Animas and the San Juan. But once ice-out hits, which can be anywhere from March to April, those in the know head for Vallecito.

That's because ice-out pike tend to move up into the shallows right away, as soon as the ice lid is off, in a pres-pawn prep feeding frenzy. This is the time when both shorebound anglers and boat anglers will work any structure they can find in shallow water, throwing offerings like oversized Rapalas, water dogs, and big streamer flies. The fishing is particularly good in the stump fields and ledges around the north end, between Lost Creek, Grimes Creek and Vallecito Creek. Fishing can also sometimes be good in the shallows around the incoming Los Pinos River, located roughly midway up the reservoir on the east side.

"When the ice comes off is always a big question," Choate says. "I don't ice fish it, but I sure fish it the rest of the year. I'm guessing the ice will probably be off late this year, but it all depends. If we get an arctic blast late in the year, it just prolongs the ice. Usually, we're able to fish it by early April. But it just depends."

The ice is typically off the north end of the lake first, and anglers will hit this end just as soon as they can to take advantage of the pike moving in to the newly opened shallows.

Biggie pike: While huge pike are not an everyday, normal occurrence here, there are enough of them to keep the local faithful always trying. "There are some really nice pike in there," says Choate. "We have a couple hanging on the wall here in the shop from Vallecito that are 40 inches. That'll weigh 10 to 12 pounds."

Choate says a good day on the water in the early, early spring might be only

---

AT a GLANCE

What: Plan now for ice-out trophy pike fishing on Vallecito Reservoir near Durango.

Where: Fish the shallows, fish the shallows, fish the shallows. Big pike will be up shallow as soon as the ice lid is off, particularly around structure like stumps and ledges.

How: If you're on foot, cast oversized Rapalas or waterdogs, or throw big streamer flies. If you're boating or float tubing, stay off structure and cast or troll into it.

When: Just as soon as the ice lid allows for open water fishing, that's when you need to be there.

three or four pike, but any one of them could be a whopper. "I caught one last year that was in the 15- to 18-pound range," says Choate. "We do a lot of our own fly rods here in the shop, and a fish like that will really bend a rod. While you won't catch fish that big everyday, it's a consistent deal throughout the season. People are catching big pike all the time, every year, that are 4½ feet long."

Choate says the critical component to this fishing is to fish as early as you can, just as soon as the ice is off, and always be on the lookout for shallow structure. "They'll be up on the flats, and all around the stumps," he says. "Hands-down, that early spring season is the best time to fish for them. It's best at the north end, but it's not restricted to just that part of the lake. Anywhere there's structure in shallow water, that's where you need to fish."

Says Glenn Tinnin with the fly shop Duranglers in Durango (970-385-4081), "we don't guide up there, because we're so busy guiding on the rivers. But a lot of the locals fish it, primarily for those pike."

Tinnin recommends that if you're fly fishing, walk the shoreline. Anywhere you see rocks, some submerged structure or grass beds on the upper end of the lake, "that's where the pike will be. Up there in the shallows, getting ready to spawn." Tinnin says most local fly anglers just park their trucks and walk out to wade the edges of the lake.

Vallecito is a big hummer of a lake, at 2,700 acres. It's located at an elevation of 7,750 feet. The deepest end is at the south end, near the dam.

Other fish, too: In between casting for pike, bank anglers and boat anglers who are willing to soak Power Bait on the bottom will be amply rewarded by Vallecito's resident rainbow population. Says Choate, "on any given day up there, you can wade out with a little

Power Bait and catch rainbows." The lake also has browns, kokanee, smallmouth and crappie.

Directions: From Bayfield, go north on County Road 501 approximately 15 miles. From Durango, go northeast on County Road 240 approximately 20 miles.

Contact: Contact the US Forest Service, San Juan National Forest, (970-884-2558). Lodging is available at Bear Paw Lodge in Bayfield (970-884-2508). For fishing information, supplies and tackle, try Garden Swartz Sporting Goods in Durango (970-247-2660) or Durangler Fly Shop at (970) 385-4081. **F&H**

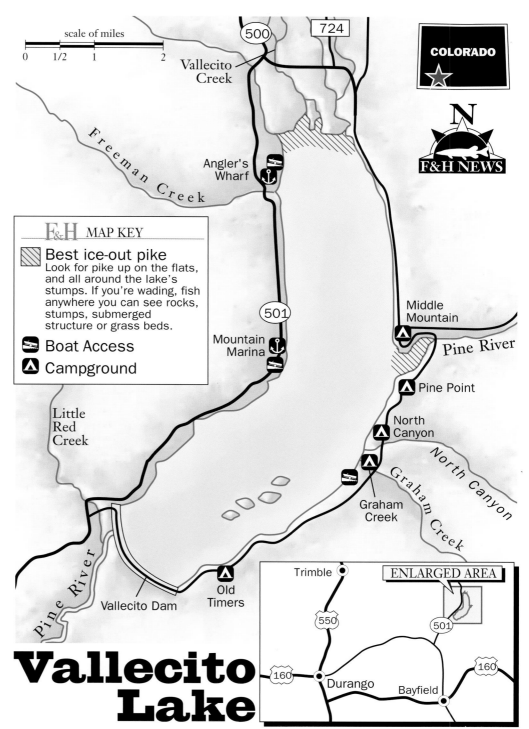

scale of miles
0   1/2   1   2

500   724

COLORADO

N
F&H NEWS

Vallecito Creek

Freeman Creek

Angler's Wharf

F&H MAP KEY

Best ice-out pike
Look for pike up on the flats, and all around the lake's stumps. If you're wading, fish anywhere you can see rocks, stumps, submerged structure or grass beds.

Boat Access

Campground

Little Red Creek

501

Mountain Marina

Middle Mountain

Pine River

Pine Point

North Canyon

Graham Creek

North Canyon

Graham Creek

Pine River

Vallecito Dam

Old Timers

Vallecito Lake

Trimble

ENLARGED AREA

550

501

160

Durango

Bayfield

160

MULTI-ZONE FISHING

Colorado bass — at the starting gate and ready

by Mike Kennedy

The last two weeks of May and the first two weeks of June feature some of the best bass fishing of the year. Waters are warming into the 60s, bass are in pre-spawn, spawn, or post-spawn, depending on the body of water and they are ready to bite.

While Colorado may not have the world-class bass of California, Florida, or Texas, there are a lot of bass in the state in the 5- to10-pound range. The state record largemouth bass is 11 pounds, 6 ounces, caught at Echo Canyon Reservoir by Jarrett Edwards in 1997 and the state record smallmouth was caught at nearby Navajo Reservoir in 1993 by Carl Dewey and was 5 pounds, 12 ounces, and 21 inches.

CHUNKY BASS like this one held by Mike Weaver are available across the state right now.

Everyone has their favorite bass lake, but in preparing for this article I wanted to identify a good bass lake in each DOW section of the state: Metro, Northwest, Northeast, Southwest, and Southeast. There is no way to mention all of the bass lakes in the state in one article; however, the following reservoirs should be representative of bodies of water in your local area.

The first bass that move into the shallows are often the largest ones, so now's the time to get after them. Please practice catch-and-release on all spawning bass.

I talked to John Kelly, a member of the

Tracker Boat Pro-Team, this week about his favorite bass lakes, and he helped me develop the following list. Kelly teaches fishing for senior citizens at the Montbello Recreation Center. For more information about joining the Montbello Senior Citizens Fishing Club or sitting in on Kelly's fishing classes, call Dallas Jackson at the Montbello Recreation Center (303-375-3852).

Metro Denver: Chatfield Reservoir, in the southwest Denver Metro area, is a great smallmouth bass lake. Smallmouth average 12 to 14 inches, but there are many fish in the 18- to 20-inch range. Try crawdad or shad imitation crankbaits, curly tail grubs, or 1½-inch salty tubes in greens or browns along the rocks by the dam, off the rocky point by the north boat ramp, the flats off Massey Draw and the riprap by the spillway. Fishing up in the South Platte or Plum Creek inlets can also be effective before snowmelt cools the water or after snowmelt and the water heats back up.

Be careful casting lures too close to shore along the dam. It is very shallow right at the shore, and there is a gradual drop into deeper water. I've lost many a lure there, and it's too shallow to use your trolling motor to retrieve your bait. I tried using Lure-Saver "O" rings, which work well when the hooks of your lure stick into brush or trees, but they don't help if the bill of your lure gets wedged between the rocks.

The best time to fish in early spring is from 1 p.m. until dark when the water is warmer. Try to locate the warmest water you can find. To get to Chatfield, take C-470 to Wadsworth and turn south to the park entrance.

For more information, contact the park office at (303) 791-7275. Other great Metro-area bass lakes include Quincy Reservoir, Arvada Reservoir, and Ward Road Pond.

Northwest: Rifle Gap Reservoir, is a great western slope bass lake. In spring, fish the backs of small coves along the north side and along the riprap at the dam using plastics and small crankbaits. Crawdad patterns

work well. Yamamoto Senkos are another lure to try. Senkos are salt impregnated plastic worms that you fish with no weight. They work well and are one of the most effective baits to come along in recent years. This lure is especially effective when fish seem to have the lockjaw, such as right after a cold front or on a blue-bird sunny day.

You can fish a Senko worm using a Texas rig weedless hook setup or a "Wacky Rig" with the hook right through the middle of the worm. A No. 2 or larger Gamakatsu G-Lock or similar hook works best. You need to fish shallow water with a Senko (10 feet or less). Cast out the worm around structure and let it sink slowly. You can fish it too fast, but you can't fish it too slow. Watch your line for the slightest tic. If you see any movement or an unexpected stop, don't set the hook immediately. Wind up the slack line until you feel resistance, then set the hook. Green pumpkinseed is one of my favorite colors; use the 4-inch size. If water is stained or fish are really turned off, I'll use a 3-inch chartreuse Senko. Nothing seems to be able to resist it. I've caught bluegill, trout and bass of every size on the 3-inch Senko.

For more information, call the state park at (970) 625-1607.

Northeast: Horsetooth Reservoir, near Fort Collins, is one of my favorite bass lakes in northeast Colorado. Kelly preferred the nearby but much smaller Dixon Lake, but you can only use small boats on Dixon.

At Horsetooth in spring, fish the backs of coves on the west side of the lake and other shallow waters that warm first. Use jerkbaits, swimbaits, Senkos and minnow or crawdad imitations. Vertical jigging blade-baits, spoons or grubs off main lake points is also effective. Fly fishermen try Clouser Minnows, Woolly Buggers, or Zonkers on sinking tip line along the rock shorelines. Try poppers or rabbit strip minnows for largemouth bass.

For more information on Horsetooth Reservoir, call the park office at (970) 679-4570.

Colorado Bass

Southwest: Navajo Reservoir, on the Colorado/New Mexico border, is the home of the state record smallmouth. Nearby Echo Canyon Reservoir holds the record for largemouth. You need both a Colorado and New Mexico license to fish the lake because most of the lake is actually in New Mexico.

The bass bite will be coming on in May with the smallmouth bite starting first then the largemouth. Bass will be moving to shallow water, especially in the afternoons as the water warms. Earlier in the day look for them in a little deeper water near spawning areas and off points. Largemouth will be in the backs of coves and near wood, weeds or similar structure. Look for smallmouth along the rocky shoreline.

Make sure that you're casting into water 15 feet deep or less. Navajo is a very deep reservoir, and you can be a cast from the bank and be sitting in 50 feet of water. It's best to sit in 15 to 20 feet of water and cast toward shore. Piedra, San Juan, Pine, La Jara and Banco canyons are good locations to look for spring bass. Crawdad or baby bass patterns work well. Try jerkbaits until the water warms, then try spinnerbaits or crankbaits.

For more information, contact the park office at (970) 883-2208.

Southeast: Neegronda Reservoir, the deepest of the so-called "Northern Lakes" — north of Lamar but south of Eads — usually produces fish all spring and summer. Largemouth bass in the 2- to 4-pound range are common and larger fish are possible. Fish around submerged logs and brush and use heavy line and equipment, at least 8-pound test line.

There is a public boat ramp on the east side and a private boat ramp on the west. Check to see if the east ramp is in the water deep enough before you launch your craft. The private ramp is deeper in the water. Water levels have been a little low in recent years.

Try crankbaits in shad or crawfish patterns and white, green or brown tubes. On the north side of the lake you'll find a campground known as Cottonwood Park (719-829-1801). By Golly Liquors in Eads sells worms and minnows and other supplies.

Editor's note: For more information, be sure to visit Mike Kennedy's Web site (www.mikescoloradofishing.com) **F&H**

2. Horsetooth Reservoir

4. Neegronda Reervoir

3. Chatfield Reservoir

F&H MAP KEY
✳ Bass   ⚓ Boat launch

1. Rifle Gap Reservoir

5. Navajo Reservoir

AT a GLANCE

What: Statewide Colorado bass.

When: Now through mid-June. Remember to release spawning bass.

Who: Rifle Gap State Recreation Area (970-625-1607), Chatfield State Park (303-791-7275), Horsetooth Reservoir: Larimer County Parks (970-679-4570), Neegronda Reservoir: Cottonwood Park (719-829-1801), Navajo State Recreation Area (970-883-2208)

Colorado's tailwaters offer best winter river fishing

COLORADO SPRINGS

by Dusty Routh

BUNDLE UP AND NYMPH THE ICY BANKS of some of Colorado's tailwaters for trout like this one caught by Van Barron.

Baby, it's cold outside. And that means a lot of things for Colorado's legions of fly anglers who like to get out in the winter to chase trout. Winter fishing offers more solitude than you'll find during spring, summer or early fall months; less pressured fish; and the opportunity for what can sometimes be very, very good fishing. But it also means adjusting your approaches and fishing times in order to keep the negative effects of winter at bay.

Keys to winter river fly angling include fishing "banker's hours" between 10 or 11 a.m. and 2 or 3 p.m., in order to be on the river during the warmest parts of the day, when fish will be most active.

Another important key, says Art Rowell with Fryingpan Anglers in Basalt (970-927-3441), is to keep your offering small. "In the winter you've got really limited hatches, mostly midges," he says. "So dress warm and fish with small flies. If you can fish with midges, you can catch fish."

Because river mainstems can often be a tough proposition to fish in the heart of winter, with skim ice around the edges and blocks of ice floes coming down with the currents, another good strategy is to stick to dam tailwaters for your fishing.

Tailwater benefits: None of us like the fact that dams intrude on some of our favorite rivers. But a benefit to dams are the terrific tailwater fisheries they create. Steady current, lots of food sources flushing down from the reservoirs above the dams, and a lack of ice in the water make tailwater fisheries perfect places to pursue winter trouting. Add to that the fact that a wide variety of trout — rainbows, cutthroat, cuttbows, browns — call tailwater fisheries home because of the constant supply of oxygen and food, and you've got a terrific combination for excellent fishing.

Tailwater top spots: Colorado is "blessed" with a lot of dams, and thus with a lot of tailwater fisheries, too. "I think one of the best tailwater fisheries in the state is right here on the 'Pan," says Rowell. "It's good most of the time, but it's even better when we get a little warm weather in the middle of winter. You'll want to fish from the dam halfway down to Basalt. When conditions are good, the fishing is great."

Rowell says he likes the Fryingpan River's tailwaters because of the variety and sizes of the fish. "Rainbows, browns, cutthroat, cuttbows, we've got them all," he says. "Those that prepare themselves

well will do really well."

• Another tailwater hot spot in the winter is just below Spinney Reservoir, on the South Platte. In fact, fishing can be very good in this tailwater as well as the tailwater located just below Elevenmile Canyon Reservoir. Both areas have undergone stream rehabilitation and habitat improvement projects over the years, mostly as a result of how popular these fisheries are in the warmer months. In the winter, you'll still have company, but not nearly at the level of the crowds in spring and summer. These South Platte tailwater fisheries can offer some big fish on occasion too, made up of browns and rainbows.

• Another incredibly popular and equally productive tailwater fishery to consider in very, very early spring, like in late February and early March, is the short, trout-infested Williams Fork River just below Williams Fork Reservoir. It can be achingly cold in this part of Colorado even at the start of spring, but early spawning rainbows moving up from the Colorado River can be found here, along with lots of browns. What they come for are good food sources, excellent pocket water and lots of oxygen. As with other tailwaters in the state, nymph fishing is king here during the cold weather months.

• Another outstanding tailwater fishery, less known and less popular among the state's fly fishing faithful, is the Arkansas River below Pueblo Reservoir. The Ark can fish well all winter long, but skim ice and cold temps can keep mainstem trout activity at a minimum. Instead, fishing up closer to the dam provides more open water, and even some winter time midge and BWO hatches, particularly on overcast days.

Tailwater tactics: As Rowell points out, winter means midge time, and that means fishing with small flies. Dry midges will work during the very warmest parts of the day, but at other times you may be better off using tiny mayfly nymphs and emerger patterns of dry midges and mayflies. If you're going to nymph, go with a short leader, with or without a strike indicator at your discretion. Strike indicators can be very effec-

---

AT a GLANCE

What: February means winter trout fly angling on dam tailwaters throughout the state.

When: Fish the middle part of the day, when temperatures are warmest, in order to find the most active trout.

How: Fishing small midge dries with dropper nymphs is killer, as is nymphing the bottom or fishing attractor patterns like streams and Buggers.

Where: Top tailwater fisheries include the Fryingpan, the South Platte and the Arkansas.

tive at detecting the subtle take of a winter fish, but in clear, shallow pools they can also be a potential detriment by way of spooking wary fish.

A double-whammy of a dry fly up top and a nymph, emerger or attractor pattern down below as the dropper is always a good strategy for winter fly fishing. And solo attractor patterns like Woolly Buggers in olives, browns, purples and blacks are standard winter fare if there's no visible insect activity.

Unlike in summer, winter trout tend to "keg" up in slow-moving pockets and holes rather than in riffles and faster tail-outs. These deeper spots can be the perfect place to nymph close to the bottom, or drift an attractor pattern through.

Top tailwater flies: Proven fly patterns in the winter include the Griffin's Gnat for midge work, or a Biot Midge. Other good dries in the winter include the Parachute Adams, a Brassie and Hare's Ears. A Pheasant Tail Nymph, Prince Nymph or Beadhead Prince Nymph are good dropper choices. And Woolly Buggers, of course, are excellent for winter attractor work, though you'll need to experiment with sizes in order to determine the preferences of the fish. Another option for attractor fishing is Bucktail streamers.

Stay warm: Fishing in winter is a matter of being

well prepared for the elements. This isn't a time to wear leaky waders or thin socks. Bundle up good, complete with long johns, layers of shirts and hooded sweatshirts, a heavy jacket or parka, and be sure to wear a knit cap or other warm lid on your head, where most of the heat from your body escapes. Fingerless wool gloves will help keep your hands warm while still allowing you the free use of your fingers for casting and stripping line. If ice forms in your rod guides, simply dip the rod in the river. *F&H*

Colorado Tailwaters

F&H MAP KEY

▨ Best winter trout

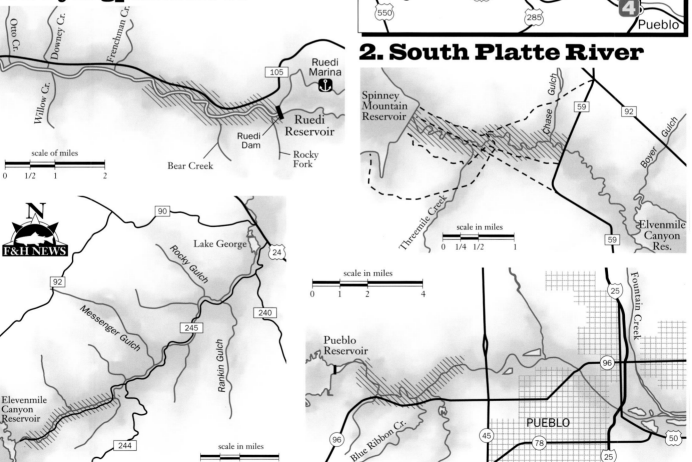

1. Fryingpan River

2. South Platte River

3. South Platte River

4. Arkansas River

Northeast
HUNTING

Banner year for Banner Lakes waterfowl?

HUDCON

by Joel Shangle

So far this young season, it's been anything but a banner year for waterfowl at the Banner Lakes State Wildlife Area. This collection of ponds just east of Hudson is one of the closest public marshland hunt areas for Denver gunners, but don't expect the shooting to take a turn for the better until the weather takes a turn for the worse.

"It's been relatively slow up to this point," reports wildlife area technician Mike Smith (303-546-4608). "We've had nice weather and the local birds have already been shot at enough that they've moved on. The hunting has really slowed down since opening day, and I don't expect to see many birds coming down until it gets really cold and unsettled up north."

Ah, yes, you've heard it before: no weather means no birds. But that's especially true at Banner Lakes. Situated in a lowland valley surrounded by farmlands, the wildlife area's ponds and marshes are the only wetlands for miles. The South Platte River is roughly 20 miles to the north and you'll find a few scattered irrigation reservoirs scattered around Greeley, Hudson and Strasburg, but Banner Lakes' ponds collectively serve as a major stopping point for birds headed south.

"The worse the weather, the better the hunting here," says Smith. "Birds will be looking to get out of the wind and hunker down in the ponds. We're really kind of an oasis of wetlands here — the ponds offer shelter in a lowlands area, with some tree cover around."

Lay of the land: The wildlife area is broken up into 13 hunt sites, covering 934 acres on 11 major ponds and two "satellite" marsh areas, laid out in a northwest/southeast line across Highway 52, 4 miles east of Hudson. Four of the 11 major ponds lie south of 52, while seven other large ponds and the two satellite hunt spots stretch out north of the highway. The Denver/Hudson Canal snakes between Ponds 1 and 2 and alongside Ponds 2, 3 and 4 on the south end, and runs adjacent to Ponds 12 and 13 (the satellite hunt spots) on the northern section.

"Most of the ponds are several acres in size, with varying water levels," says Smith. "Vegetation is mostly cattails, and there are some woodlands immediately on the west side of some of the ponds. There's some willow vegetation at the ends and along some of the sides of the ponds, but it's all pretty typical wetlands environment."

Blind luck?: The majority of the duck hunting at Banner Lakes is done out of 19 ground blinds scattered

BANNER LAKES SWA offers hunting out of ground blinds for a wide variety of duck species. Steve Walters, Mark Steel and Brad Coon show the kind of birds you can expect.

AT a GLANCE

What: Banner Lakes SWA waterfowl

Where: Northeast of the Denver metro complex, roughly 4 miles east of Hudson.

Why: The WA's ponds offer one of the only wetlands stopoffs in the area. When weather pushes birds down from the north, mallards, gadwall, teal, etc. will use the ponds as resting spots.

How: Hunting is done mostly out of ground blinds located along the shorelines of the WA's ponds. The ponds on the far north end of the complex require a hike to get to the hunt sites, so you may want to pack fewer decoys if you're hunting them

When: Don't even think about hunting Banner Lakes until the weather turns. The local birds have already been pushed out of the area by early season hunting, but the shooting will improve this month as weather starts pushing more migrants into the area

Rules/regs: Open Saturday, Sunday and Monday with reservations only until the Nov. 22 pheasant opener. From then on, hunting is open all week, and hunt sites are assigned at the check-in station

Information: Banner Lakes SWA headquarters (303-546-4608)

around the ponds. Most of the blinds are kidney-shaped culvert structures built for two people, but there are a couple of box blinds on property as well. Hunting on the wildlife area is reservation-only on Saturday, Sunday and Monday until the Nov. 22 opener of pheasant season, when it opens seven days a week. After that, you can register for a hunt/blind site at the headquarters check-in board just off the highway.

Points to pond(er): Water levels on the ponds are all good this season except for 1, 6, 7 and 9. Pond 1 is completely dry and won't be filled without breeching . The other three have water this year after laying dry for two years for a wetlands restoration project, but they've been overtaken by vegetation.

"Those ponds sat empty for two years, so cattails have invaded the open water," Smith says. "We plan to drain a couple of those ponds, mow and refill them to drown those cattails out stop them from completely boxing in those ponds. But right now, they're not very attractive for waterfowl hunting."

Prime ponds: While all 13 of Banner Lakes' hunt sites will produce fair to good gunning on any given day, the blinds located around the perimeter of the wildlife area's bigger ponds are the most consistent producers. That means that Ponds 5, 8, 10 and 11 (all located north of Highway 52) should be your first choices.

"I suspect those ponds are the best because there's more shoreline and more open water to hunt," says Smith.

Here's a rundown of the best duck spots on the wildlife area:

Pond 3: The best option of the three filled ponds south of the highway, Pond 3 has four blind sites (13, 13, 15 & 16) on the east and west shores.

Pond 5: The largest pond at Banner Lakes, covering some 11 acres when it's full. There's only one blind here (Blind 11, located on the west shore, on the south end), but this is the closest hunt location to the check-in station.

Pond 8: The WA's second largest body of water, this pond covers 6 to 8 acres (depending on water level), with Blind 6 situated on the east bank and Blind 7 tucked into the west side of a

Banner Lakes State Wildlife Area

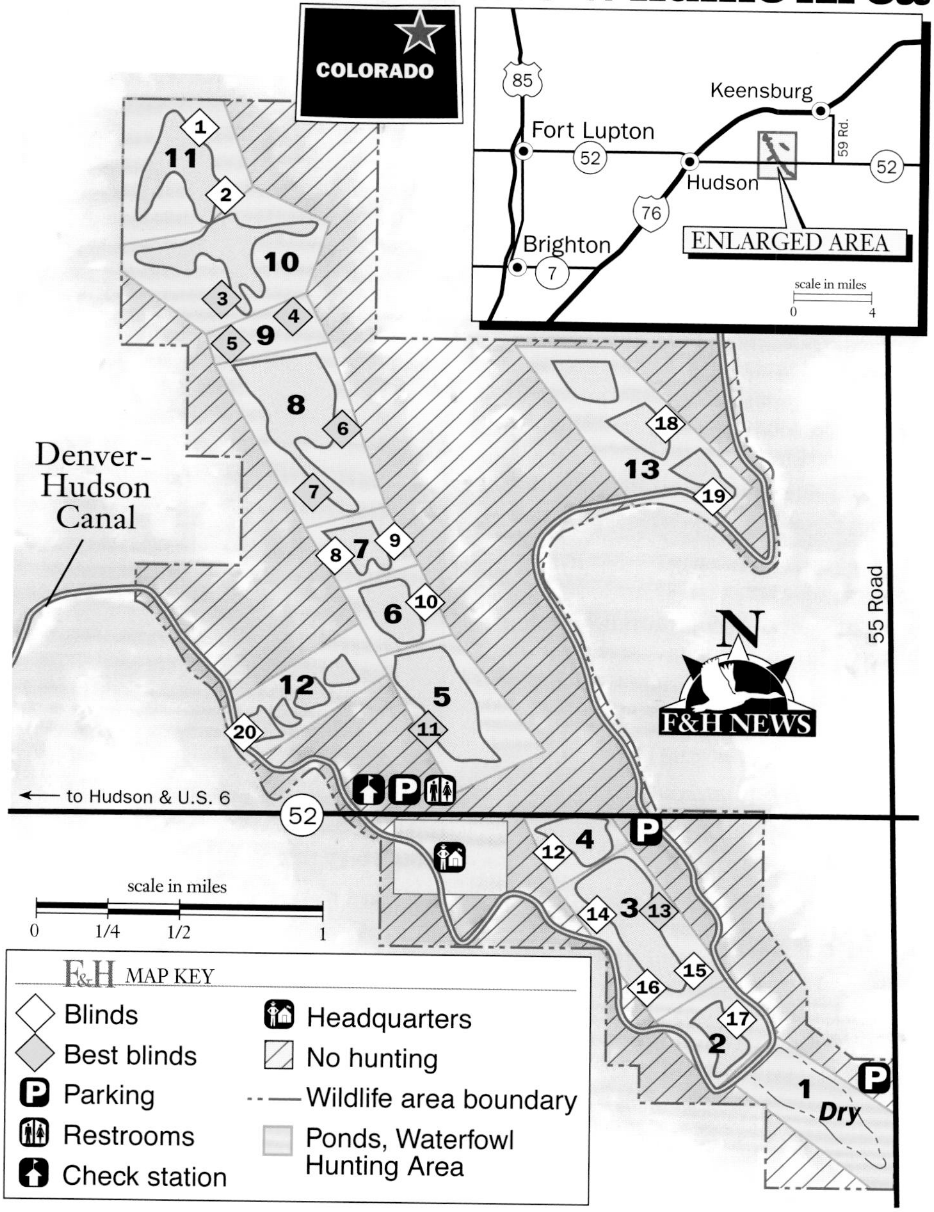

Denver-Hudson Canal

← to Hudson & U.S. 6

scale in miles

| 0 | 1/4 | 1/2 | 1 |

F&H MAP KEY

◇ Blinds
◆ Best blinds
P Parking
🚻 Restrooms
⬛ Check station

🏠 Headquarters
▨ No hunting
--- Wildlife area boundary
▢ Ponds, Waterfowl Hunting Area

long, narrow "leg" on the south end.

Pond 9: Pay special attention to the blinds (4 and 5) on Pond 9, which lies between Ponds 8 and 10. While this pond is one of the smallest on the wildlife area and is almost completely covered by cattail this season, the two blinds located on the east and west ends are perfectly situated to target birds flying between the two bigger ponds.

"(Pond) 9 gives you a chance to hunt off a point that dissects the south end of 10, and it can be pretty good for ducks," says Smith.

Pond 10: Features one blind (No. 3)

on the southwest shore. This offers a good mix of open water and shoreline vegetation.

Pond 11: Lying at the extreme north end of the wildlife area, this pond requires a 45-minute hike from the check-in. Consequently, you'll probably want to pack in only a couple dozen decoys to hunt out of either of the blinds (1 and 2) located on the east shore.

"There's some smartweed and Russian olive around that pond," Smith says. "It can be pretty good, but the hunting is limited by how ambitious you are. It's quite a hike from the parking lot."

F&H

Belly up to Barr Lake's middle blinds for pass shooting

by Joel Shangle

Before we even start talking about the meat and potatoes of the waterfowl hunting at Barr Lake State Park near Brighton, here's a warning to those of you who judge your duck hunt by the number of decoys you lay out: dekes aren't even an afterthought at this state park northeast of Denver. Second warning: calls are, by and large, in the same category. Bring 'em if you have to, but don't count on using them much.

If you're still reading, you've probably already figured out that a hunt at Barr Lake is a pass-shooting proposition. It's a low-tech, limited-gear hunt where, on a good day in December, you'll have a shot at mallards, shovelers, the odd light goose and droves of dark geese as they traffic between Barr Lake and a series of fields and potholes lying just adjacent to the hunt site. There's enough shooting for hardcore gunners and it's a simple enough hunt for neophytes. Belly up to the Barr, boys. Here's how it's done:

Blind luck: All waterfowl hunting at Barr Lake is done from a series of 13 blinds stretching out in a diagonal line just north of the dam on the

YOU DON'T NEED DOZENS of decoys or the best caller to bag geese like this one at Barr Lake. Pass shooting's the name of the game here, with the middle blinds (6,7,8 and 9) providing the best action.

north end of the lake. The blinds lie in the middle of a series of canals controlled by the local irrigation district, but they're all at least 300 yards from the waters of Barr Lake proper, with no standing water to speak of. Hence, the absence of need for decoys.

"The birds flying off the lake are passing over on their way somewhere else," says park ranger Steve Williams. "There are some marshy areas, cattail, prairie grass and some Russian Olives, but birds aren't really stopping to feed in the immediate area around the blinds. You'll occasionally see some guys use decoys, but I don't really think it helps." Actually, there's nothing lucky about how you choose your blinds at Barr Lake. Birds tend to lift off of the lake on the west side and head in a diagonal toward a series of small potholes located just north of the hunt boundary, bringing them over the middle of the line of blinds. Consequently, if you're sitting in the four blinds in the middle, you're probably going to see a lot more action than the shooters on the ends of the line. "I would suggest that blinds 6, 7, 8 and 9 are the most effec-

AT a GLANCE

What: Barr Lake State Park waterfowl

Where: On Barr Lake near Brighton, northeast of Denver

When: Hunting is allowed on Wednesdays and Saturdays only during the waterfowl season (closes January 23, 2005, for ducks and Feb. 13, 2005, for dark geese). Pintail and canvasback season ended Dec. 16.

How: Barr Lake features 13 three-man blind sites located north of the dam on the north end of the lake. All hunting must be done from these blinds, which are assigned on a reservation basis. All blinds left unreserved are assigned on a first-come, first-serve basis on hunt mornings. There are also two handicap-access blinds near the check-in station on the east shore.

Get there: From Denver, take Interstate to the Bromley/152nd exit and go right for roughly a mile to Picadilly Road. The check-in/headquarters is on Picadilly.

Who to call: Barr Lake State Park (303-655-1495); Colorado Division of Wildlife northeast region (303-291-7227) Blind reservations: (800) 846-WILD

tive," Williams says. "Since it's all pass shooting, the birds seem to come off the west side of the dam and fly over those middle blinds on the way to wherever they're going to stop to the north. They don't go far past the blinds, either — maybe a couple of hundred yards — but they still have to fly over." If you can't get one of the four middle blinds, shoot for blinds 12 and 13, which are located several hundred yards north of the rest of the blinds, on the extreme northern fringe of the hunt area. Blind 12 sits in a straight diagonal from Blind 5 and 13 is similarly located diagonally from Blind 4, so they see plenty of fly-over traffic from birds who make it past the guns in the middle blinds.

Getting your blind: The lake's blinds are assigned on a reservation basis by calling (800) 846-WILD at least two days before your desired hunt date. Once you've made your reservation, you simply check in at the headquarters station off Picadilly Road at 5 a.m. the morning of the hunt. Once blinds are vacated, they can be re-filled by hunters arriving at the check station on a first-come, first-serve basis. If you arrive at the check-in to find any blinds unreserved or left open by no-shows, you can claim them for the day after 7 a.m. Each blind holds a maximum of three hunters. There's one handicap-access blind located east of the parking lot. This blind is not operated on a reservation system.

Still to come: While the duck season will likely play itself out as a slightly below-average year, the late-season goose gunning will likely hold out right up to the February closure. Barr Lake isn't known for its numbers of light geese, but there are more than enough Canada geese in the area to provide limit-style shooting through the winter. "We have an enormous amount of dark geese," Williams says. "There's a tremendous abundance of opportunity for them. They could stand some additional harvest."

Water worries?: At presstime, Barr Lake was at full capacity, and should remain that way through the hunting season. Until water is released from the dam, there won't be much water in Speer, Beebe and Neres Canal, or in West and East Burlington ditches, which run north from the base of the dam, through the hunting area. That lack of water in the canals won't affect the waterfowl hunting much.

"The birds that come off the dam won't stop off in the canals," Williams says. "They're headed to the ponds further north." **F&H**

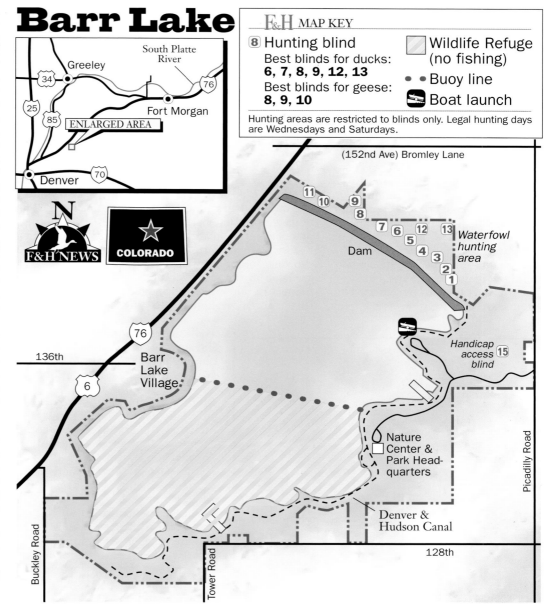

Barr Lake

F&H MAP KEY

⑧ Hunting blind
Best blinds for ducks:
6, 7, 8, 9, 12, 13
Best blinds for geese:
8, 9, 10

Wildlife Refuge (no fishing)

• • • Buoy line

Boat launch

Hunting areas are restricted to blinds only. Legal hunting days are Wednesdays and Saturdays.

Prewitt, Jumbo offer late season goose chances

STERLING

by Tom Behrens

Some exceptional public hunting opportunities for geese exist in northeastern Colorado, including Prewitt and Jumbo reservoirs and a host of other State Wildlife Areas (SWA) in the South Platte River area. Actually, no geese hunting is allowed on Jumbo, but the lake provides a vital function in the hunting scheme: It serves as a roost area for thousands of geese during the winter months.

Prewitt and Jumbo carry the classification of Plains reservoirs, shallow bodies of water used for irrigation. The bottoms are relatively structure-free,

PREWITT AND JUMBO RESERVOIRS are two of your better bets for late season geese. Don Haberer took this photo of his son Cole, loaded up with "110 pounds of geese" taken by himself and other hunters.

shaped similar to a salad bowl. Prewitt is the larger of the two — 2,924 acres to 1,703 — when full. During December, Canada geese are the predominant bird.

Prewitt and Jumbo both have firing lines. If you get caught shooting or hunting on the wrong side of the line, it'll mean a trip to local justice of the peace. Firing lines are a conservation practice put in place to allow a safe resting place for ducks and geese. Maps showing locations of firing lines are available in the same locations where hunters can purchase the $3 daily pass fee required to hunt on SWAs. An annual pass for $5 is available to hunters showing proof of a hunting license. As of Nov. 1, the lakes are closed to motorized boating. Hand-propelled boats can be used to put out decoys and pick up downed birds. Hunting from a boat is prohibited.

Because the lakes are used for irrigation, at times the lack of water can present some challenges to the goose hunter. "Unless the lake is completely full, it can be really tough hunting," says Brad Jackson, who lives about 10 miles from Prewitt. Jackson hunts Prewitt on his free days and guides in other areas. "Last year they did not fill Prewitt all the way after they drew it down. There was no water beyond the firing line." This year the lake does hold water and there have been reports of good duck hunting earlier this hunting season.

As mentioned earlier, Jumbo is not open for goose hunting during the December–February season, but duck hunting is allowed. Jumbo, like Prewitt, has a firing line, located south of another pond called the Annex. The first late goose season lasts until Feb. 13 for dark geese and Feb. 20 for snow geese.

"During the regular goose season, the ponds south of the firing line, any of that area, is the only place you can hunt geese," says Jackson. "In the past they have opened the Annex during the late snow geese season during March. That can be really good hunting. You still can't hunt Jumbo Reservoir for snow geese. Hunting is from the shore of the lake or the edge of the water, depending on how full they are. It's a lot of pass shooting."

Setting up to catch the bird's movements is the tough question. Where on the shore of the reservoir or pond are the birds going to pass over?

"On Prewitt and Jumbo both, the birds can go just about any direction to feed," says Jackson. "Come out the evening before the day you hunt to watch the birds' movements. Typically they will go to the same fields that they did the evening before. If possible set up in the area where they will cross when they are coming back and you will have a pretty good chance of getting them."

Pay attention to weather as well. "It also depends on the wind," Jackson says. "If the wind is blowing really hard you'll be able to tell which way they'll be flying, how high and low they're going to be when they leave or come back. The wind definitely plays a big role in the pass shooting at those places."

Besides wind speed and direction, temperature is another factor in the hunt. "Wait five minutes and it could change," says Jackson. "I think the biggest thing to remember at this time of the year is that these lakes and ponds freeze over. By mid-December the lakes are frozen over. The geese will sit there right on the ice. They almost seem to prefer it; the ducks will stay around as long as they can keep a hole

1. Prewitt Reservoir SWA

2. Jumbo Reservoir SWA

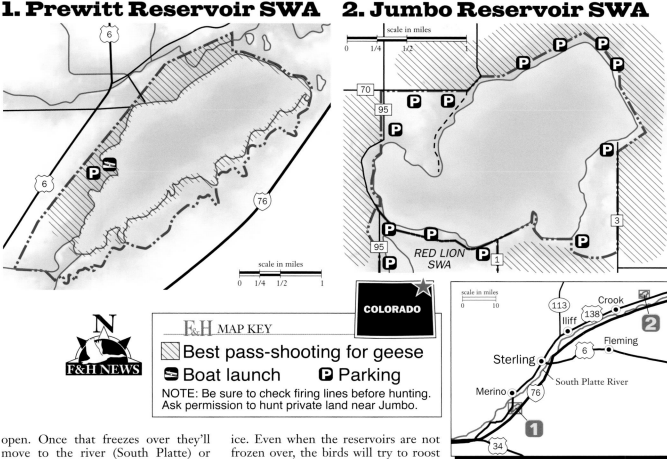

COLORADO

F&H MAP KEY

▨ Best pass-shooting for geese

⛴ Boat launch   🅿 Parking

NOTE: Be sure to check firing lines before hunting.
Ask permission to hunt private land near Jumbo.

RED LION SWA

open. Once that freezes over they'll move to the river (South Platte) or head south, one of the two options."

Dan Rieves, owner of Outdoor Connection (970-580-1560; *www.hasslefreehunts.com*) agrees that pass shooting works at this time of the year, but he would recommend spend some time knocking on doors and getting permission to hunt on some of the fields that the geese are feeding in after they leave Prewitt, Jumbo or the other SWA ponds and reservoirs.

"Let the reservoirs concentrate the birds and use them as stopovers during migration," he says. "That's what holds the birds in the area. The really exceptional hunting would be on the agricultural fields around there. Use as many decoys as you can carry if you decide to do a shore hunt. Big spreads are a must, especially during the later part of the season when they've been pressured. Hunt during the week. The amount of pressure during the week is maybe 10 percent of the hunting pressure as on the weekends."

Don't let a little ice stop you. "You can still get by hunting the edge of the

ice. Even when the reservoirs are not frozen over, the birds will try to roost in the middle of the reservoir, but they're somewhat susceptible to decoying along the shoreline with kind of a mixed spread of both ducks and geese. Decoys are placed the first 40 to 50 yards from shore on the ice."

Hunting the SWAs is primitive. "Build your own blinds," says Jackson. A lot of the hunters use the layout blinds, and they work well. A lot of guys just take camo material and arrange it and natural materials for a blind.

"Jumbo is walk-in access only," says Jackson. "It's not a very far walk, I would say about ¼-mile to the first

pond. Then at Prewitt, depending on how full the lake is, there are quite a few roads you can drive on. Right now I would say that it is ¼-mile to ½-mile walk to the water."

Prewitt and Jumbo reservoirs and other SWAs along the Platte River in northeastern Colorado can offer the ingredients for some good late season goose hunting. Prescouting the area to hunt is necessary whether you're pass shooting or asking permission to hunt on private land. Dress warmly and keep your face down; birds will be winging your way soon.   ***F&H***

AT a GLANCE

What: Public goose hunting near S. Platte River.

When: December and January. Hunting really gets good in March.

Where: Jumbo Reservoir is located about 30 miles northeast of Sterling. Prewitt Reservoir is about 15 miles southeast.

Who: Outdoor Connection (970-580-1560, *www.hasslefreehunts.com*); DOW Field Office in Brush (970-842-6300).

Walk-In Access Program offers late-season pheasant

CLARKVILLE

by Sam Grothe

WALK-IN ACCESS can provide you with hot pheasant action. Pat Ruzzo after a successful pheasant farmland hunt.

Four years into the Colorado Division of Wildlife's Walk-In Access Program is plenty of time to determine whether it is paying off for hunters or not.

The Walk-In Access Program has really become the darling of pheasant and upland game hunters, who before the program had driven out to the Eastern Plains, only to be turned around at the end of a long day of road hunting without having much luck getting permission to hunt on private property.

"Now guys are extending their trips," Gorman said. "We're tending to see a lot more younger people out early, like adults with their kids. And, we're even seeing them come out late season like in December or January."

"We're about at our maximum with 162,000 acres, which is quite a bit," says Ed Gorman, Small Game Manager for DOW.

Last year, according to the DOW, an estimated 18,541 hunters were out hunting ringneck pheasants.

The Walk-In Access Program probably won't grow much more in terms of the number of acres enrolled in the next few years, but those who purchase the program's stamp can be sure that the DOW is working hard to acquire better quality habitat, according to Gorman.

In terms of the bird count, DOW officials say conditions are nearly the same as last year, or perhaps a little bit better. But Colorado is definitely rebounding from the Y2K draught that slaughtered pheasant broods across the state. Harvest counts went from roughly 70,000 in 1999 to approximately 44,000 in 2000. The harvest numbers bumped a little in 2001, but then sank to only 34,000 bagged roosters in 2002. Last year's harvest by hunters was approximately 48,000 ringnecks.

"Our breed counts for 2004 were real good," said Gorman. "We had some cool weather in June (during pheasant broods), but I don't think it will have a negative effect. Guys are going to find birds out there."

Colorado's top five pheasant counties this year should come as no surprise: Yuma, Phillips, Kit Carson, Logan and Prowers. Those counties generally battle it out for the top spot and rotate a bit.

"As recently as two years ago Kit Carson County was challenging Yuma for best harvest," says Gorman, noting that Kit Carson had some trouble bouncing back from the draught, but is in decent shape now.

Here's a Walk-In Access county-by-county roundup of conditions hunters can expect this year for acreage enrolled in the program.

Weld County: Nearly all CRP enrolled acreage. Weld is pretty much an unknown factor as far as being a hunting success. For that reason it may be overlooked by many hunters heading to the plains. Areas include tall grass, wheat patches, and some seasonal (probably empty) lagoons with thick weeds. For a short day hunt, try hitting the areas up near Raymer and Stoneham.

Morgan County: Areas around Fort Morgan and Brush mainly contain weed and grass cover, but hunters can hit a few crop plots. Morgan County has pretty decent pheasant numbers up north. The sleeper area is down south.

Logan County: This county is fairly stocked with corn fields as well as some good wheat plots. It's worth taking a look at the areas around Fleming. This could be an excellent county to hit after a snowstorm, when the birds are seeking shelter in tall grasses, thickets, and along fence rows.

Sedgwick County: This county has a bounty of crop land to access. If hunting wheat strips and stubble is your bag, then this is the county for you. The pheasant numbers are decent in areas, but there were also some areas damaged by summer hail storms. Areas south of Ovid could be a good morning warm up just before heading into Phillips County.

Phillips County: There is a fair amount of cropland and grass pastures to hunt in Phillips County. Areas around Holyoke are normally packed with hunters early in the season. It's nearly impossible to pass through Phillips County without seeing a pheasant. Scout this county out early, if you want early success. Also, don't overlook field corners that may look undervalued, but have enough cover to hide a stealthy bird.

Washington County: This county has a fairly uneven distribution of habitat quality. There's lots of CRP, grasslands, and corn stubble. Pheasant populations in this county are on the rise because of improved cover. There's not much access in the south half of the county, so the action will probably be north.

Pheasant walk-in

Yuma County: The top spot this year has plenty of CRP, wheat, some real thick weeds, and corn. Just remember: Yuma may be the No. 1 county for harvest numbers, but it's also guaranteed to be the No. 1 crowded hunting spot this year as well. Areas right around Yuma and Wray are pretty decent, but most of that is private property. So, you'll have to go north or south of Yuma. Don't overlook taking a trip to the southern portion of the county. Try hitting the Walk-In areas around Joes, before tackling some of the fields at the Bonny State Recreation Area.

"There can be a pile of pheasants and you wouldn't even know it," says Gorman about how deceiving the Yuma County cover can be.

Kit Carson County: This county is still recovering from the draught that savaged it in 1999. Most of the cover on these areas will be grass, but there is some wheat and corn. However, the DOW outlook for this area this year is optimistic. It's still not going to approach the quality of Yuma County, not yet anyway. A good number of hunters do fairly well in this county in the middle of the upland game season. Any area around Stratton should be worth checking out.

Cheyenne County: You'll find wheat, CRP and grass cover to be predominant in this county.

"It's been the equivalent of a rain forest this year," says Gorman of Cheyenne County's habitat. "The cover quality is awesome."

In fact, the cover quality may be too good here and could make flushing birds burrowing below and running through tunnels harder to flush.

Kiowa County: Lots of lakes in this county. Most waterfowl hunting will be around the west side of Neesopah Reservoir.

Prowers County: Normally, this county hits within the top five harvested counties. This county has mostly irrigated ground with grass and wheat stubble. Hunters willing to scout this county will find pheasant, bobwhite and rabbit. Don't overanalyze the cover; just hunt it. Better quality cover and habitat lies in the eastern portion of the county.

Baca County: For those who like standing milo and milo stubble, this is the ticket for you. Hunters will also find CRP, corn stalks and grass in this county. In the southern part of the county, hunters may have a chance of running into pheasants, and scaled and bobwhite quail.

The access permit costs only $20 for hunters 16 years and older, and can be purchased at DOW offices and license agents. The stamp must be signed, and attach small game licenses before hunting. Hunters 16 years and under are can hunt these properties for free, with a small game license. *F&H*

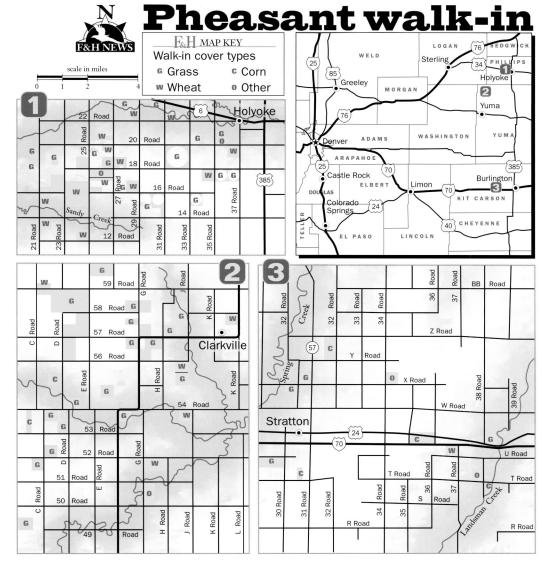

F&H NEWS

F&H MAP KEY
Walk-in cover types
G Grass   C Corn
W Wheat   O Other

scale in miles

AT a GLANCE

What: Over 160,000 acres of walk-in access pheasant hunting.

When: You can find good hunting all the way through January.

Where: Kit Carson, Yuma and Philips counties offer some of the best hunting.

Who: For more information about the Walk-In Access Program, contact the DOW Headquarters (303-297-1192).

SOUTHEAST HUNTING

Pueblo Merriam's in the thick stuff

by Dusty Routh

Ah, springtime. The Rockies crank up their bats, daytime temps finally creep up, trout put on the feedbag, and spring turkey hunting opens with a blast.

It's an especially awesome time of year if you live in south-central Colorado in or around Pueblo. There's outstanding opportunity for turkey action pretty close to home — in some cases, no more than 20 minutes from town. If you aren't a resident of the area, it can be worth your time and hunting effort to give these south-central gobbler hot spots a shot.

Why here? Because there's lots and lots of habitat ideally suited for Merriam's. Thick undergrowth adjacent to river bottoms, particularly along the Fountain River, provides hiding, feeding and roosting spots for wary birds. These birds are bent on not becoming lunch for the coyotes that are so pervasive throughout the area. You'll also find lots of Russian thistle, a favorite of turkeys. While public land access can be challenging, there's enough of it around to hunt, especially west of Pueblo in the Wet Mountains area.

Listen to the expert: You can get all your turkey dekes, calls, camo, scatterguns, advice and everything else you might need for the spring season at Big R Sporting Goods in Pueblo (719-542-1835). That's also where you'll find Brodie Gratiot, who's been wailing on turkeys for the past 42 years. A former Wisconsin guide who started his turkey campaign back in 1969, Gratiot now makes his home in Pueblo. He knows as much as anyone about turkey hunting in this part of the state.

"We've got mostly Merriam's down here," he says. "When you get up towards Salida there are some crossbreeds up there. Probably because at one point or another someone may have unleashed some farm-planted birds. There are areas of the state that have trouble with that. And down south towards Trinidad you'll encounter Rio Grandes."

The Merriam's can get thick in this portion of southern Colorado. "The forecasts that I get come mostly from predator hunters," Gratiot says. "They'll come in after they've been hunting coyotes, and tell me about all the turkeys and turkey sign they saw while they were in the field. In a general kind of way, based on what I've been hearing, we should have a really great spring season."

Still a challenge: While there may be plenty of turkeys, there are two inherent difficulties hunting birds in this area: the high population of coyotes, and the vast amount of land that is in the hands of private owners.

"There's lots of predation," Gratiot says. "The coyote population is way, way up. Especially south of San Isabela and south of Rye. We're still seeing good-sized flocks of turkeys, but not like we used to. The areas down there east and just west of Highway 25 have tons of coyotes."

For whatever reason, the coyotes seem to be intensely concentrated in that area just south of Colorado City down to just north of Walsenburg. The predation is enough that you'll want to avoid that area, Gratiot advises, unless of course you'd

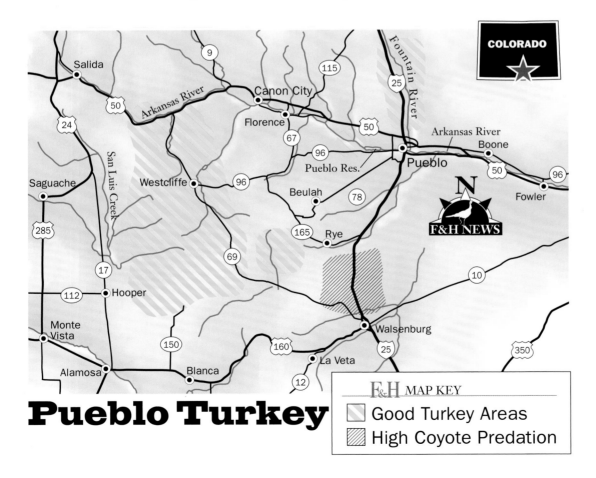

Pueblo Turkey

F&H MAP KEY

▨ Good Turkey Areas
▨ High Coyote Predation

like to do some coyote plinking.

The better news is that "around San Isabela north, and around Beula, it'll be real, real hot this spring," says Gratiot. "Lots of birds in that area, and they don't seem to be as affected by the coyotes. If I were to hunt right now, I would look at the Rye/Beula area, mid- to upper San Isabel, and west of that, and on up to Salida."

In terms of SWAs, Gratiot recommends giving the western end of Pueblo Reservoir a try. "We were doing some duck hunting there last fall and came across a lot of turkey sign out there. It might be a real good spot. The problem is going to be the hunting pressure. It can get hot and heavy. I mean, it can be like Vietnam out there when there's a lot of hunters."

The other real challenge is private land ownership. Some of the best turkey ground around is on private land. "All along the Fountain River, that's got real rich undergrowth. It's got plenty of food and cover for these birds. It's just a real turkey area. But it's mostly private, there's no public hunting without permission. But if you can get it, man, that's just a tremendous area to hunt turkeys."

The area immediately to the east of Pueblo holds turkeys, also, but Gratiot says it can be spotty. "You'll want to be sure to look for Russian thistle. They like that. There's lots of grazing land over there. If you hunt it, remember the turkeys will be down in the thick stuff."

Load 'em up: When it comes to arms and ammo, Gratiot goes simple. "Believe it or not, even with all the guns I've owned I always go back to my Browning Auto 5 (12-gauge). I like it the best for turkey hunting. I shoot it with a full choke, and No. 5 shot in a 3-inch mag."

Gratiot points out that he'd like to eventually experiment with an extra full. "I think it would be worth a try," he says, "but I'm real particular about distance when it comes to shooting turkeys. I absolutely will not take a shot if I think it will cripple that bird instead of kill it outright. So most of my shots are 20 to 25 yards at the most, and no more."

Gratiot also prefers a box call. "I just can't use a diaphragm call," he says. "My gag reflex and all. But I've never had any trouble calling birds in. A screech call will locate birds."

Tale of the tape: Spring season means you can take one one bearded jake (as opposed to two either-sex in the fall). The season opens up April 12 and runs to May 25 statewide except in closed units (1, 2, 15, 21, 25, 26, 27, 30, 34, 35, 36, 44, 45, 47, 80, 81, 90, 93, 95, 98,106, 111, 115, 120, 121, 201, 371, 444 and 471). If you carry a limited spring license for all units or parts of units east of I-25, you can bag two bearded turkeys. One must be harvested with a limited license in the limited area. The second must be harvested with an unlimited license in an unlimited area. If you take two turkeys in spring, you cannot take a turkey in the fall. (Our advice: Read your regs *very* carefully.)

You'll need an access permit to hunt on the Higel and Rio Grande SWAs. New hunts have been established in units 91, 92 and 96 in the spring season with licenses that are not valid on SWAs. Each unit maintains some licenses, which can be used throughout each unit. (Our advice: Make sure you're legal.)

The application deadline for limited hunting units was Feb. 13 (something you'll want to note for next year if you missed this one). DOW will begin accepting apps for fall limited turkey hunts as of June 3, with an application deadline of July 10. Lucky turkey hunters will be notified by Aug. 12. (Our advice: Try to be one of the lucky ones.) ***F&H***

SPRING TURKEY! Ronald Nutter took this turkey in May a few years ago. He shot the 17-pounder at 26 yards near Trinidad.

AT A GLANCE

What: Springtime gobbler hunting.

When: Season opens up April 12 and runs to May 25. There are a number of closed units and limited entry units, so be sure of where you're headed before you go.

Where: Areas north, northwest and west of Pueblo in south-central Colorado. Watch out for the area directly south of Pueblo which is having trouble with coyote predation.

Gear, tactics: Camo up, grab your scattergun, your calls and dekes. Look for river bottoms, the real thick stuff, and anywhere you can find Russian thistle.

Species: There are big Merriam's north, Rio Grandes south, and some cross-breeds (Merriam's and farm birds) up near Salida.

Who: Call Brodie Gratiot, area turkey guru, at Big R Sporting Goods (719-542-1835).

Head southeast for late-season ducks, geese

La JUNTA

by Tom Behrens

John Martin and Rocky Ford State Wildlife Areas in southeastern Colorado offer waterfowlers a chance at late-season goose and duck hunting, each offering two different shooting opportunities. Rocky Ford SWA is river bottom hunting, while John Martin SWA offers reservoir shooting action.

Both SWAs can produce some good late season waterfowl action if you're there at the right time. Watch the weather projections and time your hunts with the passage of "nasty weather." Dress warm and score on late season waterfowl hunting.

Rocky Ford SWA consists of two different blocks of land, one consisting of 552 acres and another of 660 acres, connected by a 96-acre strip of land on the Arkansas River. "We probably have a little over 3 miles of continuous property along the river," says Don Lewis, Property Technician for Rocky Ford SWA. "Usually during the late season, it can be a good place to try your luck."

The cold weather that usually accompanies this time of the year can help

1. Lake Meredith

2. Rocky Ford SWA

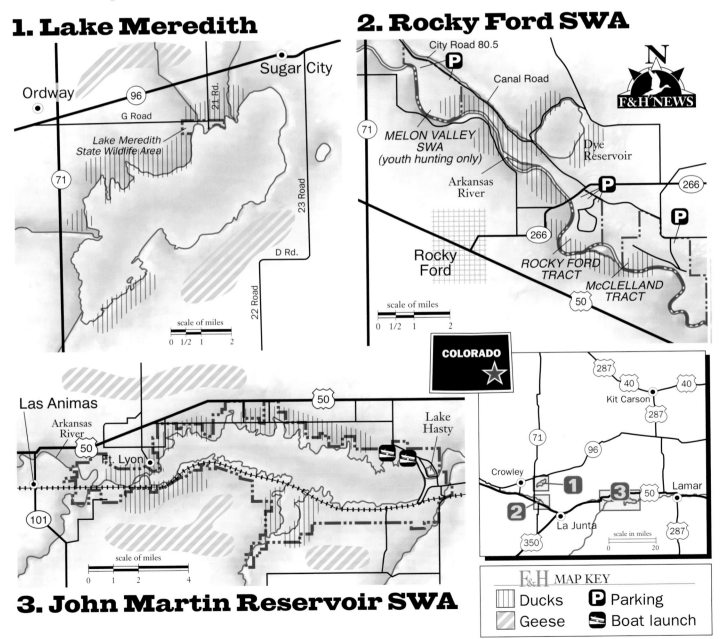

3. John Martin Reservoir SWA

F&H MAP KEY

▦ Ducks	🅿 Parking	
▧ Geese	⛵ Boat launch	

load up birds in the SWA. Reservoirs in the Rocky Ford area, such as Lake Meredith, freeze over, forcing ducks to seek open water that can be found on the Arkansas River in the SWA. Of course, even without ice conditions the river bottom provides lots of small ponds and backwater areas for ducks to rest and roost.

"There is always a little water (in the river), some years a little bit more than others," says Lewis. "We have 11 ponds on the wildlife area. Ducks like the smaller ponds. Historically, until the ponds freeze over, hunters usually have done real well on them. Good duck hunting areas have been in the La Junta and Las Animas areas. Hunters put out three or four dozen decoys, hunker back into the weeds or tamaracks and wait for the ducks to come in."

"Occasionally we will pick some geese up coming down, landing in fields adjacent to Lake Meredith," says Lewis. "Normally there has always been a lot of grain for the geese in the close proximity. The geese come and stay for a little rest and they're off again. They usually go further south to the big agriculture fields, wheat fields and corn stubble. There is some pass shooting that goes occurs on real ugly days," cold days with low clouds and wind, maybe some rain or snow mixed in. "They (geese) are low enough to get some shots at. If it is a real nasty day, instead of going back to the reservoir, they will go ahead and pull into the river and rest there."

Dave Williams, who lives in the area, hunts the Ford SWA regularly. "We normally hunt fields, scattered around the area," he says. "Most of the geese in this area stay on Lake Meredith. The fields that they feed in are from Pueblo to Lamar, along the river bottom."

Williams and six of his regular hunting buddies rely on massive decoy spreads, consisting of a mixture of shells and rags, to lure the birds into shooting range. "We put out about 1,000 rags," says Williams. "To get the numbers you need for snow geese you almost have to use rags or be a

YOU AND YOUR DOG can find late-season waterfowling at John Martin and Rocky Ford SWAs in southeastern Colorado.

millionaire. Between the beginning of the season and now, there is not much of change in the way we place the decoys. It's pretty much a numbers deal. Wherever the first bird sits down, that is where they all go. They are tough to decoy.

"Weather is a big factor for snow geese also," Williams says. "When it's a clear day, they fly so hard it's hard to decoy them. If you can get some wind or some clouds then the guys have a pretty good shot." He and his buddies garb themselves in white and settle in among the white rags and wait for the birds.

John Martin Reservoir SWA can be very good duck hunting. "It's a reservoir that was created by the damming of the Arkansas," says Steve Keefer, District Wildlife Manager. "When we have a lot of water it is the largest lake — surface-acreage wise, 12,000 surface acres — in Colorado."

Like many reservoirs in Colorado, the water is drawn down for crop irrigation. "Right now there is a large marsh at the west end of the lake that has several areas of open water that has been holding ducks off and on," says Keefer. "Consistently there have been a few thousand ducks, sometimes closer to 10,000, sometimes to 1,000."

The Fort Lyon area has ponds that are ice-free pretty much all winter that often hold birds. "The river, depending on the weather, will often hold birds," says Keefer. "If it gets real cold you have a lot of ice floating through it, pushing them out. But ordinarily, the river has birds. The river actually tends to be better hunting late in the season. Those warm water sloughs and open areas created by the river really hold the ducks."

Keefer hunts early morning and evening hours over decoy spreads. "Definitely try to go in early, using decoys, to bring them in. Decoys are real effective, especially in the marsh areas. A canoe or jon boat, something like that, is a much better way of getting in and out instead of trying to wade through. You have a marsh that is over a mile wide and it has a real soft bottom. That mud can be pretty nasty. There are a lot of little puddles, some of which you can walk in on pretty easy. Midday we do a lot of jump shooting around here on the ponds."

According to Keefer, the best goose hunting tends to be on private agricultural land, where the birds are feeding off the farm fields. "They move around to what is available," he says. "Another thing that does influence where the geese fly is that we have Queens, Neenoshe, Neegronda to the northeast of John Martin in Kiowa County that often hold a lot of geese. We get movement between those lakes and John Martin. Hunting depends more on where they are feeding more than anything else. *F&H*

AT a GLANCE

What: Late season ducks and geese at John Martin and Rocky Ford SWAs

Where: John Martin and Rocky Ford SWAs are located east of Pueblo on Highway 50 near the towns of Las Animas and Rocky Ford.

Who: Pueblo DOW Office (719-561-5300), Southeast Region Service Center (719-227-5200).

NORTHWEST HUNTING

Plenty of public land for antelope season

COLORADO SPRINGS

by Ed Marsh

I love watching wildlife, even when I'm not hunting them. I could sit for hours, watching, observing, admiring and, most importantly, learning.

With all the time I spend in the outdoors, I see plenty of animals and one of my favorites are pronghorn antelope. I've hunted and harvested 'lopes in Montana and Colorado. So far, all the meat I've had from these beautiful creatures has been choice. I'm seriously thinking about applying again and giving them a go!

Because of my travels, I get to see a lot of country where all kinds of animals are found, and a lot of this country is antelope country. Wyoming is supposed to be the antelope capital of the United States, and I'm sure that's true, but I bet Colorado runs a very close second.

In GMUs north of Craig, there are huge herds of pronghorns, and I bet they wander back and forth between the states. I do know that driving up through these units, antelope are almost everywhere, including a lot of public land open to hunting.

GMU 4 (which I'm familiar with) and GMUs 5 and 441 (which I'm not) are all open to hunting from Sept. 14 to Oct. 11. I know GMU 4 is loaded with 'lopes, and I'm sure there are equal numbers in 5 and 441. There is a lot of private land in most of this region but maps are available showing where public land is.

GMU 80 has a lot of BLM land in the foothills west of Monte Vista. I've seen many antelope in this country while hunting cottontails, and some of the bucks in there had good horns. The season runs from Sept. 28–Oct. 4, which isn't a very long season, but I've seen enough animals here to know that taking a pronghorn shouldn't be a problem. This is a buck-only unit.

Also in GMU 80, Hot Creek SWA offers more than 3,000 acres of public hunting. This area may not have the numbers of antelope found to the west of Monte Vista, but it only takes one buck to fill a tag. (Check out the cottontails here too!)

GMU 68 and half of 681 are really loaded with antelope. The only place where I've seen more antelope is GMU 4. It's another short, buck-only season, but with large areas of public land, both BLM and national forest. A little preseason scouting will really pay off.

GMU 68 and the west half of 681 have the most public land, while the east half is combined with GMU 82. There is public land north and east of US 285. I've seen animals here, sometimes in good numbers.

On the west side of 681 along CO 114 north of Saguache, there's plenty of public land — and antelope. I would suggest getting Rio Grande *and* San Isabel National Forest maps because of all the public land, especially BLM. As usual, preseason scouting is an absolute must for a successful hunt.

GMUs 69, 84, 85, 86, 691 and 861 have some prime antelope country, especially west of Walsenburg. This is all private land, but considering the pronghorns in these units, it could well be worth the time to seek permission to hunt here. The season dates here are Oct. 5–11, another short season. Antelope are easy to hunt — I've never needed more than two days to fill a tag, and I've never been skunked on antelope.

Other areas offer good hunting, including South Park in GMU 58. There's even some public land to hunt here. There all kinds of antelope along US 24 east of Colorado Springs. This is all private land, but this is where I've taken all my 'lopes, and I never had trouble getting permission. Just don't be knocking on a landowner's door at 0-Dark-30 to ask permission to hunt. **F&H**

Colorado Antelope

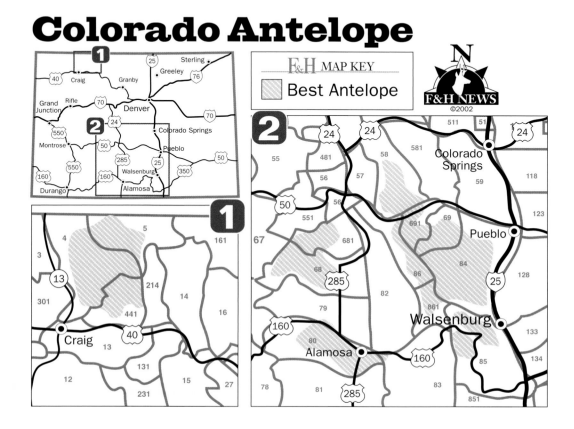

F&H MAP KEY — Best Antelope

F&H NEWS ©2002

Go (north)west, young man, for trophy elk

DINOSAUR

by Tom Behrens / F&H News contributor

From all indications, northwest Colorado could produce some great trophy elk hunting this coming season, specifically in units 201, 2 and 10. They could produce an opportunity to harvest a bull that would measure 300 Boone & Crockett points, and the possibility of taking an even bigger bull.

"There are a few bulls that are killed in these units that will go better than 350," says John Ellenberger (970-255-6182), Big Game Manager for Colorado Division of Wildlife.

Units 201, 2, and 10 are limited access hunting areas specifically designed to produce quality elk. "The reason we have big bulls there is because we have restricted hunting pressure," says Ellenberger. "If we did not restrict hunting pressure, it would be like our units where the majority of the bulls harvested would be 2½-year-old bulls."

Hunters enter their names in a drawing for the opportunity to hunt in these units. "If you draw for a license and are not successful, you receive a preference point," says Ellenberger. Hunters can accumulate points. More points increase the chances of being drawn for a hunt the next year.

Lay of the land: The area is described as high plateau country. "It's not the high Rockies with peaks going up to 14,000 feet," says Ellenberger. "This country tops out at 9,000 to 10,000 feet. Most of the areas that you will be hunting are 7,000 to 8,000 feet."

Ellenberger hunts Unit 201. "It's drier than what you would expect to be good elk country," he says. "There are spruce and fir trees mixed with aspen at the higher elevations, but then a lot of the country is open sagebrush grassland." It's not uncommon to find elk frequenting the open sagebrush areas. "Some of the sagebrush is located in pretty steep canyon country where elk use the topography for escape cover instead of using heavy timber, heavy cover," says Ellenberger.

Elk hunting season for 201, 2 and 10 starts Oct. 1 and continues for 11 days.

"The first of October is still fairly warm," says Ellenberger. "The elk like to draw up in the middle of the day so

Nice rack: It's hard to draw a tag in units 201, 2 and 10, but if you beat the odds you'll have a great shot at a trophy. Stan Grebe of Arvada took this 7X7 bull in 2002.

they'll be in aspen groves or in the timber, one or another. You just have to start covering some country on foot or on horseback, glassing early morning, late afternoon, reading tracks and signs to tell how recent the animal has been in the area. Almost the entire mountain is elk habitat. There are portions which are obviously better than other parts, such as combinations of aspen and timber with some grassy open parts, but you'll see that when you get there."

Taking a trophy: "A lot of guys drive the roads early in the morning," says Darby Finley (970-878-6064), a Colorado Division of Wildlife biologist who works the northwest part of Colorado. "A lot of the times that's when they'll see bulls or hear the elk bugling. Some guys will go scout the area and get a specific area they want to hunt. Some will use more of a spot-and-stalk type of method. Some will sit and try to pattern elk activity at water holes."

"For instance a hunter may be sitting on a rim where they have a good vantage point, glassing the area," Finley says. "They see a bull they want to go after and figure out how they're going to stalk the animal. I know some individuals who I talked to last year that were driving up the road in the morning to an area where they thought might be good. They spotted a bull silhouetted on a rim, took off after him and ended up getting him. But it all depends on how far that elk is away from you when you're glassing, whether he's still going to be there when you get there."

Besides glassing the open area and cover, a hunter should listen for the familiar bugle of the male elk. The 11-day season takes place during the rut.

"Most of the time you can locate elk by just listening for them to bugle," says Ellenberger. "This country is dry, and so water holes are kind of at a premium. The elk will congregate at water holes."

"Unit 10 is certainly in a dry cycle," says Finley. "The Browns Park National Wildlife Refuge area, which is up in unit 2 and 201 area, seems to be getting some consistent moisture from passing thunderstorms. Some people who have been hunting there for years say it has some of the best conditions they've seen."

Shooting distances are going to be between 75 to 200 yards. "You could be shooting 500 yards, but that's really on the outside," says Ellenberger. "That's probably the extreme. I shoot a Remington 7mm mag. Any big game rifle from 270 on up is an adequate rifle for elk. The main thing is that the hunter be proficient with the weapon, be able at 100 yards to hit an areas the size of a saucer. If you can't do that you'll be tracking the animal for a long way."

"There is a road system through the area," says Ellenberger. "You can camp at a lower area and drive in to prime hunting locations daily, or there are places to camp at some of the higher elevations that will put a hunter into closer proximity with some elk. It is not a situation where you have to pack in 10 miles to get in elk hunting country."

Maps are available to show topography and land status. The Bureau of Land Management controls most of the land.

Topographical maps can be obtained by contacting the state office of the BLM (303-239-3600).

If your name is drawn for units 201, 2 or 10 in northwest Colorado, your chances of getting a bragging-rights bull is going to be good this hunting season. Look for water, especially if hunting Unit 2. Glass whatever area you're checking out early and late when the elk are moving, and listen for the call of the lovesick bull.

Last, but a very important point, take into consideration the distance between you and the elk if you choose to stalk him. He could be gone when you finally get there, or it could be a long carry out with that new trophy. **F&H**

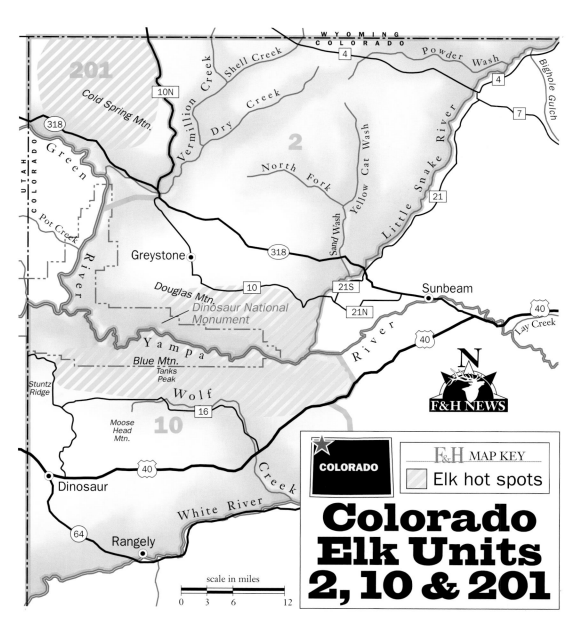

F&H MAP KEY — Elk hot spots

Colorado Elk Units 2, 10 & 201

Where to go in northwest Colorado for turkey

STERLING

by Louis Bignami

BOB FRALEY crossed some rocky terrain for this bird. Expect to do the same in northwestern Colorado, but if you work at it, you can expect similar results.

The numbers show that turkey hunting is getting more and more popular in Colorado. "There are about 35,000 to 40,000 birds in Colorado, and about 5,000 (NWTF) members," says Michael Storey, the Volunteer State Chapter President of the NWTF. "Bird and member numbers seem to be growing about 10 to 15 percent a year. We're moving birds every year, but they're still scattered when you compare Colorado to other states. So hunters need to know prime habitat for each species."

"This is especially the case up in the northwest where you need to put in a lot of miles — and vertical miles — to get birds."

As a rule, the old elk hunting adage is also the best turkey hunting advice in this area: "Go down in the steepest, deepest or most inaccessible spot from which no hunter would wish to drag a turkey home, and that's where the elk – and turkey — hold."

Both Merriam's and Rio Grande turkeys are available in this part of Colorado. Their preferred habitat differs. The former, according to local wildlife biologist Dan Prenzlow, "hole up at elevations from 6,000 to 8,500 feet in pine country, unless winter weather drives them down into the river bottoms where the latter lurk."

Not for the weak at heart: Much of the turkey hunting in this part of the state is at elevation and on the steep. So come fit, and with a pair of broken-in boots! However, you probably won't be able to get much above 6,000 feet until the snow melts. Oh, and come equipped for rain and snow, too.

As a rule, Merriam's — *Meleagris gallopavo Merriam's* — are tougher to find because they move more often and further in tougher country. During summer they gang up in scrub oak and ponderosa pine foothills and up into the meadows. So if the warm spring continues, check for Merriam's at altitude up into elk terrain, where glassing can work better than calling. To narrow your search for current flocks, talk to locals. Most will report flock sightings. School bus and truck drivers and mailmen are other good sources.

While Rio Grande turkeys tend to hang out in open country near heavier cover along bottomland, canyons and creeks with water, food and roosting trees, they do move up to 6,000-foot and higher elevations. Roost trees can be a limiting factor, so glass for big snags as well as walking birds. Calling early and late in the day seems the best approach for this subspecies, and can produce Merriam's turkeys as well early in the season before mild weather sends them back up into pine country.

Where to go: The best chance to fill a tag is enjoyed by holders of one of the five tom permits on the White River east of Meeker, as this is the hot spot if you can get a draw.

NWTF member Bruce Johnson attempts to hunt here often. "Bruce tries every year, but only manages to get on every third year or so," says his wife.

"The area just east of Meeker is Unit 23 with five-tom draw," says Dan Wyatt at Wyatt Sporting Goods (970-878-4428) in Meeker. "But you need to get down to BLM land and unposted private land down around Rifle. April is, however, a good time to fish for our trout as snowmelt isn't until May."

NWTF spokesman Charles Stockstill agrees. "The best bet in this area is in

AT A GLANCE

What: Scouring the northwest corner of the state for the new and growing population of turkey. Rios and Merriam's are there. It's not the best location, but with some work you can get into birds. And you'll be hunting pretty much by yourself.

Where: The public lands between Highway 70 and Highway 40 offer hunting where units are open. Focus on the waterways in the Meeker area for the best action.

When: Seasons kick off April 12 and run into late May.

Who: Wyatt Sporting Goods (970-878-4428); DOW Meeker (970-878-2197); Colorado NWTF President Michael Storey (719-686-0563; *www.nwtfcolorado.org*).

the BLM lands north of Rifle Gap Reservoir; that's about 12 miles north," he says. "It's an over-the-counter tag and there are birds there. Otherwise, there's far better turkey hunting in the southern half of the state. I'd head for southwest and south-central Colorado. If you can afford hunter access fees, consider the ranch hunting down south for sure birds"

Most of the rest of northwest Colorado has scattered pockets of birds, and many are in protected zones or available only by draw.

Otherwise your best shots are off a couple of turns north or south off the freeway along the I-70 corridor towards Grand Junction and east

towards Glenwood Springs. In the open plateau and high desert, the key to action is considered scouting. Over in ski country, the keys are access to national forest or private property and open hunting zones.

In three or four years, there should be all sorts of new spots. For example, the NWTF moved 100 birds over into Douglas Mountain last year. These relocating efforts, plus a series mild springs the last three or four years, are gradually increasing both the population density and distribution. Storms at the end of February should green up the area and improve survival for this season's hatch too.

Limited draw applications are a

rather low-percentage operation: In 2002 there were 3,787 applications submitted (85 by nonresidents) and 501 applications drawn (9 by nonresidents). The odds of drawing were even higher in the most popular areas like that around Meeker.

Units closed to all spring turkey hunting are: 1, 2, 15,21, 25,26,27, 30, 34, 35, 36,37, 44, 45, 47, 80, 81, 90, 93, 95, 98, 106, 111, 115, 120, 121, 201, 371, 444 and 471. Units open for limited spring turkey licenses: 23, 31, 43, 59, 91, 92, 96, 102, 103, 105, 107, 109, 124, 125, 129, 126, 146, 127, 132, 120 North of US-50, 128, 139, 140, 444 and 851 with other restrictions in state wildlife areas.   **F&H**

Northwest Colorado Turkey Hunts

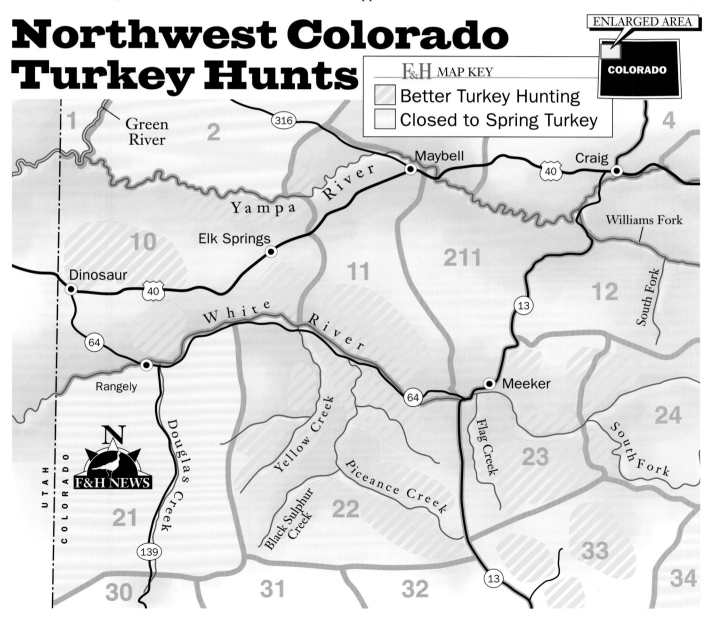

Expect excellent elk between Craig, Meeker

CRAIG

by Dusty Routh

When the state's top big game manager says that one area of the state offers an incredible density of elk, you'd better believe that region is worth checking out. Such is the case with the areas around northwest Colorado, between the small towns of Craig and Meeker. John Ellenburger

points out that the state lands and other public lands in these areas, such as BLM land and forest service land, offer what he calls "our best elk populations in terms of densities."

Specifically, Ellenburger says that the White River area near Meeker, all around Craig, north of Craig and anywhere north of the Yampa River will likely provide some excellent hunting this fall during elk season.

Because not all elk hunting in these areas is managed by a draw permit system, Ellenburger cautions that hunters may not find huge trophy bulls, because escapement numbers can be low from season to season. So most hunters are going to come across elk that are in the 2- to 3-year-old range. But what these areas may lack in trophies, they more than make up for with herd numbers.

Gimme land, lotsa land: There are not only healthy numbers of elk in this region, there's also a wealth of public land opportunities on which to hunt. Starting at Craig and heading east on Highway 40, you'll find a good number of state lands centered around the Elkhead Reservoir area. Hunting northeast of the reservoir can be good. There are also a smattering of state lands directly east and southeast of the reservoir, including the Maynard Gulch STL.

Heading north out of Craig, there are state land holdings along Highway 13 around Ralph White Lake (most of this is just west of Highway 13), and further north along Fortification and Blue Gravel creeks. There's also a large swath of state land just south of the Wyoming border, also along Highway 13. And heading west from there, hunters can access a large tract of state land centered around the Pole Gulch STL. This is an expansive piece of state land just south of the Little Snake River.

Heading west from Craig, there are more state lands available along the north side of the Yampa River, around the Triangle STL and Boston Flats STL, and up north from there at the larger Little Snake SWA. Further north, there's a huge state land holding

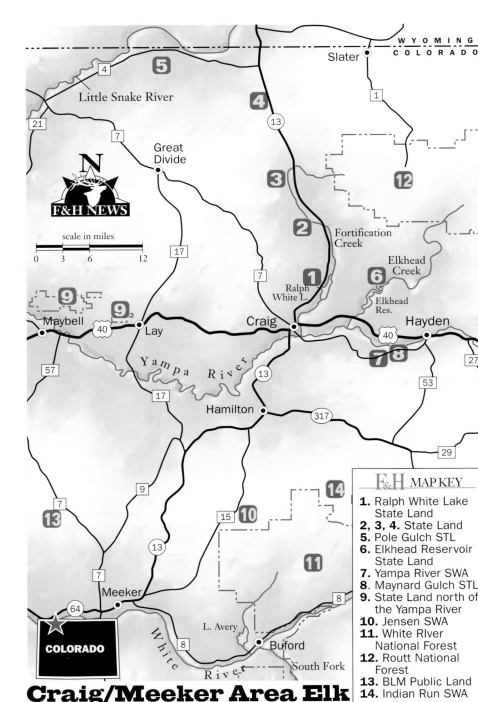

F&H MAP KEY
1. Ralph White Lake State Land
2, 3, 4. State Land
5. Pole Gulch STL
6. Elkhead Reservoir State Land
7. Yampa River SWA
8. Maynard Gulch STL
9. State Land north of the Yampa River
10. Jensen SWA
11. White River National Forest
12. Routt National Forest
13. BLM Public Land
14. Indian Run SWA

Craig/Meeker Area Elk

with the South Nipple Rim SWA marking the far western edge.

In addition to these, the state has smaller single tracts of public land dotting the landscape, some accessible by road, some by foot. Your best bet for these harder-to-find, harder-to-reach areas is a good BLM map and the Colorado Atlas & Gazetteer. Also, be sure to have a good state game management unit (GMU) map, since of course different units carry different regulations.

Closer to Meeker, hunters will find lots of forest service land offered by the White River National Forest, just east of town. North of Meeker, you'll find the Jensen SWA and Monument Bluff and Box Elder STLs. To the far northeast of Meeker, there's the Indian Run SWA and Yampa River and Stokes Gulch STLs. Closer to Meeker are the Morapos and Monument Butte STLs.

Or go private: If you'd prefer to hunt on private land with an outfitter, you have a lot of options in the Craig area. These include All Seasons Ranch, (Bruce Rhyne, 970-824-4178). All Seasons offers high-country horseback hunts in GMUs 4, 441 and 21. Or try Bigrack Outfitters & Horseback Adventures (Eric Hamilton, 970-826-4468).

For drop camps into the Routt National Forest, try The Craig Wild Bunch, Inc. (Mary Funkhouser, 970-824-5463). For the Flat Tops area (GMU 231), call Dunckley Peak Outfitters and Pack Service (William Terrill, 970-824-8257). Another option is Elkhorn Outfitters (Dick Dodds, 970-824-7470). For the Williams Fork Mountains, try Myers Hunting Service, Inc. (Don Myers, 970-824-9317).

For hunts in GMUs 1, 2, 201, 3, 301, 4, 10, 12 and 13, call S&K Guide & Outfitting Service (Kyle Revelle, 970-824-4932). If you're a bowhunting fanatic, call Triple Track Hunting (Brandan Stewart, 970-824-6045). Triple Track offers bowhunts, both guided and unguided, on more than 10,000 acres of private land in the region. In Unit 301, call Walz Guide Service (Mitchell Walz, 970-826-9814). Walz offers elk, deer and antelope hunts on 25,000 acres of private property in this unit.

In Meeker, try Buffalo Horn Ranch, Inc. (Jim Walma, 970-878-5450). They offer guided deer and elk hunts in the area.

SOME of the best elk densities in Colorado are on the BLM land around the White and Yampa Rivers. It might be your best bet to harvest a nice bull with a bow like this hunter.

Season dates: The archery elk season will run this year from Aug. 28 to Sept. 26 west of I-25 and in Unit 140. Muzzleloading rifle for combined deer/elk (by drawing only) runs Sept. 11 to 19. For the first general rifle season, the separate limited elk dates are Oct. 9 to 13. The second season for combined deer/elk runs Oct. 16 to 24, the third season runs Oct. 30 to Nov. 5 and the fourth season runs from Nov. 6 to 10.

Limited permits on the rise: DOW reports that roughly 17 percent of the elk hunting in Colorado is managed by limited draw entry permits, but that number may increase as much as 30 percent in 2005 to. The Colorado Wildlife Commission recently received five proposals to add additional limited elk units in the state. These were for GMUs 43 and 471 near Marble; GMU 551 southwest of Salida; units 54, 55 and 551 near Gunnison; units 80 and 81 in the San Luis Valley; and 75, 751, 77, 78 and 771 south and west of Wolf Creek Pass. All of these units now offer over-the-counter regular season bull elk licenses.

The Colorado Wildlife Commission received five proposals to add additional limited elk units for the 2005 big game seasons. "The individuals or groups that have proposed managing these additional units for limited bull hunting must now provide supporting documentation showing support from local stakeholders in those areas," says Mike King, DOW's regulation manag-

er. "These include local chambers of commerce, livestock producers, the local farm bureau, Habitat Partnership Program committees, local governments, outfitters and local and state hunting organizations."

For more information: The Craig Chamber of Commerce's Sportsman Information Center (970-824-5689; 800-864-4405) has topo maps and Forest Service and BLM land maps.

There's also a DOW submission station for checking deer and elk for chronic wasting disease (CWD) located at the Craig DOW Warehouse (970-824-2502) in Craig. Hours are 8 a.m. to 10 p.m. during the season. Last year's cost was $15 per animal. Checking is voluntary, but it's a great idea to do it with any animal you harvest in this area. *F&H*

AT a GLANCE

What: Expect big numbers of elk in northwest Colorado this season. The Division of Wildlife reports some of the state's highest densities of elk are in this region.

Where: There's a wealth of public land around the towns of Craig and Meeker, and lots of outfitters and guides who offer access to private land hunts.

When: Things will get rocking with the archery opener starting on Aug. 28.

Colorado rabbits: The in-between season

GRAND JUNCTION

by Tom Behrens

At this time of the year, the outdoor scene normally looks kind of bleak. There's not a whole lot of things to check out. Big game hunting seasons just finished up and fishing is on hold, unless you're one of those frostbit guys or gals that likes ice fishing. But there is a hunting season that lasts until Feb. 28. It's popular with a lot of Colorado hunters.

It's rabbit season.

For the cost of a small game license, hunters can pick up their shotgun or small caliber rifle and head for Bureau of Land Management land and start looking for cottontails, snowshoe hares or white or blacktailed jackrabbits.

"Rabbit hunting in general is pretty popular in western Colorado," says Randy Hampton, a public information specialist for the Colorado Division of Wildlife. "We have good habitat, brushy draws, high desert habitat and a fairly good population of rabbits. Liberal limits are an indication of the plentiful amount of rabbits available." Daily bag limits are 10 cottontails, 10 snowshoe hares and 10 jackrabbits.

"Rabbit hunting is fairly popular," says Brian Gray, district wildlife manager for Colorado Division of Wildlife

and an avid rabbit hunter. "People enjoy doing it. It's not as popular as big game hunting, but fathers and kids can go rabbit hunting pretty easily and for not much expense."

"This year we have a pretty good population of rabbits," says Dean Riggs, an area wildlife manager for Colorado Division of Wildlife. "Probably in 30 to 45 minutes you can have a limit of rabbits."

DON'T PUT the gun away yet. Rabbit season is open for another month in Colorado. Anthony Zuber, age 4, holds a rabbit taken last November.

Where to go: "I've been hunting in some places up by Rangely," says Gray. "You hunt for half an hour, and you're done hunting because you run into quite a few rabbits. But some places around the Rifle area and up toward the Roan Creek area north of Grand Junction, you might get a couple and call it a day. The area by Grand Junction is pretty arid, desert type of area, but if you get into some of the areas that have draws with some good brush cover you will find rabbits."

Some good places to go are north of Grand Junction, about 60 or 70 miles, heading down from Douglas. "There are some really good rabbit hunting places north of Douglas Pass area toward Rangely," says Gray. "Once you get up higher in elevation it's less arid and then you'll start finding rabbits."

Riggs typically hunts north of Grand Junction, west to the Utah border,

"probably the best rabbit hunting area in the state," he says. A lot of the area is BLM land that hunters don't require permission to hunt on.

"Anywhere you go out of the valley here around Grand Junction, you're going to run up on public land," says Gray. "If you go up to Glen Park or north to Douglas Pass, or up toward Roan Creek area, there is BLM land all over the place."

Don't waste your time on forest service land. "There are not a lot of cottontails up on the forest service land because usually it is higher in elevation and there will not be any cottontails up that high," says Gray.

How to do it: Hunting techniques are simple. "The best luck I have hunting rabbits is just walking along with my rifle and a couple of people flushing the rabbits out ahead of me," says Gray. "Sometimes sitting and waiting for a few seconds to see if one is going to pop out where it looks like a good spot works too. Matter of fact, about a month ago I was with a couple of kids of mine and we were in this small area for about an hour and a half, maybe two hours, the same area just kicking out different rabbits. We would just sit there and wait for one to pop out and run around. I think they kind of feel uneasy when someone is around and tend to want to run away. If you don't end up seeing them, they'll pop out again later on."

Riggs looks for sagebrush flats. "On cooler days the rabbits will come out on south-facing slopes (in the draws), to get in the sun and warm up. Go up through a draw on foot and look for the rabbits underneath the brush that are on the slope facing south."

"The BLM country around Grand Junction is pretty open, not a lot of

AT a GLANCE

What: Rabbit hunting.

Where: Near Grand Junction and Rangely.

When: Now through Feb. 28.

Why: Because big game seasons are closed, and you don't like ice fishing.

Who: Colorado DOW Grand Junction Office (970-255-6100).

Rangley area rabbits

fencing and most of the vegetation is down in the draws in the bottoms," says Gray. "What helps sometimes is to have someone down in the draw walking and kicking rabbits out ahead while another hunter walks along the top of the draw."

Choice of weaponry boils down to what a person likes to shoot, shotgun or small caliber rifle. Riggs notes that some hunters forsake a rifle or shotgun for bow and arrow.

"Personally, I like to use a .22 rifle so that I can shoot them in the head and not blast them up with a shotgun," says Gray. "But in checking some of the hunters around the area, it seems to be an equal amount of people who are using a shotgun and .22s. They use both 12-gauge and 20-gauge shotguns. Some guys use an over-under that has a .22 on the top and 20-gauge on the bottom. If you get a rabbit that is a ways out there you can select the .22 on the top. On some of the close-up stuff that they're flushing, then they can use the 20-gauge. I haven't seen the .22 Hornet or .223 being used that much. People seem to stick to the .22 or the shotgun loads."

"Sometimes you get lucky and one flushes out 30 yards in front of you where you can get a clear shot," says Gray. "I went a couple weeks ago and every rabbit we flushed took off and you never saw it again. Early on in the season, around mid-November, it seemed like the rabbits were running off and stopping and not getting too spooked."

Rabbits are generally numerous and not that hard to find. Look for brushy areas. Focus on BLM land and start your hunt. It definitely is something to explore during those winter months when it's too late for one hunting season and way too early for fishing. ***F&H***

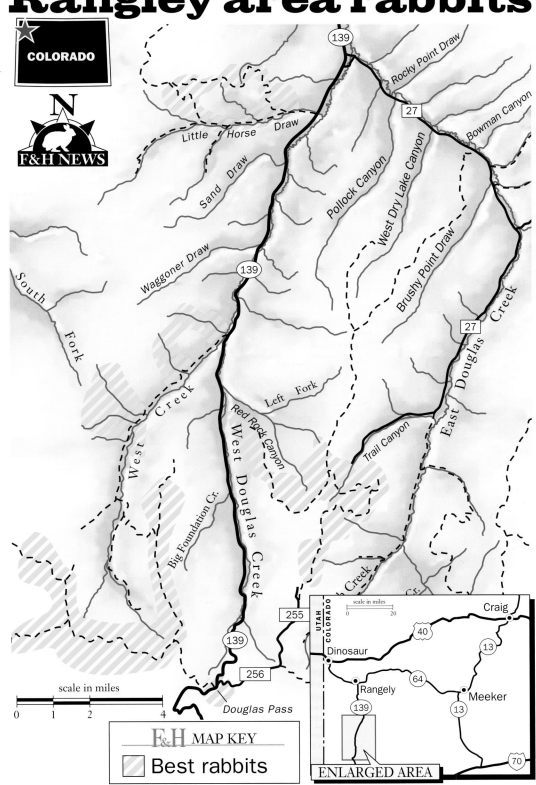

COLORADO

N
F&H NEWS

MAP KEY
Best rabbits

ENLARGED AREA

Douglas Pass

scale in miles
0   1   2   4

SOUTHWEST HUNTING

Head to Hotchkiss to hunt blue grouse this fall

by Dusty Routh

There's a lot to like about the far western side of the Western Slope if you happen to be addicted to fall scattergun action for infamously flushing blue grouse, also known as forest grouse. A lot of the area around the small town of Hotchkiss holds good concentrations of birds, and this year should be a good one for finding them.

In addition to the blues, there is also a rare, holdout population of sage grouse around the nearby town of Crawford.

The excellent habitat in this region — a mix of rolling hills and forestlands with lots of creeks and water sources, and with plenty of elevations to choose from, and a heady variety of berry crops — is an ultra-rich source of birds. While the grouse populations can have up years and down years, with a lot of that having to do with precipitation and overwintering, this year is expected to be a good one for grouse gunners.

"It should be especially good this year," says Gloria Kendall with Weekender Sports in Hotchkiss (970-872-3444). "I think hunters will find pretty good numbers of birds. We had more water this summer, it sure wasn't as bad as some other summers we've had. The grouse hunting

IN SEELEY AND SWAN VALLEYS, you can find grouse in high and low elevations. XXX XXXX shows the spoils of a day's effort.

should be good."

A lot of this range is forest land, and the cover isn't too thick. "You don't always need a dog for this kind of hunting," she says. "I'd tell anyone who asked where the good hunting for grouse is, to go to the BLM lands around here."

According to bird biologists at the Division of Wildlife, blue grouse typi-

cally winter up high in stands of Douglas Fir and lodgepole pine. In the spring they move to sub-alpine areas and creek bottoms for breeding, but their preferred areas are where sagebrush and aspen meet. These transition areas are perfect places for the blues to strut their stuff.

In the area around Hotchkiss, look for these transitional zones, with adjoining stands of chokecherry, serviceberry and oakbrush. At lower elevations, this means hunting edges, benches and draws. At higher elevations, DOW recommends climbing as high as you can and hunting the birds downwards. If you're at higher elevations, remember that if you're seeing lodgepole pine you're probably hunting too low, and keep going up until you get into spruces and firs. Search for berries at high elevations with a nearby water source, and you should be in business.

There's considerable debate about the effectiveness of hunting dogs on forest grouse. At lower elevations where the land is more open and the birds more prone to sitting tight, a dog is a definite asset. But at higher elevations, a dog certainly isn't a necessity.

Lay of the land: The town of Hotchkiss on the Western Slope is in the North Fork Gunnison River Valley, or what's simply called the North Fork Valley. Two other towns are close by: Crawford, and Paonia. The larger town

AT a GLANCE

What: Excellent hunting for blue (forest) grouse when the season opens up this September.

Where: Head to the small town of Hotchkiss and hunt the BLM lands in the area.

How: Look for blues in higher elevations around spruces and firs, and in lower elevations around transition areas between aspen and sage brush.

When: This season should be a good

one, given the wet summer and a good spring. Hunting should be excellent from the opener on.

Contact information: Weekender Sports (970-872-3444) in Hotchkiss is open from 7:30 a.m. to 6 p.m. Mondays through Fridays, and 7:30 a.m. to 5 p.m. on Saturdays, closed on Sundays. For lodging and general visitor information, contact the Hotchkiss Chamber of Commerce (970-872-3226). Or try these for overnight accommodations: Above the Law Bed and

Breakfast (970-872-3126); the Hotchkiss Inn (800-817-1418); Leroux Creek Inn (970-872-4746); Leroux Creek Lodge (970-835-7903). For camping and RV sites, call Rogers Mesa Store and RV Park (970-872-2262) or Mountain Valley Meadows RV Park (800-782-4037). If you need hunting dog information, contact Ted Hoff at Cottonwood Kennels (970-921-7100).

Regs: Colorado's blue grouse season officially opens on Sept. 1, and runs to Nov. 10 west of I-25.

Colorado Grouse

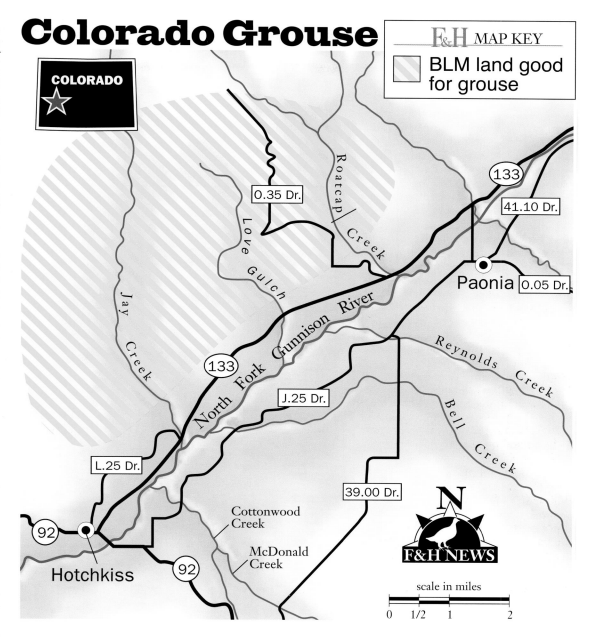

COLORADO

F&H MAP KEY

BLM land good for grouse

Roatcap Creek

0.35 Dr.

133

41.10 Dr.

Love Gulch

Paonia

0.05 Dr.

North Fork Gunnison River

Reynolds Creek

133

J.25 Dr.

Jay Creek

L.25 Dr.

Bell Creek

39.00 Dr.

Cottonwood Creek

N

F&H NEWS

McDonald Creek

92

Hotchkiss

92

scale in miles

0   1/2   1   2

of Delta is just to the west of these three. Out of Denver, you can get there by taking I-70 west, and turn south at Glenwood Springs on 82. From the southern part of the state, take Highway 50 west, then turn north at Montrose into the town of Delta, then head east on 92.

While it's a remote part of the state, the area offers a good assortment of public land hunting, private land outfitters and good lodging options.

Public land aplenty: While there are some excellent private hunt opportunities for upland game birds run by local outfitters, the North Fork Valley area is really noted for lots of good public access on nearby BLM lands.

For example, there are some excellent BLM spots just north of the town of Hotchkiss, situated on the north side of Highway 133. To the south of Paonia, hunters will also find good BLM land access as well as the McCluskey and Roeber state wildlife areas. Further up the North Fork, there's also BLM land located along the Paonia Reservoir.

One of the best areas in this region is along Leroux Creek, which runs out of the Grand Mesa National Forest south and then southeast into the North Fork of the Gunnison.

In the early days of this area's settlement, coal mining was the driving economic force. A number of old mines are still in the area, and a lot of the small creeks around these old mines are worth exploring for grouse, especially early and late in the day. The birds have a reputation for being fast flushers in more open areas, and for being pretty easy to spot in more forested areas. Since the cover isn't too thick, a medium load like 7s in a modified to improved cylinder choke setting should work just fine.

Or, go private: If striking out on your own in search of public land access isn't your cup of tea, or you don't have time for the exploring that it takes to find birds, another option is to book with an outfitter in this area. One of these is Hubbard Creek Outfitters (970-872-3818), located in Hotchkiss.

The contact there is Larry Allen. Hibbard Creek runs 5,000 acres of pines and conifers loaded with grouse.

Or, for a more upscale adventure, book with Orvis-endorsed Scenic Mesa Ranch (Alan DeGrange, 970-872-3078). Scenic Mesa offers 9,000 acres of private land and a host of different upland game bird opportunities, including chukar, pheasant, quail and Huns. For a really unique experience, be sure to ask about the European-style driven pheasant hunts.

For later in the season, keep in mind that Scenic Mesa also offers duck hunts, primarily for mallards, and they report excellent success rates. **F&H**

Rabbits plentiful around Durango and Cortez

DURANGO

by Tom Behrens

The grouse populations were unbelievable, best grouse hunting I have seen in my life," says Patt Dorsey, (970-375-6770), Area Wildlife Manager, Colorado Division of Wildlife, referring to the blue grouse hunting in the area around Durango.

"So far this year we have snow, so I am assuming potentially, depending on what happens this spring, we could have another fantastic year as far as grouse hunting goes." Blue grouse is just one of the types of small game or varmint hunting that is available in the Durango area.

Locating places to hunt small game and varmints is more good news. "We just have a lot of public land...BLM land, forest lands," says Dorsey. "On the west side, the area around Cortez, there is some BLM land that is a little lower in elevation that gets a little less snow around Durango. A lot of the higher mountain stuff at this time of the year is fairly difficult to access. Opportunities on private land are different. One of the things different about it is the type of terrain. Private land is a lot of the lower elevation kind of stuff. There is a lot more prairie dog and coyote hunting opportunities." Check the DOW Web site, *wildlife.state.co.us* for the prairie dog season and hunting areas. Coyote hunting is open year-round.

"Blue grouse are kind of interesting because they actually come down in elevation in the spring time to have their chicks and to feed them along the river bottoms," says Dorsey.

"Then they start heading up in elevation. About September they are kind of in the area that we like to be, where the aspen are turning colors. They eat

CHRIS STORENG of Montrose shows a snowshoe hare taken 8 miles east of Montrose a few seasons back.

a lot of raspberries, buffalo berries and that kind of thing. So, a lot of the time where you find them are on the edges of trails, edges of old clear cuts, old burns, that kind of thing. You normally find them on the edges of their feeding area and their cover."

Hunting with a dog can be a help. "I have a German shorthair and we take him. They can benefit you because a lot of times grouse are very well camouflaged. So a lot of times they think you can't see them, so they will be hiding in the bushes." Grouse season was Sept. 1–Nov. 10.

Rich Lopez, (970-882-4911), District Wildlife Manager for the Delores District, hunts blue grouse and cottontail rabbits in the Cortez area. Delores is about 10 miles north of Cortez, which is near the four corners area.

His favorite hunting season is blue grouse. "I hunt blue grouse and cottontail rabbits on occasion in this area," says Lopez. "Grouse is a longer season; you can shoot three grouse a day. I don't hunt every day, but I usually try to get out once a week during the grouse hunting season." He uses a 20-gauge shotgun for hunting grouse and .22 rifle for the rabbits.

"We just go out into the sagebrush country, usually where you find them. Just walk through the sagebrush and hopefully kick out a few ahead of you a ways. These cottontails tend to run 10 to 20 feet real quick in the brush and then just freeze. If you walk carefully you can get close enough to hit them in the head with a .22." Cottontail rabbit season is Sept. 1–March 31. Lopez hunts rabbits any place he can get permission. "This so far has been pretty much a bumper year for cottontails. Pretty much anywhere in and around the proper habitat which will give them food, cover, and water. Sagebrush in the mountain ranges, elevation from about 4,000 feet all the

Cortez area rabbits

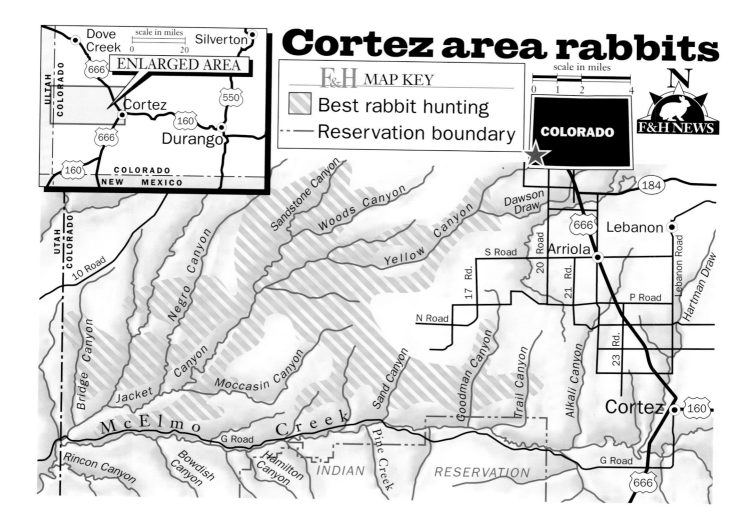

F&H MAP KEY
- ▨ Best rabbit hunting
- --- Reservation boundary

way up to around 8,000 to 9,000 feet. Most are in the PJ type country, Pinion Juniper, from about 5,000 to 7,500 – 8,000 feet.

You could look at a map and hunt in all directions from Cortez. Sometimes you find localized areas that have higher populations, but actually most guys hunt where they have permission or public land. Finding a place to hunt is not a problem."

Does he ever use dogs in hunting for rabbits? "Dogs, beagles in particular, have never become popular for hunting rabbits around here. I guess this terrain is more conducive to just walking and kicking out rabbits; you really don't need a dog. Get a couple of guys out there on a draw, put one guy down in the draw and brush and some guys up on the sides and it normally works out pretty good."

According to Dorsey, the type of rabbit you are hunting dictates the area you will be hunting. There are four types of rabbits to hunt, including the cottontail, snowshoe hare, white-tailed, and black-tailed jackrabbits.

"Rabbits toward the end of February are going to be a little bit harder to get to," says Dorsey. "Rabbits prefer brushy areas; cottontails at lower elevations and snowshoe hares at higher elevations.

Snowshoe hares are interesting species to hunt because in the wintertime they turn sold white. In the summertime they turn brown. They are also a little bit larger than a cottontail.

"You know what I found interesting about the snowshoe hare was being able to see them. I had been walking through the woods and I would see an eye. I was telling somebody about it and they said that is what everybody sees when they see a snowshoe rabbit. You don't see the outline of a rabbit. You see an eye sitting under a bush. Their eyes are real round, shiny and black. For some reason that's what stands out.

Blue grouse season is over for this year, but be sure to pencil it in on the calendar for next September. For the present, pick up the .22 rifle and head out for some rabbit hunting. Check the Department of Wildlife Web site, *wildlife.state.co.us* for a complete list of what small game and varmint hunting are available and their respective seasons. **F&H**

AT a GLANCE

What: Rabbits and Blue Grouse in the Durango and Cortez areas.

When: Now through Feb. 28 for rabbits and Sept. 1 to Nov. 10 for grouse.

Who: DOW SW Region Service Center (970-247-0855), Rich Lopez, (970-882-4911), District Wildlife Manager for the Delores District.

Info: Department of Wildlife Web site: *wildlife.state.co.us*

Plenty of turkeys in Durango — but they're spread out

by Dusty Routh

If you're accustomed to hitting the public Forest Service and BLM lands around the Durango area for your spring turkey hunt, you might just find that the old standard method of "hunt the snowline for big concentrations of birds early in the season" strategy isn't going to work this year.

With Colorado's unusual winter in this area — lots of snow, followed by lots of rain — the vast numbers of Merriam's in this part of the state are showing early signs of dispersing and scattering well ahead of their normal spring schedule.

While the drought wreaked havoc with all kinds of game birds in southwest Colorado, from grouse to turkeys, the snow-followed-by-rain of late winter will have a real impact on where hunters coming to this area are going to find their birds.

"We've been having some ongoing discussions about how the turkeys have overwintered here this year," says Pat Dorsey with the Durango office of the DOW. "In some e-mails we were sending around, we were saying things like 'it looks better for turkey numbers in this district than it did the past two years.' We're seeing more turkeys. But it's still nothing like it was 10 years ago, on account of the drought. But it should just get better and better as we continue to come out of this drought."

Snow burning off fast: "The one real key thing about the spring turkey hunt around Durango this year," says Dorsey, "is that it just might be that, at least as far as I've noticed, the snow is really burning off fast. What will happen is, with that rain coming in and the snow melting off, the turkeys are going to break up into smaller bunches. They'll be distributed everywhere instead of right on the snow line."

Dorsey says that hunters are accustomed to seeing early spring season turkeys in big, concentrated bunches, but that likely won't be the case this year. "You probably won't see those big, large concentrations in just a couple of hot spots," she says. "We're expecting that hunters will see smaller numbers of birds distributed all over the place. That means you can expect to run into them almost anywhere. The chances of just one area being real hot, a real guarantee of birds and better chances for success, probably isn't going to happen this year."

The positive side: The upside to this expectation, however, is that hunters may have a better shot at seeing birds as turkeys break into smaller groups and move into their springtime areas. And, as Dorsey points out, "the hunting pressure hopefully will be better distributed. You're less likely this year to reach a trailhead and find 55 cars already parked there."

This also means that hunters are really going to have to hoof it to find birds, Dorsey says. "You'll have to hunt for them, instead of just walking up to the snow line. They could be anywhere by the time the season opens."

Where to find 'em: Dorsey points out that the public lands around the Durango area are plentiful, and provide near-perfect habitat for turkeys. "There's a *lot* of places to hunt," she says. "The good turkey habitat is spread from Pagosa to the Dolores Rim. The turkeys will be spread out across this area, and they could be anywhere, basically. That's what's great about this corner of the world.

YOU'RE GOING to have to put in some legwork for turkey around Durango this spring. The weird weather this winter has already scattered birds, and you won't find them in big concentrations. Dingo Holtz shot this turkey last spring.

Anywhere is turkey habitat, from the snowline on down, on BLM and Forest Service land."

Dorsey says this is all over-the-counter turkey license hunting. "These are not permit areas," she says. "And I would say that most of the good public land is going to be west of Highway 160, and on any of the forested lands north of Highway 160, between Pagosa and Durango. And then there's a lot of stuff further west, north of Cortez and Dolores on Forest Service land. There's just a whole lot of public land. I'd suggest hunters pick up a San Juan National Forest Service map and find those boundaries."

Dorsey has some further advice if you're planning to hunt in this area. "The one thing I'd tell hunters is that if you've never hunted birds in the mountains, it's different. I've hunted them, for example, in the river bottoms in

Durango area turkey

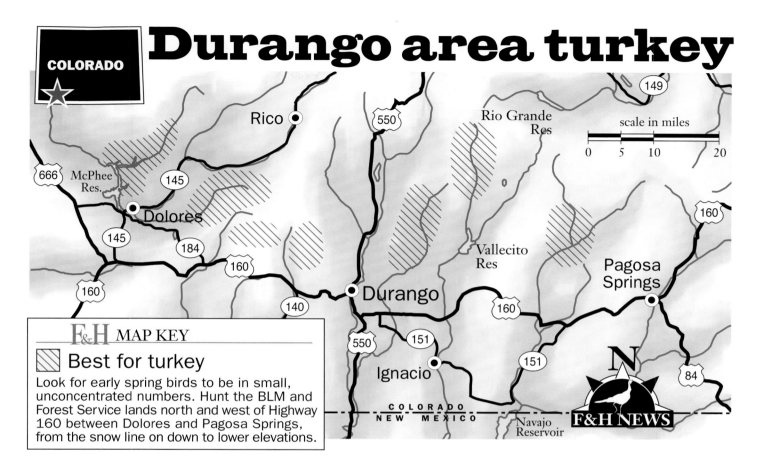

COLORADO

Rico

550

Rio Grande Res

149

scale in miles

0   5   10   20

666   McPhee Res.

145

160

Dolores

145

184

160

Vallecito Res

Pagosa Springs

160

160

140

Durango

160

N

550

151

151

84

Ignacio

F&H NEWS

C O L O R A D O
N E W   M E X I C O

Navajo Reservoir

F&H MAP KEY

▨ Best for turkey

Look for early spring birds to be in small, unconcentrated numbers. Hunt the BLM and Forest Service lands north and west of Highway 160 between Dolores and Pagosa Springs, from the snow line on down to lower elevations.

Nebraska. There you set up a decoy and call the birds. You know they're traveling the river bottoms. But here we have a *lot* of good turkey habitat. So being able to pick that one spot, you really can't do that. There's 40,000 acres of land with turkeys. It's pretty hilly terrain, and for the most part it's steep terrain. As opposed to knowing just one specific place, these birds can be just about anywhere. So it's better to call and try to locate birds and then move in on the birds."

Dorsey says road hunting isn't going to help you this year. "I would advise people who drive in their cars and call from their car, that's not a good strategy. Get out and hoof it in, and find out where that bird is."

Turkey numbers: Dorsey points out that turkey hunting in Colorado is becoming a much more popular sport, but it hasn't built up as fast in Colorado as it has in other states, like Missouri.

"I think, for one, the turkey populations here were slower to build, and traditional turkey hunting wasn't a big thing because we didn't have that many turkeys," she says. "But it's a real marvel

of wildlife management. There are more and more birds, and so there's higher hunter interest. But we're still one of the states where there's less turkey hunting pressure than in some other states. But it's building up. People are becoming more aware of it. Our work on reintroducing birds — they're doing so well on the habitat we have, and they're protected during the off-season — I think it's going to get better and better in future seasons. The drought may have hurt the populations, but they're bouncing back. We're not back to the 'good old days' but we're getting there."

Rain effect: While the drought really did a number on game bird populations, too much rain this spring can hurt chick production. "How the chicks fare this spring will really depend on conditions when they nest and sit," Dorsey says. "If we get a lot of late rains, and late freezes, that could hurt the chicks. What we saw last year with grouse, though, was we had rain at first followed by a great spring. It got warm and it stayed warm. So we had a bumper crop of chicks." Hopefully that's the case with the turkeys, too.   ***F&H***

AT a GLANCE

What: Springtime turkey hunting in southwest Colorado.

Where: Consider Highway 160 from Cortez to Pagosa Springs as the turkey's central highway in this part of the state. Hunt the BLM and Forest Service lands in this area.

How: Don't rely on just hunting the snowline this season. Early warm weather and lots of rain has burned off a lot of the snow, and turkeys are showing late-season movement into small, scattered bunches early in the year.

Best tip: Call to locate your bird(s), then move in on them. Traditional hot spots with big concentrations of birds won't be the norm this season.

Deer, elk, trout abound in famed GMU 61

REDVALE

by Dusty Routh

YOU CAN FIND plenty of mule deer in northeastern Wyoming, and about twice as many whitetail. Brian Azevedo is shown here with his first muley, a 4X3, taken last year.

Deer and elk hunting in Colorado these days can best be defined as "pick the best places, and be patient." With more and more elk hunting falling within the limited draw/permit system (The DOW expects up to 30 percent of elk hunting to move into the limited license permit system in the coming seasons) and all deer hunting now managed under this system, big game hunters have to pick their spots, build up their preference points, and sweat it out to await drawing the area they want to hunt.

One of the game management units (GMUs) most deserving of your patience and persistence in drawing for tags is GMU 61, located in the southwestern part of the state. This unit is located due south of Grand Junction, and southwest of Montrose. GMU 61 is categorized as a Quality Unit, meaning the deer and elk herds in this area are being managed to produce trophies.

Elk harvest in this unit was quite good in 2003. During the fourth rifle season last year, 80 hunters took 41 elk, for a success rate of 51 percent. Of these, 11 elk were bulls and 30 were cows. By comparison, in neighboring GMU 62, 464 hunters took 70 elk, for a hunt success of only 15 percent, and a lot more hunters in the field. With the exception of GMU 64 (52 percent), GMU 61 posted the highest hunting success percentage of any elk units in the southwest region during the fourth season.

GMU 61 fared just as good last season in the earlier rifle seasons too, more evidence that this is one of the best units in the state for quality elk. During the first rifle season, 179 elk were harvested by 387 hunters for a success rate of 46 percent (62 bulls, 100 cows, 17 calves). During the second, 448 hunters scored 216 elk for a success rate of 48 percent (86 bulls, 114 cows, 16 calves). And during the third rifle season, 234 big game hunters brought down 104 elk for a success rate of 44 percent (30 bulls, 70 cows, four calves).

Muzzleloaders did amazingly well too, with 88 hunters harvesting 52 elk for a whopping 59 percent success rate. Archers managed an impressive 60 percent success rate, with 84 hunters harvesting 50 elk.

Deer hunters also managed impressive success rates in this quality unit. In the second rifle season, 158 hunters scored 81 bucks (51 percent success rate), and in the third 158 hunters took 120 bucks for an incredible 76 percent success rate. That kind of hunting is tough to beat. Muzzleloaders also did well, but with far fewer hunters. Only 20 muzzleloaders hunted, scoring 13 bucks (65 percent success rate), and 23 deer were taken by 69 archers for a 33 percent success rate.

It all adds up to make this unit one of the most productive and highly prized of the quality units in the state. Preference point requirements are understandably high. Seven points, for example, are required for resident elk archery and rifle, eight for muzzleloading and seven to eight for deer. But the work and wait to draw for this unit are more than worth it.

GMU 61 is managed out of the Montrose Service Center (970-252-6000). One of their wildlife technicians is Gene Hunt (970-327-4455) in Redvale, who helps manage things around the Dan Noble State Wildlife Area.

"We've seen quite a few guys coming up to hunt this season," Hunt says, "but it's hard to tell if we're getting the same number of hunters as last year. I think the wildfires in some of these units in this part of the state in the past seasons may have scared some people off."

Hunt says the area continues to suffer from the effects of long-term drought. "Personally, I'd like to see about 6 feet of snow on the ground right now, but we don't have it," he says. He points out that GMU 61 "is a pretty big unit. That are lots of forest service roads

GMU 61 deer & elk hunts

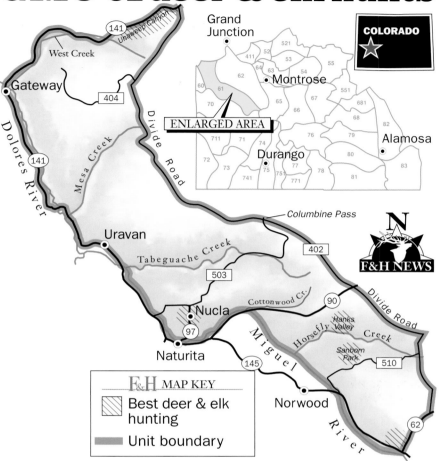

that go into it. But if you're on an ATV, you need to be careful. We've had some road closures because guys are going in on ATVs and tearing up the habitat."

Hunt says the weather has been a factor in hunting this season. "It's been dry," he says, "and that's no good for hunters. But we're finally getting some moisture, we've had some clouds hanging over us, which is good."

Hunt says the weather has scattered both elk and deer. "They're pretty spread out right now," he says. "The drought has placed them in different areas because of the feed. The elk are still in pretty big herds, I saw a herd of about 400 of them in the Wildlife Area. I haven't seen that many mule deer this season, but the ones I've seen are some really nice bucks. Big racks, big weights, real healthy."

Hunt says your best bet for finding animals is to find the feed. "Look for broadleaf stuff, like forbes, which is a kind of alfalfa. And patches of bluegrass, they really love to feed on bluegrass." Hunt says he's also seeing a few grouse around, so if you like to grouse hunt, bring a scattergun for afternoon hunting.

Better yet, Hunt recommends hunters coming to this area be sure to bring a fly rod or a spinning rod. "The fishing has been excellent at Dan Noble, Hunt says about the water formerly known as Miramonte Lake. "It's a man-made lake, about 460 acres." Hunt says the good fishing should continue until ice-up, and then hardwater fishing can be equally good.

"I usually see 35 to 40 hunters fishing it this time of year. They're bank fishing, mostly. I saw one boat out on it," Hunt says. "The lake has two boat ramps. They're fishing for rainbows. Most guys are bank fishing with lures, spinners and spoons."

What's great about this lake is that the DOW stocks it heavily, and holdover fish are common. "The fish are big," Hunt says, "They probably average 3 to 4 pounds. You can keep four fish, no minimum size."

Hunt says these trout are delectable. "They're excellent eating. After they've been in there for two years or so, feeding on crawdads and freshwater shrimp, they turn real bright pink, like a salmon. They don't have that trouty smell, and they have a real sweet taste to them."

Hunt favors jigging for them using a black Woolly Worm. When the water turns colder, he switches to a white Woolly Worm. You can also float tube this lake, Hunt says, to reach spots away from bank fishermen.

This quality unit is considered part of the Uncompahgre Plateau. Combined with neighboring GMU 62, the area represents more than 2,300 square miles of land ranging in elevation from 4,600 feet to over 10,300 feet. Within 61, DOW recommends hot spots including Hank's Valley, Sanborn Park, Craig Point, the Nucla area and Unaweep Canyon.

The closest town to the unit is Montrose, where hunters can find lodging and restaurants. To get there from Denver, follow I-70 to Grand Junction, then south out of Grand Junction to Montrose. Continue to proceed south out of Montrose to Ridgway on Highway 62 to Highway 145. To get to the lake, come out of San Miguel Canyon (12 miles long) onto Norwood Hill. It's the second left before you get to Norwood. Stay on that road for about 17 miles. *F&H*

AT a GLANCE

What: GMU 61, one of the finest quality deer and elk units in the state. It takes a lot of preference points to get in, but it's worth it. And the trout fishing on nearby Dan Noble Lake is awesome, too.

Where: This GMU is located due south of Grand Junction. Hot spots include Hank's Valley, Sanborn Park, Craig Point, the Nucla area and Unaweep Canyon.

When: The fourth rifle season runs Nov. 6–10.

How: Deer and elk are scattered because of the lack of weather. Look for feed like forbes and bluegrass. The elk will be in large herds, but the mule deer are more scattered.

High success predicted for southwest deer, elk

DURANGO

by Dusty Routh

If you're pondering which area of the state will provide the best success on deer and elk this upcoming season, you might want to put your money and time into southwest Colorado. In fact, if you hunt this region you may very well find the buck (or bull) stops with you.

All signs for the nearing deer and elk season in southwest Colorado are absolutely positive, says Scott Wait, big game biologist for the Department of Wildlife. "We expect hunter success to go up," over last year's strong season, says Wait.

Hunters scoring on deer and elk last year topped an admirable 40 percent. If Wait thinks this year will be even better, that's exciting news, since his big game expertise is devoted to the San Juan and Dolores River basins. These include Game Management Units 71 through 78 (except 76) and 711, 741, 751 and 771.

One critical factor sure to affect hunter success in these units is the drought, of course. "The real impact of the drought is an unknown," says Wait.

"It will have some impact, but the animals are still there."

Wait points out a pretty interesting meterological phenomenon that hunters might want to pay attention to. "Down low it's real dry," he says, "and way up high it's real dry. But in that midrange elevation, 9,000- to 10,000-feet elevation, there's a lot more green than there is low or high."

There's been some "monsoon precipitation" at that level, Wait says, accounting for greener meadowlands and richer food sources, as well as more water for the herds.

Archery season will open the end of August and run through the end of September, says Wait. There will then be a two-week break before rifle season opens in early November. A number of units will also likely have late season cow elk opportunities, but these units are mostly comprised of private land. For a complete breakdown of regulations and seasons, consult the DOW Website (*wildlife.state.co.us*) or regulations pamphlet.

Elk lookout: "We've got a bunch of elk," Wait emphasizes. "We're over objective, and we want to reduce the populations in all of the units. One tool we'll use is either-sex licenses in a couple units, and anterless in all the units." GMUs 74 and 75 will have "additional elk" cow licenses as an option.

Wait believes the best units to hunt for elk will be 71, 74, 77 and 78. "Units 75 and 751 have good elk populations, too, but the fire impacts will have an effect," says Wait. "The unknown entity will be access" because of the fires.

Still, he believes most units will be open for business as usual, and there are large portions of them not affected by the fires.

Deer time: This is muley country. And while the DOW considers muleyes in these units to be "sub-trophy," Waits says they're still big animals of a very respectable size.

"'Big' is a relative term," Wait says. "Five years ago a hunter might have taken a deer that this year he'll pass up for something bigger."

The underlying message here is that the herds are producing bigger and bigger deer, and hunters are becoming more selective in their harvest decisions. "Some of our units will produce trophies, but just wait two years," Wait says. In a couple years those "sub-trophy" animals will definitely be trophy class.

Wait advises that units 711, 741, 751 and 771 will offer the best deer hunting. Fortunately there's been no evidence of chronic wasting disease among the herds any of these southwest units. "We've got good numbers of bucks, and buck hunters will have a great opportunity this fall," he says.

Be legal: Wait says that for the most part hunters have been good about following game regulations in this part of the state. But he points out that every year the state bags a few hunters on a variety of "typical" game violations, such as carrying loaded firearms in a vehicle, party hunting and overbagging. Wait says there will be game wardens out, some of them in unmarked vehicles and plain clothes. *F&H*

Southwest Deer & Elk

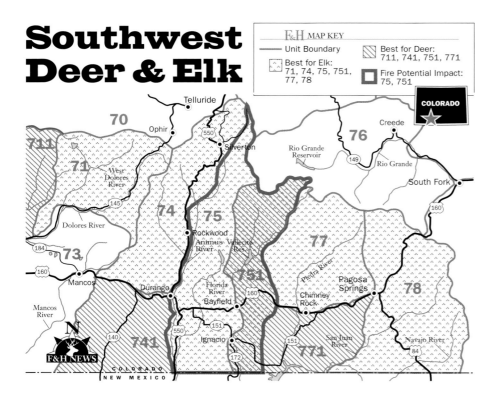

F&H MAP KEY
— Unit Boundary
Best for Elk: 71, 74, 75, 751, 77, 78
Best for Deer: 711, 741, 751, 771
Fire Potential Impact: 75, 751

Uncompahgre Plateau rich in elk, muley bucks

MONTROSE, Colo.

by Ed Riser

Bring a 4-wheeler to southwest Colorado's Uncompahgre Plateau for this fall's elk hunt, but you'll fill your tag faster if you park it at camp.

This sprawling public-land plateau that stretches from the Gunnison River over a 9,000-foot divide to the Dolores River is one of the most elk-rich spots in a state that has too many elk. In Units 61 and 62, hunters can shoot a bull plus an additional cow as long as they buy the appropriate tags.

If you're hunting mule deer and didn't draw a permit in the spring's lottery, you're out of luck. But if you scored a tag, chances are good you'll see plenty of deer, thanks to the fourth year of low hunter pressure and a rebounding herd. And game managers expect southwest Colorado mule deer hunters to do well on trophy bucks.

"I think we're going to see a case where folks can see enough deer that they'll feel comfortable passing on forkhorns and being selective about shooting larger deer," says John Ellenberger, big-game manager for Colorado's Division of Wildlife. "By limiting permits, we've not only boosted hunter success, but the buck component of our herd is increasing. We're either at or over our objective of 25 bucks per 100 does, post-harvest, in many of our deer units."

But success for elk will be especially dependent on climatic conditions this fall. Unless the persistent drought eases, hunters may be closed out of broad swaths of public land, and dry, crisp conditions can make hunting for elk especially difficult. The other end of the spectrum is heavy snowfall, which tends to boost hunting success, but a whopper of a storm in the second or third seasons would close much of the Uncompahgre to highland hunters.

Which brings us back to the issue of 4-wheelers. Much of the Uncompahgre is laced with jeep trails. In fact, this aspen-and-pine highland is one of the few large swaths of public ground that's not managed as a roadless area. But while ATVs allow hunters to access fairly remote ridges and promontories, they're likely to be frowned on by land managers as vectors for fires, so don't bet on being able to drive them anywhere on the plateau you want this fall. And while

they'll allow you to access the big country, the plateau's elk are likely to be in areas inaccessible by machine. The Uncompahgre has a broad table-top plateau that's bisected by Divide Road, but most of the highland's shoulders are nasty: steep, brushy, remote. In other words, elk country.

Start on the top: Colorado's first rifle elk season runs Oct. 12-16. The combined second season runs Oct. 19-25, the combined third season is Nov. 2-8 and the combined fourth season is Nov. 9-13. Note that Unit 62 has a number of restrictions on hunting, primarily limiting hunters to shooting cows on private land south of Transfer Road, which includes much of the Shavano Valley and the west side of the Uncompahgre River Valley south toward Ridgeway. Unit 61 is more straightforward, with standard bull and cow regs, except for a

late hunt on private land that runs through December.

Unit 61's deer season is also simpler than its northern neighbor. Rifle hunters in the first season can kill a buck from Oct. 19-25. The second rifle season is Nov. 2-8. In Unit 62, the seasons are similar, but there's a private-land restriction on some license types.

If you're serious about bagging a big buck, spend a lot of time glassing the plateau's high sagebrush basins and get away from the motorized trails.

Info: For local information, check in with DOW's terrestrial biologist Bruce Watkins (970-252-6025) in Montrose, Gene Taylor's Rod and Gun (970-641-1845) in Gunnison or True Value Hardware (970-327-4238)

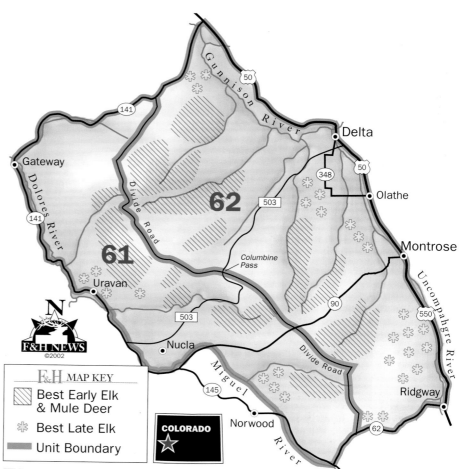

MAP KEY

▨ Best Early Elk & Mule Deer

✳ Best Late Elk

▬ Unit Boundary

Units 61 & 62 Hunts

West Elk Wilderness: tough hunt

by Steve Nelson

The West Elk Wilderness is difficult, physical hunting, but it holds fairly good numbers of elk, according to Brent Carlson at Gunnison Sporting Goods (970-641-5022). "You have several major drainages coming off the south side and many access roads that either go up to the top or the bottom. Red Creek, Rainbow Lake, Soap Creek and East Elk Creek are some good ones. There is some hunting on the top, but the majority of it starts at the bottom wherever the road ends. The elk go where the pressure isn't; they'll either go up or they'll go down."

During early seasons you can expect to find elk at higher elevations at or above timberline. But not all the elk. "Some of them will be down in that heavy dark timber, the thicker forest where there's a lot of vegetation and water," says Carlson. "The best hunting is usually during the early seasons and in the late season if there's enough snow where you can catch those elk coming down."

Carlson says that while there are some good bucks in the West Elk Wilderness, their numbers are not high. He doesn't recommend it as a good deer hunting unit. "I think it would be a good unit for bear, and there are a few lions in there," he says. "Bear hunting can be good depending on the berry crop. Find the berries and you'll be into bears. As far as lions, I don't recommend it because it's such rugged country it would be a very difficult hunt."

There are no roads into the West Elk Wilderness Area, and trails are restricted to foot or horse traffic only — no vehicles permitted.

Hunting in the West Elk Wilderness (GMU 54) is over-the-counter for bull elk; cow licenses are by limited draw. All deer licenses are by limited draw. For map info, call the USFS (970-641-0471).

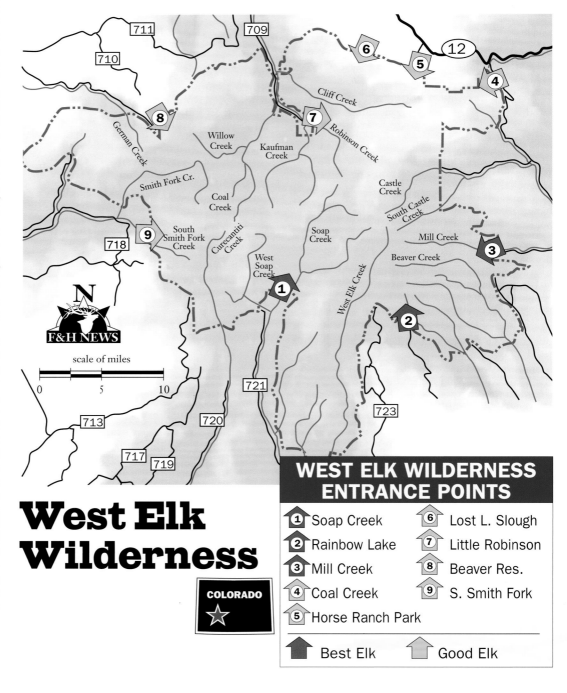

West Elk Wilderness

COLORADO

WEST ELK WILDERNESS ENTRANCE POINTS

1. Soap Creek
2. Rainbow Lake
3. Mill Creek
4. Coal Creek
5. Horse Ranch Park
6. Lost L. Slough
7. Little Robinson
8. Beaver Res.
9. S. Smith Fork

Best Elk   Good Elk

MULTI-ZONE HUNTING

LAMAR

Do your part for conservation: Harvest late light geese

by Steve Nelson

Snow goose populations continue to increase in North America despite liberalized bag limits and longer hunting seasons. Their population has grown so much in recent years that arctic habitats are being degradated and biologists fear disease outbreaks because huge numbers of birds are concentrated on small areas.

Winter population counts indicate that the combined population of lesser snow and Ross' geese in the United Sate has more than tripled in the past 30 years from just over 800,000 in 1969 to 2.8 million today. Biologists believe that the total spring breeding population may be at least 4.5 million.

It's bad news for the environment and other species, but hunters can take advantage of special late light goose season in eastern Colorado. The season opens Feb. 26 and runs through March 6 with a bag limit of 20 light geese per day and no possession limit. And by harvesting these birds, you will be doing your part for conservation.

The vast majority of snow geese are hunted in southeastern Colorado and, unfortunately, the best hunting is almost always found on private farmlands. But that doesn't mean that there aren't public hunting opportunities around. "The two places where public hunters do best are Queens and Meredith state wildlife areas," says Colorado Division of Wildlife biologist Jeff Yost (719-336-4852). "They killed a lot of geese at Queens during last year's late light goose season. Meredith Lake is private but you can get limited access through the Junction in Ordway for a fee, and they usually do pretty well there."

The Junction charges $10 per gun or $40 for the season. For more information, call (719) 267-3262.

QUEENS SWA: This is the largest and certainly the best goose hunting property in the southeast. With more than 70 blinds, it can accommodate a lot of hunters and chances are you won't be turned away because it's full. The blinds are open on an even/odd day system. Hunters must check in and check out at the check station. For more information, check your 1999 Waterfowl Regulations

GEESE GALORE: Snow goose populations have increased so much that a special late light goose season in eastern Colorado opens Feb. 26 and runs through March 6. Bag limit is 20 light geese per day. There is no possession limit.

booklet or call the Colorado Division of Wildlife.

JOHN MARTIN SWA: As for snow geese on the John Martin, Yost says, "Hunting on the John Martin State Wildlife Area can sometimes be good too, but you just don't see the concentrations of birds on it. I think the reservoir is just too big and deep and the birds won't use it as much."

THE THING ABOUT SNOW GEESE: The number of hunters who target white geese and take advantage of this special late season continues to grow, but it has taken some time. Hunting white geese is quite a bit different that hunting Canadas in that it requires more scouting, more decoys and a willingness to change plans at the last minute.

"The difficult thing with the snow geese is they move around so much," says Yost. "You can scout a field for a couple of days and watch the birds use it, but when you come back the next day to hunt, they're on the field a mile away. So you have to be ready to move. The snows are continually moving. They use their habitat more like a duck than a goose. When they land in a field they are continually moving.

"Last year I watched them coming into Nee Noshe for a day and then they flew to a field 10 miles to the east."

Which makes the birds very difficult to pattern. "But the people who are figuring them out can do very well," Yost continues. "You do have to hunt them differently from Canadas. Use lots more decoys and try to make that movement work for you.

"And I think it's important to use calls. Sometimes when I hunt Canadas I don't even use a call; they'll land right in my decoys. But you need to use a call for snows. The real key is decoys. You have to use lots of them — big spreads like 700 to 800 or more — and try to place them in front of the birds. Scout out the direction they are flying rather than a particular field and set up so that you'll bring the birds in that way. Windier days seem to be best for hunting and the people who use kites or decoys on poles seem to have more success."

GETTING PERMISSION TO HUNT: As we mentioned earlier, there are limited hunting opportunities on public land, with the majority of the hunting in the southeast, which is also where the majority of birds are. There can be huntable populations of snow geese in the northeastern part of the state, but the birds are usually tucked in along the eastern border. But because the birds travel in such large groups, they can be very destructive when they land in a field of winter wheat. White geese are grubbers and can really do a lot of damage. That means farmers may be much more receptive to granting hunters permission to hunt on their property.

Arranging permission requires that you do a little prehunt scouting . . . something you should be doing anyway. Take a few days to scout an area, locate fields that the birds are using, the direction they are moving. Then present yourself to the landowner a day or two before you plan to hunt. Your chances of getting permission are better than you think. Several guides and outfitters are offering their skills and leases for this special season as well. For information on them, you can also call the DOW.

REGULATIONS CHANGES: Because of the overpopulation problem with white geese, the feds have attempted to make it easier to hunt them by extending the season and liberalizing the regulations. President Clinton recently signed legislation to reinstate the use of electronic calls and extended hunting hours in the Central Flyway. The Arctic Tundra Habitat Emergency Conservation Act legislation is designed to reduce the impact snow geese are having on habitat and agricultural crops.

The Colorado Wildlife Commission will consider adopting these special regulations at their Jan. 13 meeting in Denver. Assuming that they adopt them and there is no reason to assume that they won't, the regulations would not take effect until March 1. The new regulations would allow hunters to use electronic calls during the later portion of the special season. In addition, Colorado will likely be adopting a conservation order under the Migratory Bird Treaty Act which would allow hunters to take light geese after March 10, outside the traditional migratory bird hunting seasons. Electronic calls and hunting half an hour past sunset would be

allowed from March 11 through March 31. No bag limits would be in effect while the conservation order is valid.

AT A GLANCE

Location: Special late light goose hunting season runs east of I-25. The best hunting is in the southeastern part of the state.

Species: Light geese.

Season dates: Feb. 26-March 6. If the Colorado Wildlife Commission implements the conservation order, an extended season would run March 10-March 31.

Bag limits: Daily bag limit is 20 light geese, no possession limit. Under the conservation order season, there would be no daily bag limit.

Tactics: Snow geese fly in large numbers and continually move around. Hunters must try to anticipate the direction the birds are flying and set up a large decoy spread to draw them in. Kits and decoys on poles are very effective. Calling is also helpful, especially with electronic calls (if the Commission approves them).

Information: Call the Colorado Division of Wildlife in Lamar (719-336-4852) or Sterling (970-521-0233).

Public Access
1. Tamarack Ranch State Wildlife Area
2. Red Lion State Wildlife Area
3. John Martin State Wildlife Area
4. Queens State Wildlife Area
5. The Junction

Late Light Goose Season

☐ Open Areas
Season: Feb. 26-March 6, 2000
Daily Bag Limit: 20 light geese
No Possession Limit

Colorado hunters are doing their part to reduce the light goose populations but the birds have really only had huntable populations here for about 15 years. Last year 1,638 Colorado hunters participated in the conservation order and harvested 13,000 birds.

West best for Colorado mountain lions

MONTROSE

by Tom Behrens

Hunting mountain lions may not be as popular as the pursuit of deer or elk in Colorado, but it certainly has an active following. The long-tailed cats are spread across the state, with the heaviest population density in the western two-thirds of the state. Different outfitters and Department of Wildlife officials give different opinions on the average size of a male cat, but DOW estimations are from 100 to 160 pounds. Females range from 80 to 120 pounds.

Depending on the time of the year, lions can be found in very diverse topography in Colorado, with the exception of way up in the alpine, up above timberline and up in some of the heavy coniferous forests, 8,500- to 10,000-foot elevations. You won't find many lions at those elevations. Some cats can be found in the aspen, oak brush, mahogany type of communities. A lot of lions are found in the pinion, juniper and sagebrush communities.

In matter of fact, the DOW has an ongoing study of mountain lions to learn more about the big cats. "First of all we're trying to find out movement patterns, how they're using the landscape, which ones are leaving, younger males versus younger females," says Bill deVergie (970-252-6000), wildlife manager for the Montrose area office. "We are looking for density and numbers available. Mountain lions, because of the wide area they roam, are the

THE WESTERN TWO-THIRDS of Colorado hold the most mountain lions. Scott Spear took this 145-pound cat in 2004.

hardest species to do any counts or inventories. By going out there and marking them, you know where that animal is." Marking refers to the fitting of tranquilized lions with telemetry collars.

The study is taking place in the northwest portion of the southwest part of the state. This area has been closed to all lion hunting. The southern portion of game management unit 61, all of 62 and a portion of unit 70 are included. The rest of the state is open for hunting.

"We want to see how high we can let this population go," says deVergie. "We're going to try to estimate what the population is for the next five years, see what kind of increase we can get without hunting, see how many lions we can get. Then after five years we're going to open it up to hunting and bring that population back down."

Through the use of watching the population growth and harvest figures, the department is trying to measure the effects of harvest so that they can establish yearly hunting quotas.

For more on this study, please see the story on p. 45.

Hunting for mountain lions is accomplished predominantly through the use of dogs. "Some people can call them and

spend a lot of time without dogs, but it's not nearly as efficient," says deVergie. "People drive around with their dogs looking for tracks in the snow along the sides of a lot of the forest service/BLM private roads. If they find some that look fairly fresh, they turn the dogs out and start following them. The dogs are barking and the cats go to the tree. They're basically hunting them by scent until they're treed, caved or ledged out where the hunter has a chance to take the lion, if they want it. Without a dog you can find tracks, but you'd be walking forever."

Lawrence Zeldenthuis hunts lions in the west-central part of the state. "We start looking for tracks," he says. "Once we find track we do our best to warm that track up to one to two nights old. Then we start trailing through with hounds. Lions travel. An old tom may have a 200– to 300-mile radius that he travels. If we find his track three or four days old, then we're going to start looking in the direction that he is going and cutting way out front of that track. We try and find where he has come through someplace, warming that track up to a night or two nights old. Generally we catch up with him in the same day, but sometimes it takes a couple of days."

"Lions move at night," Zeldenthuis says. "During the day we're actually trailing that lion where he's been through the night. Out here you catch a lot of lions on the rims, in the rocks. A lot of trees are not big enough to really hold a lion."

Walt Isenhour (512-273-2520) of Lone Star Outfitters hunts a private ranch in south-central Colorado. "We like to wait until we get a good tracking snow, then our guides will go out and cut fresh tracks," he says. "We like to measure those tracks to know that we're looking at a lion the size we want to take. Then we call our clients to see if they can be at the ranch in 24 hours.

AT a GLANCE

What: Mountain lions in the western two-thirds of the state.

Where: GMUs 12, 21, 23, 30, 33, 42, 58, 61, 70, 85, 851 and 86 all had 10 or more cougars taken in 2002 or 2003. Keep in mind that portions of GMUs 61 and 70 are closed for a study.

Who: Walt Isenhour (512-273-2520) of Lone Star Outfitters, Bill deVergie, (970-252-6000) wildlife manager for the Montrose area office.

From the rear foot to the front foot, the distance is measured. We can estimate how long the cat is. A good cat will go 7 feet and that's what we're looking for, a 7-foot stride.

"We take the dogs out with the hunters and work the tracks from the freshest point," he says. "Turn the dogs loose and let the dogs trail again. Hunt time varies, anywhere from 30 minutes to three hours, depending on how far the cat is."

Good dogs are the most important part of the hunting equation. "A dog is measured by his heart and willingness to hunt," says Isenhour. "Most hounds, black and tans or red bone hounds, or a mixed breed of those type of dogs, do very well. We like the red bones and what we call 'blackmouth cur' dogs. They do pretty well when they're really interested. It's based on a dog's personality. Is he interested in hunting, is he is interested in running a cat versus a deer or elk? We want to make sure the dogs stay on the cats and not run big game animals."

"To be able to keep a cat treed, I like four dogs, anywhere from three to six, says Isenhour. "You got to have enough dogs to keep the cat occupied. Don't have so few dogs that the cat can focus on any one particular dog. These cats are lethal. They can kill a dog in a heartbeat. They get bit quite often. These cats get pretty smart. They'll tree and then jump out of the tree as the hunters and guides approach and the chase is on again. Sometimes they get cornered where there is no tree, and there a pretty good fight goes on. The dogs get slapped, bit and beat up pretty good."

Hunting mountain lions in Colorado requires a good set of dogs. Sometimes the hunt can be physically demanding tracking down the big cats, but the adrenalin rush as you hear the dogs' barking intensify, signaling a treed cat, is worth the effort. As Zeldenthuis puts it, "we've run them into caves and holes, just about every crevice and crack you can think of. If you're fortunate you get them in tree." **F&H**

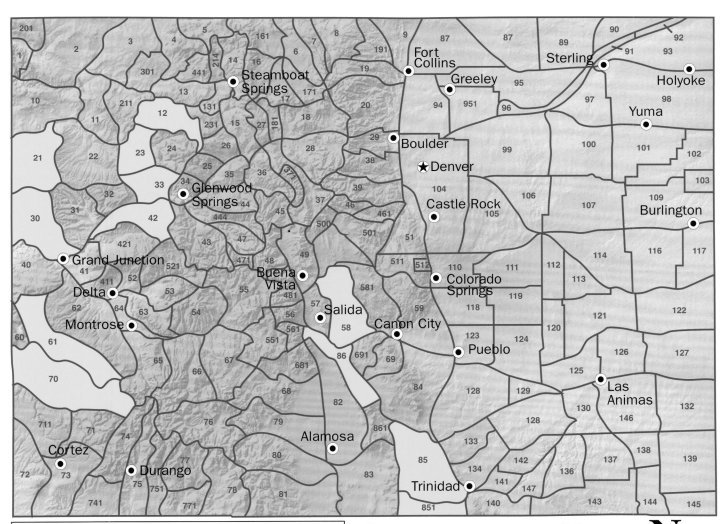

F&H MAP KEY
GMUs with 10 or more cougars taken in 2002 or 2003

Colorado Cougars
F&H NEWS

Looking for ringnecks? Check out these preserves

Naturally, we'd all like to hunt wild ringnecks on wild land. But the reality of it is that sometimes there's not enough time to scout and hunt public Walk-In lands, and only a small percentage of us can afford leases and exclusive pheasant club memberships. More than anything, we're all time-challenged.

So for those of us who work for a living and like to see birds when we hunt, and for those who want to bring youngsters into the sport, consider that Colorado has some of the finest pheasant hunting preserves in the country.

This list is by no means the quintessential authority for best-of-the-best hunting preserves in Colorado. We made our list of primo ringneck ranches based on their ability to provide the best bang for the buck, decent amenities like a clubhouse and cleaning stations, adequate quality of cover and habitat, and good customer service.

Rocky Ridge Sporting and Conservation Club

Established in 1984, Rocky Ridge is the second oldest pheasant hunting preserve in the state; only Stillroven Farm is older, and they only allow private members. Rocky Ridge gets our "Pheasant Glow" honors for offering nonmembers a one-time "Introductory Rate" hunt for $140 for quality-raised birds in some of the most majestic settings in the state. The package is for two hunters. It's a self-guided hunt, and includes three pheasant and two chukar.

"One of the key things that sets us apart is we operate on irrigated ground, when at other times other (preserves) can't," says Mike Moreng,

owner. "It's quality birds, it's quality cover, it's quality dogs, and quality scenery. Our birds are fed nutritionally balanced formulas in order to develop the full potential of the bird."

Rocky Ridge only claims 1,000 acres of pheasant range on four hunting fields, but it boasts some of the finest irrigated habitat and scenic cliff and mountain views of any preserve. The two upper fields are for beginners, with tall wheat and brome grass. The two lower fields between rocky cliffs and a large reservoir are for intermediate and advanced hunters. The lower fields also have several natural waterfall terraces

PREPARATION and good shooting can produce results like these. Will Peterson took the photo, and Jon Gibbs sent it our way. (Realtree/Lowrance Photo Contest entry)

emerging from sandstone cliffs, Russian olive tree-lined draws, and cottonwoods along the banks.

Besides training hunting dogs, Rocky Ridge's staff also provide free advice to hunters with questions about their own dogs. "We have over 20 years of dog training experience of all breeds at all levels," Moreng says.

Guided hunts are also available for

$175 (add 17 percent gratuity), and includes dogs. For more information call (970) 221-4868.

Rocky Mountain Rooster

"We've been here 20 years," says Brett Axton. owner of the Rocky Mountain Rooster, located a half-hour drive east of Colorado Springs. This preserve is without question Colorado's version of "Pheasant World." Basically, everything here is super-sized, including the clubhouse, the number of birds released, and available fields to hunt.

"We're the biggest preserve west of the Mississippi, as far as volume goes," Axton says. "We kill 65,000 birds a year."

The ranch is on 5,000 acres of private rolling hills with three creek systems. The hunting habitat is spread over 27 areas comprised of corn, sorghum and milo. Although size and volume don't necessarily make a preserve the best, RMR offers extremely competitive pricing for the size of its operation; nonmembers get three hours to bag either five pheasants or seven chukar for only $160.

RMR also offers a 6,000 square foot, state-of-the art clubhouse, and will clean birds in vacuum-sealed bags for $3 apiece. "My theory is you can be a really good sporting clays or bird hunting facility," Axton says. "I chose the latter."

To make a reservation, call (719) 635-3257.

Kiowa Creek Sporting Club

This preserve may only boast 1,000 acres, but what it does with that land will astound any pheasant fan, which is why we give it the "Tower of Pheasant Power" distinction.

"We grow every year as we can afford to grow," says Mark Moore, who owns and operates Kiowa Creek with his wife Brenda. "We went from 160 acres and a five-stand when we first started, to 1,000 acres and a 120-foot tall, 20-station sporting clay tower."

If the tower doesn't get your pheasant hand/eye coordination tuned up, check out their "European-Drive Pheasant Shooting" area. Basically, it consists of a grain silo where pigeons and pheasant are released and come flying out the top. You'll be sitting in one of 12 blinds that are positioned like a tire spoke in order to intercept birds coming your way. "It's a different way of hunting," Moore says.

For more traditional hunts, the habitat on this preserve is perfect. "It's wooded creek bottom and cultivated fields with draws that are woody and bushy," Moore says. "We can do five hunts simultaneously."

The pheasant food plots consist of milo, millet and alfalfa. Hunting packages include use of a club dog, choice of five pheasants, seven chukar or 10 quail per person. Cost is $105 for three guns or $130 if fewer than three guns. Packages must be booked on Tuesday, Wednesday or Thursday.

Kiowa Creek also has one of the nicest clubhouses around. It's finished with cherry wood paneling, two fireplaces at either end of the room, leather armchairs, and a gift shop with everything from shells to clothing. The club offers hunts six months a year (Oct. 1 to March 31). It's located at 46700 East Quincy in Bennett. For more information call (303) 644-4627.

Scenic Mesa Ranch

Scenic Mesa in Hotchkiss (located between Delta and Paonia along Highway 92) is undoubtedly Colorado's most exotic and upscale place to hunt for under $500. A half-day hunt includes a round of five-stand per gun (two person minimum), field transportation, professional guides, dogs and bird processing with vacuum packaging, all for $350.

"We're the only Orvis-endorsed wingshooting lodge in Colorado," says Al DeGrange, manager. The 8,200-acre preserve is located right at the confluences of the North and South forks of the Gunnison River. Here hunters can hunt upland birds

GOT YOUR gun? Got your ammo? Then let's go shooting. (*F&H News* photo by Dale Darling)

on intensely managed habitat of tall native grasses, grains and draws, on top of a high plateau at the base of the West Elk Mountain Range.

"Looking at the West Elk Mountain Range and 11,000-foot peaks, you won't find any place like it," DeGrange says. "The majority of our chukar are wild, all of our Gambel quail are wild, and half of our pheasants are wild. We do offer strictly wild bird hunts on the west end of our property. We take a holistic approach for the birds and buffalo. We've been removing the sagebrush and reintroducing the original grass that was on the property originally. Now the wild birds are thriving."

The clubhouse has a full Orvis-stocked store and a great room for meals. Scenic Mesa also offers "Cast-and-Blast" adventures. For more information call (970) 872-3078.

Just More Coveys (JMC) Outfitters

This outfit's claim to fame — and it's a worthy claim — is that hunting here is for wild birds. For those purist pheasant hunters looking strictly for wild pheasants, then look no further. For only $150, hunters get a guide and a full day to bag a limit.

"Bar none, our cover is better than anyone else's," says Chad Leonhardt, owner and guide. "We're hunting on approximately 2,500 acres that are exclusively private. Then we have another 10,000 acres or more leased."

Some of the habitat includes CRP, corn, wheat stubble and shelterbelts. One property even has approximately 4,000 trees on 540 acres. "In my opinion our shining aspect is there are not many places folks can go (preserve) hunting for wild birds," Axton says. "We're unique for our wild birds and cover."

JMC Outfitters also offers preserve style hunting, which costs $20 per pheasant (no bird minimum) with optional $75 for guide and dog. A 50 percent deposit is required upon booking. The remainder is due the day the hunt begins. JMC is located near Otis.

Colorado Wing Shooters

This operation gets our nod as the "Most Accessible Pheasant Preserve in the Denver Metro Area" with locations near Fort Collins and Brighton. However, shooting pheasants this close to the Front Range won't last forever.

"Housing (developments) will eventually run us out of here," says Tim Brough, owner and guide. Colorado Wingshooters will eventually be relocating to the Pawnee Sportsmen's Center, located out in Briggsdale.

"Total, we have an active 1,500 acres to hunt and another 1,000 we can expand on (at Pawnee Sportsmen's Center)," Brough says.

"Our cover is better than most." The northern properties have mostly CRP cover and grazed river bottoms with knee- and hip-high grasses. The properties near Brighton are mainly traditional agricultural fields that are cultivated and have ditch rows.

"We do mostly non-guided hunts, so we're geared to guys with dogs," Brough says.

A half-day hunt includes standard release of four pheasants or five chukar and costs $95 per person. Limit of two visits per season. Guided hunts (with hunting dogs) runs an additional $60. To schedule a Fort Collins area hunt call (970) 482-7574; for the Brighton area call (303) 637-0008.

Wolf Creek Sporting Clay Club and Pheasant Preserve

Wolf Creek's pheasant preserve gets our highly esteemed "Preseason Pheasant One-Stop, Dial-in Shop" honors for providing a build-a-hunt and warm-up session at an affordable rate. Wolf Creek's build-a-hunt packages include $20 for pheasant, $15 for chukar and $13 for quail. The club is open for hunts Sept. 1 through March 31. They're located at 42360 RD 53 in Kiowa.

"Our bird fields are considerably larger than other preserves. They're 35 acres, so we can accommodate large groups," Wolf Creek's owner Doug Benoit says. "Our fields are not mandatory-guided. A lot of oth-

DINGO HOLTZ, Severen Pedersen and around 20 of their closest friends had a successful hunt in December. (Realtree/Lowrance Photo Contest entry)

er clubs it's non-negotiable. Here you can take your own dogs and be your own guide."

Nestled on 840 acres, Wolf Creek's habitat ranges from open areas with tall grass, to wooded areas and farm land. The preserve touts its facility as having one of the finest sporting clays courses in the state. "We probably have three-quarters of the guys coming in go through our five-stand (course)," Benoit says.

A round of 25 sporting clays from the five-stand costs only $6, or 100 for $25. The club also has a National Sporting Clays Association instructor onsite to field all your shooting questions.

Wolf Creek is located 19 miles south of I-70 off Exit 305; 11 miles north of Highway 86 from Kiowa; or 40 miles southeast of Denver. For reservations call (303) 621-2841.

Longmeadow Game Resort

Longmeadow near Wiggins gets our "Farmer Pheasant" honors for turning in their plow and hiding a pile of pheasants in their cover.

"I'm a farmer and there just isn't any money in farming anymore," says Glenn Stencel, owner and guide. "We just started it up this year."

Rather than see all the land nearby get developed, Stencel prefers to try and acquire the land or lease it and use it for hunting.

Longmeadow's prime section on 500 acres consists of a dry creek bottom with grass in it, surrounded by food plots of corn and sedan grass mix, with milo and millet mixed in as well. They also have another 320 acres of CRP near Byers.

"Next year I'll plant more ground like that," Stencel says. "The (creeks bottoms) run 300 yards wide and run for 1½ miles."

Here, don't expect anything too fancy, accommodations-wise. "Not yet," Stencel says. "But I have a place in my shop where I make soup and sandwiches."

The half-day hunt costs $100 per gun, with add-on of as many birds as you like: $20 for pheasants, $18 for chukar, $15 for quail. Guided hunts cost $150 and group discounts are available. To get to Longmeadow Game Resort, from Interstate 76 take Highway 52 south for 8 miles and 1 mile east. For reservations call (970) 768-2508.

— Sam Grothe

Spring season brings turkey hunters out

by Steve Nelson

SPENCER NICHOLL of Ohio City with a gobbler shot near East Spanish Peak.

Spring turkey is the first of the year's hunting seasons and one of the more challenging. It's also drawing new fans every year. Colorado has two species of turkeys: merriams, commonly referred to as the mountain turkey and found primarily west of I-25; and Rio Grande, found east of I-25 out in the cottonwood riparian habitat.

The Colorado Division of Wildlife has been actively transplanting birds for years, and they now estimate that there are between 18,000 and 20,000 Merriams and 2,000 to 3,000 Rio Grande. In recent years, they have been selling about 7,000 licenses for the spring season with an annual harvest of about 1,500 birds. Last year, however, both the license sales and the harvest jumped dramatically. "I don't have the exact figures, but I think we sold about 9,000 licenses last spring and the harvest shot up to 2,500 birds," says Rick Hoffman, DOW avian bird researcher (970-472-4300) and their resident turkey expert. "That was quite a jump, and

we're not really sure why it happened."

One possible reason is the influx of people moving into Colorado from states that have a tradition of turkey hunting. "We now have 24 different chapters of the National Wild Turkey Federation in Colorado," says Hoffman. "So the interest is definitely there. And also, I think that spring turkey hunting fills the bill for all those hunters out there who are looking for something to do in the spring."

Of course, the growing popularity of turkey hunting is not without its inherent problems, mainly overcrowding. Despite large amounts of public land to hunt on — particularly in the southwest — complaints of overcrowding are becoming common place. Public lands within easy driving distance from metro areas are heavily pressured. "We've transplanted turkeys into a lot of places around the state, and wherever there is a small track of public land with birds on it, it does get pressured," says Hoffman. "I think that overcrowding is a legitimate concern, most turkey hunters would rather have a quality hunt."

WHERE TO HUNT: In terms of harvest the southeast still dominates, but the southwest is coming on strong. It has excellent turkey populations, offers the best public hunting in the state, and the harvest figures are climbing. "Last spring we shot 125 birds in Archuleta County and 130 birds in La Plata County," says DOW biologist Scott Wait (970-247-0855) in Durango. "We shot 75 birds in Montezuma County and 80 in Dolores County. We've come off two good years in a row, our turkey populations are excellent, and the same old

areas that were good in the past will likely be good again this year. Our birds are doing great, but they are slow to pioneer into new areas on their own."

Come opening morning, the birds will be ranging from 7,500 to 9,000 feet. "Generally in the broken country they'll be found on the upper third on top of the ridges, and in the rolling country they'll be down on the lower third but they'll still be roosting on the upper end. I don't see them being very far down in the drainages," says Wait. "Basically, they follow the snow line up the mountain as it recedes."

In the southwest, the birds are spread out between Dolores on the west and Durango on the east, and they run north up the Dolores River drainage and on up onto the Uncompahgre Plateau. There is a tremendous amount of public land (San Juan National Forest), but access to much of it can also be dictated by the weather. The past couple of winters have been fairly dry, so access conditions in the spring have been good. This winter is a more normal one so there may be access problems with snow or snow melt. It could restrict hunters to specific areas.

Some of the more popular turkey hunting spots are McPhee Park, Haycamp Mesa, the upper Mancos Creek drainages, Missionary Ridge, Chimney Rock and the upper Cherry Creek drainage. Key on the oakbrush and ponderosa pine regions. Going north, you'll find birds up the major drainages coming off the Uncompahgre Plateau.

AT A GLANCE

Spring turkey season: April 14-May 27 statewide except in units closed or requiring a limited license. See regulations for details.

New closures: Units 1, 2, 21, 25, 37 and 201 are closed to turkey hunting so that new populations can become established.

New units open: Units 112, 113 and 114 are open to unlimited turkey hunting.

Youth turkey seasons: Flagler SWA in GMU 107 is open for youth and one youth mentor hunter with unlimited licenses.

Bag and possession limit: One bearded turkey. Hunters with a limited spring turkey license may also take a second turkey on an unlimited license.

For more information: Contact the Colorado Division of Wildlife (303-297-1192).

Gaining access to them can be an exercise in map reading and door knocking, as some public lands access is blocked by private lands.

Further north and east, there are birds up the Plateau Creek drainage, Kannah Creek and Chalk Mountain, all the Rifle Creek drainages hold birds, and the area north or Rifle is fast becoming a popular spot for turkey hunters. East and West Divide creeks in GMU 33 hold turkeys, and there are birds up on Garfield Creek (GMU 42).

"We're starting to see a real increase in birds in the northwestern part of the state around Rifle and clear up towards Meeker along the White River drainage," says Hoffman. "There are some public places to hunt up there, but you have to do your homework to find them. Usually during the early part of the season they're all on private land, but as the snow melts and they move up they move onto public land."

There is a great deal of public land to hunt turkeys on in the San Isabel National Forest between Canon City and Salida and south down into the Wet Mountains. Popular areas include Babcock Hole, Hardscrabble Creek, Locke Mountain, Indian Creek and Smith Creek.

East of I-25 offers some of the better turkey hunting in the state, both in the northeast and the southeast. The problem is access — 90 percent of the turkey hunting is on private farmlands and permission is required. In addition, almost all of the hunting is by limited draw only, and you need to secure permission to hunt before you can apply. There are several state wildlife areas along the South Platte and Arkansas river drainages, and almost all of them hold birds. Should you be lucky enough to draw a license you'll likely do fine. "In general, our turkey hunting success rates run right around 18 to 20 percent (over-the-counter units). Some were as high as 26 percent last year," says Hoffman. "But in our limited draw units, it runs more like 80 to 90 percent."

Public hunting areas that are draw-only such as Spanish Peaks, Beaver Creek, Lake Dorothy and the James M. John SWAs are difficult to draw unless you have some accumulated preference points but well worth the wait. And the new Bosque del Oso SWA shapes up to be another great place to hunt turkeys. If you're serious about turkey hunting and don't have access to private lands, you should apply for one of these units or at least a preference point every year. It shouldn't take too many seasons before you draw a license.

STRATEGIES: "Opening weekend I think they are going to be down pretty low," says Hoffman. "They'll (merriams) be down in that pinion juniper, ponderosa pine interface. I'd start with the snow line where the break is. They need access to the bare ground. If there's 100-percent snow cover, they're not going to be there. The Rio Grandes will be along the creek bottoms, and they'll probably be pretty spread out."

The season is set up so that the majority of the hens are already bred before the season opens. By late April, many of the merriam hens are on the nest and the rest are on them by early May. And when the hens are on the nest is the time you want to be out there calling. The Rio Grandes usually go to the nest a week to two weeks earlier than that. "We really try to time the season so that the hens have been bred and already on the nest or close to it by the time the season opens," says Wait. "That way the gobblers are much more vulnerable."

Hoffman agrees. "I still think that the best time to hunt turkeys is much later in the season. I wouldn't even think about starting hunting (merriams) until the last week in April or the first week in May. If I was hunting Rio Grandes, I'd go a little earlier, a week to two weeks depending on the weather. I think that the opener is a little too early. Many of the birds will still be in their winter flocks. You'll see one or two singles, maybe get one by ambush, but if you're really serious about calling them in, having an enjoyable time out there seeing a lot of birds, you'll be better off waiting until later in the season."

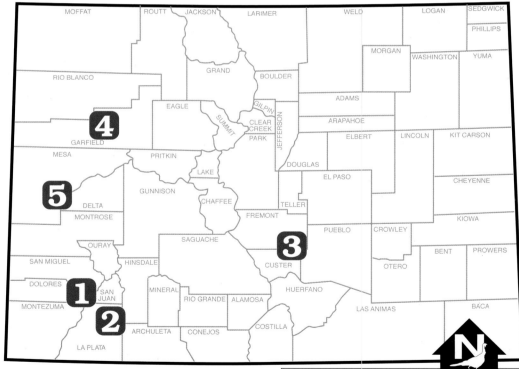

COLORADO TURKEY ROUNDUP

F&H MAP KEY

F&H NEWS Map Feature

1. Dolores River
2. Missionary Ridge
3. San Isabel National Forest
4. Rifle
5. Uncompahgre Plateau